Liturgies

on the

Holocaust

Liturgies

on the

Holocaust

An Interfaith Anthology

NEW AND REVISED EDITION

EDITED BY
Marcia Sachs Littell
and
Sharon Weissman Gutman

TRINITY PRESS INTERNATIONAL
Valley Forge, Pennsylvania

Trinity Press International, P.O. Box 851, Valley Forge, PA 19482-0851

Library of Congress Cataloging-in-Publication Data
Liturgies on the Holocaust : an interfaith anthology / edited by
  Marcia Sachs Littell and Sharon W. Gutman. – New and rev. ed.
      p.   cm.
    ISBN 1-56338-138-9 (pa : alk. paper)
    1. Holocaust Remembrance Day – Prayer-books and devotions – English.
  2. Judaism – Prayer-books and devotions – English. 3. Prayer-books.
  4. Holocaust Remembrance Day – Sermons.   I. Littell, Marcia Sachs.
  II. Gutman, Sharon W.
  BM675.H55Z5865   1996
  291.3'8– dc20
                                                     96-1862
                                                       CIP

Printed in the United States of America

96   97   98   99   10   9   8   7   6   5   4   3   2   1

*These liturgies are dedicated to
the blessed memory of*

NEHEMIAH AND SHEINDEL WEISSMAN

- *deported from Hamburg in 1938*
- *detained in the Warsaw Ghetto*
- *killed in Treblinka in 1942*

Confused!

and

GIDEON HAUSNER
(1915–1990)

- *prosecutor of the 1961 Eichmann trial in Jerusalem*
- *who opened the eyes and ears of the world to the story*
- *who opened the door for Holocaust education in Israel and North America*

Contents

This is a project of the

PHILADELPHIA CENTER ON THE HOLOCAUST,
GENOCIDE AND HUMAN RIGHTS

Post Office Box 172
Merion Station, Pennsylvania 19066

Telephone 610/667-5437
FAX 610/667-0265

DR. MARCIA SACHS LITTELL teaches at Temple University. She was the founding director of the Anne Frank Institute and is presently the executive director of the Philadelphia Center on the Holocaust, Genocide and Human Rights and of the Annual Scholars' Conference on the Holocaust and the Churches. Her publications include *The Holocaust: Forty Years After; Holocaust Education: A Resource Book for Teachers and Professional Leaders; and Liturgies on the Holocaust: An Interfaith Anthology,* vol. 1: *The Netherlands and Nazi Genocide.* Her forthcoming book is titled *Breaking the Silence: A History of Holocaust Education in North America.*

SHARON WEISSMAN GUTMAN is a rabbinic student at Hebrew Union College–Jewish Institute of Religion in New York City. She is vice-president of the Philadelphia Center on the Holocaust, Genocide and Human Rights and the international coordinator of Remembering for the Future. She is vice-president of the Annual Scholars' Conference on the Holocaust and the Churches and a director of the Post Holocaust Generation in Dialogue. From 1980 to 1989 she lived and taught in Israel.

Preface

The styles of the liturgies here published vary greatly, depending upon the type of service and the worshipers attending. In a few cases careful footnotes are given to identify for historical reasons the time and place of their first use.

The editors have presented many examples of programs appropriate for use in different settings. These include commemorations that took place in the federal and state governments as well as branches of the military. Some synagogue programs of a more traditional kind are included. We have also provided examples for church and interfaith groups, college campuses, and general civic observances.

The reader will quickly note that there are certain classical texts in the resource materials that have been used again and again over the years. They have *become* liturgy, as their repeated use has rendered them ritual, symbolic recognition. These are the descriptions and prayers that most dramatically communicate the significance of the event and give greatest promise of an honest telling and a healing remembrance. Among these resources, the poems of Nelly Sachs, the Diary of Anne Frank, the poems of the children of Theresienstadt (*I Never Saw Another Butterfly*), and the writings of Elie Wiesel are clearly preeminent.

We wish to thank all those who, over the years, have faithfully sent us copies of their Yom HaShoah programs for our files. We regret that the limitation of space has prevented us from printing all of them. We are deeply grateful to all whose publications have made the power and beauty of these liturgies accessible to men and women of differing faiths but of a shared good will.

The telling of the story of the Holocaust has gone on for a number of years and Holocaust educators are now drawing some of its lessons. But perhaps most important of all in teaching, memorializing, and never forgetting, is the use of prayers, songs and readings among people who remember. It is in these sacred hours of remembrance and meditation that the suffering of the past may be transformed into healing and hope for a better future.

MARCIA S. LITTELL
SHARON WEISSMAN GUTMAN

The Philadelphia Center on the Holocaust,
Genocide and Human Rights

Acknowledgments

The editors wish to thank all whose liturgies and publications have enhanced the meaning of this interfaith anthology:

Athenaeum House for items from André Schwarz-Bart's *The Last of the Just.*

Beacon Press, for a selection from Viktor Frankl's *Man's Search for Meaning.*

The Benedictine Foundation of Vermont, for the song "Hear O Israel."

Harry James Cargas, for a selection from *Harry James Cargas in Conversation with Elie Wiesel.*

Helga Croner of the Stimulus Foundation, for the liturgy by Eugene Fisher and Leon Klenicki: *From Death to Hope.*

Farrar, Straus & Giroux for selections from Nelly Sachs: *O the Chimneys; Chorus of the Rescued; Night, Night; In the Habitat of Death; Israel.*

Holt, Rinehart & Winston, for selections from Alexander Donat's *The Holocaust Kingdom.*

Paul Jeser of the National Jewish Resource Center, for the liturgy by Alice E. Eckardt.

Franklin H. Littell, for selections from *The Crucifixion of the Jews* and the use of the liturgy by Elizabeth Wright.

McGraw-Hill Book Company for selections from *I Never Saw Another Butterfly.*

Rabbi Charles Feinberg of Beth El Congregation, Poughkeepsie, N.Y., for his *Service for Yom HaShaoh.*

Schocken Books, for Hannah Senesh: *Blessed is the Match;* for selections from Albert Friedlander's *Out of the Whirlwind.*

Stein & Day, for a selection from Filip Muller's *Eyewitness Auschwitz.*

Elie Wiesel, for selections from his books: *Night, Messengers of God.*

Hank Knight and Tom Paxton for the words and music of *Hardly Ever Again.*

Introduction

The Days of Remembrance (*Yom HaShoah*) are observed each year on the 27th of Nisan on the Jewish calendar. This date falls on the fifth day following the eighth day of Passover. Official proclamations are issued and ceremonies conducted by the president of United States, the governors of all fifty states, the mayors of all major American cities, all major branches of the military, government and community groups, smaller towns and communities, universities and schools both public and private, and of course in the synagogues and churches.

The Days of Remembrance provide Jews and Christians in the community an opportunity for *Tikkun,* to come together and engage in healing. Yom HaShoah is the time for nonpartisan, interfaith, interreligious services to take place. This is the time for citizens in the community to unite in reflection, commemoration, cooperation, and bearing witness.

The observance of the Days of Remembrance enables people of good will to reaffirm shared values and to pledge their united commitment to democracy, liberty, and freedom. It offers the chance to examine how fragile is this web we call civilization, to understand how easily the republic can be torn apart, and to pledge again their loyalty to the common covenant.

In the early 1970s, Yom HaShoah was observed by only a few dozen congregations in America. During the administration of President Jimmy Carter, observance of the Days of Remembrance grew rapidly and marked a permanent day on the calendar. Every American president since that time has supported this endeavor.

On May 1, 1978, President Carter established the President's Commission on the Holocaust. He appointed a fifteen-member commission of "distinguished Americans, both Jewish and non-Jewish," to make recommendations for an appropriate memorial to commemorate the Holocaust in the nation's capital. The memorial was intended to serve as a reminder to all Americans of the millions who died in the Holocaust. Taking its place among the other monuments, memorials, and museums in the nation's capitol, it would stress how easily advanced technology can be turned to evil ends. It would emphasize the importance of our democratic values.

On October 7, 1980, a unanimous 96th Congress enacted Public Law 96-388, establishing the U.S. Holocaust Memorial Council, the body charged with guiding the building and development of the museum and providing for appropriate ways to commemorate the Days of Remembrance as an annual, national, civic commemoration of the Holocaust. Thus, Yom HaShoah became a public event. On April 22, 1993, the museum was opened to the public.

The United States Holocaust Memorial Museum is intended to educate all Americans about this watershed event in history and its implications for contemporary society. The educational component is underscored by the annual Days of Remembrance commemoration. The purpose of declaring an annual national commemoration was to recall the Nazi destruction of European Jewry, to point up the moral and religious issues imposed by genocide in the world today, and to indicate a better way.

The aim of the Days of Remembrance (*Yom HaShoah*) is not to place guilt, but rather through recollection of this human tragedy inflicted upon the Jewish people, to seek reconciliation and to renew faith in humanity and commitment to life. Those who offer Yom HaShoah observances share the hope that people of all faiths will gain insight and understanding of the Holocaust and the lessons of the Holocaust — an event in the death and life of the Jewish people and also an event in human history that speaks to the conscience of all peoples.

We are pleased to be able to provide this anthology to members of the clergy, both Jewish and Christian, and to civic and community leaders with whom we share the common work: to heal and repair the world-*Tikkun*.

– 1 –

The Language of Liturgy

FRANKLIN H. LITTELL

At first there was silence. The terrifying realization of the evil of which the perpetrators were capable, the numbness of the targeted victims who survived, and the shame of the spectators all combined to erect a wall of silence around the event. Then too, silence was at least a respectful tribute to the memory of the dead.

Then there was the word. Hesitantly, a few poets and novelists ventured forth into a field strewn with psychological landmines. They knew how a careless word or infelicitous phrase might hurt a survivor or someone who had lost those near and dear. They feared to approach the fire. But, like Jeremiah of old when he strove to keep silent, they found the compulsion to speak was not to be withstood. For good or for ill, the story had to be told. For the sake of the generations yet to come, the silence must be broken. The compulsion to speak came from the mandate to save life.

Then, after "forty years in the wilderness" the scriptural time span was fulfilled, and at last survivors and liberators and rescuers began to tell of what they had lived and seen.[1] The autobiographies and eyewitness documentaries became a flood. The problem became how to sift and to sort and to choose those reports that most accurately reflected the event, and to relate that event to its antecedents and to other like events in the history of humankind.

There is no religious problem with silence, provided it is the silence of respect and not the silence of denial. There is no religious problem with telling the story, provided the subject matter is respected and not made a matter of vulgar sensationalism. The problem is deeper and more subtle: the danger in using the critical and comparative method, the tools of science, in a supremely sensitive area. To lay profane hands on sacred materials is no light matter. What if the recollection and evocation are of a spirit as "ice cold" as the crime itself?

Nevertheless, the tribute to memory must be paid. Yom HaShoah ("Days of Remembrance") is, of course, a day set by the Jewish calendar. This fact is initially confusing to the gentile, who is used to another series of days, months, and years. However, Yom HaShoah almost always comes in April in the common calendar, and either the local rabbi or the U.S. Holocaust Memorial Museum in Washington, D.C., can supply the date. For the deeper issues that are raised by the place of Yom HaShoah in the Jewish calendar, a chapter in Irving Greenberg's *The Jewish Way: Living the Holidays* provides exciting information.[2]

Dr. Franklin H. Littell is Emeritus Professor of Religion at Temple University. He is a minister in the United Methodist Church.

    1. See Marcia Sachs Littell, Richard Libowitz, and Evelyn Bodek Rosen, eds., *The Holocaust — Forty Years After* (Lewiston, N.Y.: Edwin Mellen Press, 1989), chapter 1.

    2. Irving Greenberg, *The Jewish Way: Living the Holidays* (New York: Summit Books, 1988), chapter 10. The

The first Yom HaShoah observances in this country were interfaith in sponsorship. With the founding of the U.S. Holocaust Memorial Council by the Congress, many observances during the last decade have taken on a civic character. Also, many high schools and colleges have developed campus community observances. In response, to deepen the fundamentally religious nature of the event many Jewish communities have begun to hold their own services, and moreover in the sanctuary. While giving a broad assent and support to the civic, the campus, and certainly the Jewish communal observances, those releasing this handbook do so in the conviction that the observance of Yom HaShoah should be accepted as an interfaith responsibility. The perspectives are different, but both Jews and Christians need to build their memories of the Shoah into their present commitments and hopes for a better future.

In recent years a considerable number of communities and campuses have begun to hold seminars or conferences on the dates commemorating Kristallnacht (November 9–11, 1938). The first of these was held in 1978 at the University of Washington.[3] The point taken is the insight that there is a profound difference between Yom HaShoah — a time of prayer and meditation, poems, and liturgical moments, and Kristallnacht — a time when study of the lessons of the Holocaust is compelling. To remember the November 1938 pogrom instigated by the Nazi Party is to remember a very important lesson: the Holocaust was not like a flood or an earthquake, and it didn't have to happen. It was a crime perpetrated by criminals, who manipulated the most base emotions of the mob to provide cover for the cold rationality of the planning and the perpetration of the crime.

The *Shoah* must be remembered liturgically and studied scientifically, both. The Holocaust is an epoch-making event in human history, an event of the mass of which men and women thereafter say, "Before (the event)... " and "After that... " The Holocaust is an event of the critical importance that Christians and Jews assign to the Exodus, to the experience of the people at Sinai, to the Return from Exile. The Holocaust is of the measure the Jews assign the destruction of the Second Temple. The Holocaust is of the measure that Christians assign the crucifixion of Jesus. As every religious person, Jew or Christian, who has confronted the Holocaust will testify: "On this side of the mountain, nothing is ever the same again.... " For history is also a *continuum,* with our present awareness of the past (memory) a major force in the shaping of our present.

To think of the Holocaust as an event in history, in sacred history and in general human history, means already to have made comparisons and to have reached decisions. Why should the Holocaust be remembered ahead of Napoleon's defeat at Moscow or Hitler's defeat at Stalingrad? Why should the planned and systematized murder of six million Jews be considered the key to unlock the tragic mysteries of the Age of Genocide, rather than the ghastly sacrifice by dictatorial regimes of five million kulaks in Soviet Russia, or twenty million Chinese during the "cultural revolution" under Mao, or three hundred thousand Ugandans under Idi Amin, or nearly a million tribesmen in the southern Sudan? Affirming the uniqueness of the Holocaust is a moral and theological decision. Affirming its relevance to other tragedies suffered by other peoples is a decision both moral and scientific.

In an event of such magnitude, generations must pass before the lessons are drawn up

chapter is an enlargement of a lecture given by Rabbi Greenberg under the auspices of the Philadelphia Center on the Holocaust.

3. The report of the 1978 Kristallnacht Conference was edited by Lyman H. Legters (Boulder, Colo.: Westview Press, 1983), with essays by a number of Holocaust scholars.

in reasonably final form. Most important of all: premature closure must be averted. The commemoration of Yom HaShoah will greatly help to forestall the rush of intellectuals prematurely to file the event under familiar rubrics.

First, a generation and more had to pass before anyone dared to talk about "the lessons of the Holocaust," to move beyond simple story-telling. And now the task to fit the event into human history and to line out its lessons for politics and religion and other aspects of human affairs, will take the massed efforts of scientists in many fields.

Since 1959 there have been graduate seminars and courses on the subject. Since 1970 there has been an Annual Scholars Conference bringing together specialists in the different sectors of Holocaust education and study, and from several academic disciplines. The number of courses in colleges, universities, and seminaries has increased from about a dozen in 1970 to many hundreds in 1995. Religion, History, and Literature are the academic disciplines where courses have usually been lodged. The swell of articles and monographs and readers is running at full tide.

Many of the mistakes and wrong-headed interpretations of earlier years, arising from the heat of war, have been eliminated by subsequent scholarship. No informed person still blames "Hitler and his gang" alone for the tragedy. No informed person still blames "the Germans" alone for the crime. No informed person still charges that the Jews were complicit in their own destruction, because they "went like sheep to the slaughter." No informed person still thinks the Holocaust was something that happened to the Jews alone. The Holocaust was also something that happened to Christianity and Christians, and beyond that to Western civilization ("Christendom").

Being confronted by the Holocaust is not, however, primarily an exercise in analysis and critique. Because the claim is made upon the whole person, more important than the monographs and the articles and the footnotes are the prayers, the songs, the hymns, the psalms, the responses of the congregations. Until the right responses are found in worship and in the liturgies, the Holocaust will continue to burn and to hurt rather than to heal. The grief work must go forward. The healing will come when the liturgies of our congregations show that we have found the right form of words with which to address the memory of an event that cut a caesura across human history, and also across the history of practicing Jews and devout Christians.

The clergy and congregations represent the commitment to shared suffering and shared affirmation of life and its deepest meaning. They have an unequalled opportunity to develop the liturgies and prayers that will help the neighborhoods and faith communities in the American republic rightly to remember and to understand and to interpret the story and the meaning of the Holocaust. When the United States Holocaust Memorial Council was established in 1980 it was assigned the responsibility of creating a memorial and of spreading the observance of Yom HaShoah. Today the observance of Yom HaShoah — in which the president and Congress, the governors of all fifty states, the mayors of all major cities, and the community leaders in hundreds of smaller communities across America are joined — is a national calendar event.

We trust that those who use this handbook of liturgy will find their planning and observances a real contribution to the healing of ancient rifts between the peoples and to the eventual mending of the world (*Tikkun*).

Creating Christian Yom HaShoah Liturgies

ALICE ECKARDT

While Jewish observance of Yom HaShoah is an unambiguous "family" affair, Christian observance is far more problematical. The Holocaust was a Christian event and is a Christian problem in a way almost opposite to that in which it was a Jewish event and is a Jewish problem. While Jews were the certain victims, Christians were the murderers, accomplices, indifferent bystanders and only in miniscule numbers helpers or rescuers.[1] But the problem goes even deeper than this. We are faced with far more than the apostasy of a generation. Roy Eckardt states the Christian condition unequivocally.

> There is a dimension to the *Endlösung* that the Christian must know, and from which the Jew is spared.... The dark night that surrounds the Christian soul is the night of objective guilt... because here, in this event,... the "theological negation of Judaism and the vilification of the Jewish people" within the Christian tradition were, at the last, translated into the genocide of the Jews.... The annihilation of the Jews expresses, on the one side of the coin, an ultimate resolve on the part of the Nazis, and, on the other side of the coin, the final logic and application of nineteen hundred years of Christian teaching respecting the Jewish people.[2]

A Christian liturgy for Yom HaShoah[3] must bear this burden, and in some way prepare the way for this acknowledgment.

One function of corporate worship is to make the past live in the present in a meaningful way so that each generation experiences those events that help to give meaning to its own existence: acts of sacrifice, suffering, and redemption, moments of doubt, faith, and insight. Religious ceremony (liturgy and ritual) creates and keeps alive a common store of memory.

Alice Eckardt is Emeritus Professor of Religion at Lehigh University in Bethlehem, Pennsylvania. This chapter was originally printed under the title "In Consideration of Christian Yom HaShoah Liturgies" in *Shoah* 1, no. 4 (1979). It is reprinted here by permission from CLAL, The National Jewish Resource Center, 421 Seventh Avenue, New York, NY 10001.

    1. The fact that a few Christians here and there acted lovingly and sacrificially does not expunge or redeem the dreadful record of most church members and officials.

    2. Alice Eckardt, "Christian Responses to the *Endlösung*," *Religion in Life* 47, no. 1 (Spring 1978): 34–35. Gregory Baum is cited within this passage.

    3. This type of service may be observed in conjunction with the Jewish date of Yom HaShoah, or the date of Kristallnacht, or Anne Frank day, etc. See later comments regarding questions about Holy Week. A Roman Catholic priest in Memphis, Tennessee, suggested the addition of a "Feast of Atonement" to the Christian liturgical calendar.

Not only does public worship perpetuate the orienting events of faith history in new times and circumstances, but it should — if properly informed by responsible theology — build up "a significant deposit of moral reserves" on which its participants may draw when other ideologies attempt to subvert the proclaimed ethics of the community.[4]

Many of us are convinced that in this century events have occurred that must be seen and understood as new faith-orienting experiences — experiences that challenge much that we have professed and on which we have placed our trust. Therefore, even without a clear consensus about the full religious significance of these events, they must become part of the common store of memory through inclusion in the liturgical services of the churches as well as the synagogues. A new and surer "deposit of moral reserves" must be accumulated that will not evaporate when most needed, that will not include a self-destruct mechanism such as the dogmatic arrogance of the traditional Christian claim that presumed the right to destroy error.[5] These events are the Nazi Holocaust of European Jews and the rebirth of the State of Israel.

The primary task of any Holocaust memorial service is to engage the worshipers existentially in the plight of the Jewish families and communities trapped within the German Nazi state and its willing accomplices. Within my own congregation I have attempted to make meaningful the progressive denial of rights, human status, and life to the Jews of Europe by relating such denials to the congregation's own lives. Barriers of abstraction, of "foreignness," and of either overt or latent antisemitism must be overcome by the weight of the overwhelming human tragedy.

Unless it is an unusual congregation, a good deal of preparatory educational work should be done before the observance. If that is not feasible, the service should include a considerable amount of information. Even now, after the showing of the television drama "Holocaust," most gentile Christians know little about the Nazi "Final Solution," and even less about why Christians should concern themselves about it. The more informed a congregation is about the factual aspects, the more time and attention can be directed to other dimensions of the subject.

Planners of a Holocaust service must be clear in their own minds regarding its purpose and the ends to be achieved, since this will determine the form of the service and the choice of liturgical materials. This is particularly essential for this service because of the complexity of goals[6] and the psychological factors. I am convinced that no Christian service should be without a penitential confession of Christian failings and culpability. Since confession of sin and repentance are part of every Christian worship, to omit a specific confession on this occasion would be a continuation of the earlier sin. Donald McEvoy insists that the intent of a Christian Holocaust observance is not "to lay a 'guilt trip' " on the congregants but

---

4. Robert Willis, "Christian Theology after Auschwitz," *Journal of Ecumenical Studies* 12, no. 4 (Fall 1975): 494–95.

5. See the Rev. Theodore Loder, "Your People, My People," sermon in *On the Holocaust: Liturgies* (Philadelphia: National Institute on the Holocaust, 1978), 1:35–36.

6. Goals may include to educate; to share the suffering vicariously (as on Good Friday); to become sensitized to the consequences of hatred and idolatries; to remember the victims; to see the broader implications of moral issues; to help us understand our Jewish neighbors and the State of Israel; to become more aware of the past persecutions of Jews and of our own attitudes; to comprehend Christian failure to respond adequately to the needs of desperate people; to see where our teachings need changing, along with our rituals; to dedicate ourselves to Never Again; to raise theological questions.

through "acute awareness of the realities of that era [to] sensitize the Christian conscience and fortify the resolution that the mistakes of the past never be repeated."[7]

A great deal of learning and engagement come about through a congregational committee planning its own service. There are now a few helpful sources for both Christian and Jewish or interfaith groups to utilize, most noteworthy of which are the collection of twenty services and/or sermons by the National Institute on the Holocaust and "A Holocaust Memorial Service for Christians" prepared by Donald McEvoy for the National Conference of Christians and Jews.[8]

There are certain stipulations for a Christian observance of the Shoah that I believe must be insisted upon.

1. *Do not "Christianize" the Holocaust.* Hitler's "war against the Jews" was only incidentally an attack on the churches, an attack that depended on their willingness, or unwillingness, to accept Hitler's authority. The relatively small number of Christians who suffered or died on behalf of their faith and/or because of aiding the Nazis' primary victims must not be exaggerated, as if the church did not fail its test. Many Christian victims were imprisoned or killed for factors unrelated to their religious convictions or behavior. Polish clerics, for example, were often seized because they were perceived as symbols and potential leaders of Polish nationalism. Those Righteous Among the Gentiles (in this case, Among the Christians) are to be venerated and celebrated. The Dutch family of Corrie ten Boom with her father and sister, the French priests Père Marie-Benoit and Roger Braun, the German Catholics Father Bernhard Lichtenberg and laywoman Gertrud Lucknet, the Dutch Adventist John Weidner, the German Protestant pastors Paul Schneider, Hermann Maas, Heinrich Gruber, and the French Protestant congregation of André Trocmé — these are the true saints of the twentieth century. But they were the all too tiny faithful remnant. We dare not try to rewrite history to exonerate that which cannot be exonerated.

2. *Do not turn the Holocaust experience into a triumphalist demonstration of the truth of the Christian gospel.* This most monstrously evil event must *raise questions,* not support traditional answers, especially traditional answers that represent negation of Jewish existence and faith! An article in the *Church Herald* last year exemplifies Christian triumphalism applied to the Holocaust. After describing the hell that Auschwitz represented and the "psychological ploys" that inmates used to "escape the situation," the author points to "the members of one small group, Christians, [who] distinguished themselves by their refusal to turn inward. Rather they accepted the reality of their situation and lived for Christ by ministering to others." The author further asserts (as if proudly) that "in Auschwitz Protestant as well as Catholic clerics were singled out for special abuse," without any mention of the "special abuse" meted out to *all* Jewish arrivals. The author's intention is further revealed by his assertion that the martyr priest Maximilian Kolbe, who offered himself for execution in place of a fellow prisoner, did so with the words, "I'm a Christian and I'm not afraid to die." Yet Roll Hochhuth, who dedicated his play *The Deputy/Der Stellvertreter* to Father Kolbe, reports simply that the priest gave the reason that he was no longer fit for work.[9]

The love, courage, and faith of this band of Christians in Auschwitz is not being challenged here. What is being rejected is the audacity that would usurp "the Auschwitz

---

7. Donald McEvoy, *A Holocaust Memorial Service for Christians* (New York: National Conference of Christians and Jews, 1978), 5–6.

8. *On the Holocaust: Liturgies;* McEvoy, *A Holocaust Memorial Service for Christians.*

9. Roll Hochhuth, *The Deputy* (New York: Grove Press, 1964), 289.

experience" — that event most obsessionally fixated on Jews — and claim it as a validation of the Christian gospel and a demonstration of the superiority of the Christian faith: "When all else perished, Christ remained. And Christ was sufficient. The Auschwitz experience gives meaning to Paul's words to the Galatians: 'I have been crucified with Christ; it is no longer I who live, but Christ who lives in me' (Gal. 2:20). Christ lives, even in the fires of Auschwitz."[10]

By contrast to this triumphalistic misuse of the Christ figure we can offer worshipers other thoughts on which to meditate:

Had Jesus lived — or had he returned — during the Nazi era, he, too, would have been shot at the edge of a huge pit or been sent in the cattle cars to a death camp and gas chamber.[11] Just as crucifixion was the method of mass executions of Jews under the Romans, and Jesus suffered it with his compatriots, so shooting and gassing were the methods under the Nazi Germans, and he would not have been spared that death either.

"'The Christ-Messiah was in Auschwitz. With His brethren He suffered the Holocaust, once again on the Cross, as Marc Chagall has painted Him with tallith and tefillin. And we in the...so-called Christian world were the onlookers."[12] Even worse, baptized and communing Christians sent him and his people there. "Is it nothing to you, all you who pass by?" (Lam. 1:12).

"When the body of Christ is discovered at Auschwitz, it will be raised from among the victims, not hidden among the Catholic and Protestant and Orthodox guards and administrators."[13]

A Jewish poet of Vilna also links the crucified Christ to Jewish suffering:

> Close to the walls of the ghetto at Vilna there stands, blood-soaked,
>   a wooden cross.
> Endlessly suffering, the crucified Christ cries out:
> "Forgive the murderers, O Father: arouse those who are silent!"
> And as the wings of death brush by, he softly whispers in bliss:
> "Hear, O Israel..." Whitefaced, the Mother sinks to her knees:
> "O Father in heaven, you take our children, you lead us unto death;
> but if you leave some to give witness — speak then, O God,
>   speak out of their mouths."[14]

3. *Do not use readings from Jewish sources and then criticize, refute, or reinterpret them to fit Christian views.* Because we are the outsiders to the Shoah, we are particularly dependent on the testimony of the witnesses. The words, and art, and music of those who perished or survived the experience have an authenticity that must not be made the subject of disputation. Their power to disturb our consciences and awaken our spirits lies inescapably in their coming to us from out of the whirlwind.

---

10. Robert Gram, "Christ and the Auschwitz Experience," *Church Herald,* January 27, 1978, 4–5.
11. Emil Fackenheim, "The People Israel Lives," *Christian Century* 87, no. 18 (May 6, 1970): 568.
12. H. David Leuner, *Holocaust Memorial Service,* Jerusalem, 1975.
13. Franklin H. Littell, *The Crucifixion of the Jews* (New York: Harper & Row, 1975), 131.
14. Hermann Adler, quoted in Elisabeth Orsten, "Light in Darkness," in John M. Oesterreicher, ed., *The Bridge,* III (New York: Pantheon Books, 1958), 338–39.

Of the many eloquent testimonies of varying types, one of the most challenging is "Yossel Rakover's Appeal to God" by Zvi Koltiz.[15] This defiant affirmation of faith to the God whom the Hasid Rakover can only view as having veiled His countenance from the world and decided to sacrifice humankind to its wild instincts exceeds the Book of Job in both its accusations and its refusal to abandon belief. After Rakover's last words — the Sh'ma and a committing of his soul into the hands of the Lord (Ps. 31:4) — only awed silence is appropriate. We *must* reject the kind of false reading that accuses Rakover of having "the illusion that he can bang his fist on the table of the Almighty and demand answers to his complaints," the judging that faults him for desiring vengeance, or the nitpicking introduction of irrelevancies. But above all, we Christians are forbidden to do what the German Catholic editors did when they published this modern-day Job, namely, empty it of its power and undercut its challenge by a Christian apologetic that remains unchanged by the Shoah: "No, the angry God of the fathers . . . the God of Jesus Christ . . . is not an 'angry God,' even though He is Just. He is the God of incomprehensible love. . . . God's last and definitive word to the world and to history is not a word of vengeance but of love . . . spoken . . . through the passion and death of His only-begotten, his beloved Son."[16]

Too long now has Christianity taken the words of Hebrew Scripture and twisted them to fit Christian convictions. It is time we read that Scripture in its own right and for its own revelations. How much more is this true with regard to the new Torah written and being written in our own day! It is time for us to listen and to remain silent.

4. *Do not attempt to strip the Holocaust of its terrifying and awesome character.* Do not take refuge in circumlocution or abstract language. We are called to face the reality in its stark horror and in its betrayal of humanity, for only in so doing will we be forced to recoil from any kind of "explanations" or excuses. Only then will we realize that the Holocaust must be so etched in the collective as well as individual consciousness that it will become "a plumb line by which we [will] measure our response to every denial of human rights and every circumstance of tyranny."[17]

Numbers are abstractions: "six million" can become too remote to have meaning. Yet the numbers do have significance. At some indeterminate point the accumulation of numbers is indicative of a qualitative change. The murder of one person is still murder and crime against humanity. But the murder of six million people becomes something more. To give it a name, "genocide," is even more abstract. And so we must resort to two strategies. First, make the number of six million relevant by comparing it to the population of a certain number of towns or cities with which the congregation can relate. Secondly, use the building blocks of 1+1+1+ . . . : tell the stories of *this* girl Eva Heyman, *this* boy Moshe Flinker, *this* father Shlomo Wiesel, *this* mother Lena Donat, *this* grandmother and grandfather Racz. "I don't want to die, because I've hardly lived."[18] This cry of a thirteen-year-old girl wondering if she will meet the fate her closest friend had already met breaks through the walls we try to build around the Holocaust to shield ourselves from its terror and accusation.

5. *Remember the total abandonment Jews experienced.* The lack of simple and ordinary gestures of sympathy or kindness were more devastating to the victims' spirits than the cruelty of the officials and guards. We, the fortunate, must not close ourselves off from suf-

---

15. In Albert Friedlander, ed., *Out of the Whirlwind* (New York: Schocken, 1976).
16. Elisabeth Orsten and *Stimmen der Zeit* in Oesterreicher, *The Bridge*, 335–38.
17. McEvoy, *A Holocaust Memorial Service for Christians*, 6.
18. *The Diary of Eva Heyman* (Jerusalem: Yad Vashem, 1964), 65.

fering wherever it is felt. The role of indifferent bystander has been revealed all too clearly as the accomplice of those with evil intentions. We are reminded most vividly of Jesus' own words on this subject:

> I was hungry and you gave me no food, I was thirsty and you gave me no drink, I was a stranger and you did not welcome me, naked and you did not clothe me, sick and in prison and you did not visit me.... Truly I say to you, as you did it not to one of the least of these my brethren, you did it not to me. (Matt. 25:42–45)

In this account we have a compelling reason for Christian liturgies centering on the Holocaust. We dare not ignore or forget those six million lives or the meaning they have for our own.

6. *Finally, do not allow a Yom HaShoah service to become a one-time occurrence.* We are building a common store of memory, and that is accomplished only through repetition and emphasis. Every year we observe the death of one Jew almost two thousand years ago. Should we not each year remember the death of six million of his people? and ask what that says to us? Should we relate the two observances? In Claremont, California, alongside the annual service of Good Friday an ecumenical prayer vigil was held as "A Christian Witness to the Memory of the Holocaust of Six Million Jews." A statement was also issued by the participants.

Do not make this service the only time during the year when the whole area of Christian-Jewish relations is considered. A Holocaust memorial service should be the *beginning* of new awareness and sensitivity, and of efforts to build new bridges of understanding and support across the lines of faith, so that as Christians we will never again send others down the bloody path to Ponar and Auschwitz, Babi Yar and Chelmno, Buchenwald and Belzec, Terezin and Treblinka, Dachau and Sobibor, Mauthausen and Maidanek.[19]

Having considered carefully the guidelines and goals, the components of the service can then be marked out. Words can be very powerful and are central to most worship services. But they should be reinforced and brought to life by the use of other means of communication. Silence as a counterpoise is not only effective but at times almost obligatory. Appropriate music, particularly some of the songs written in the ghettos, can sometimes have an impact far beyond the spoken word. Visual images — enlarged pictures, slides, films and filmstrips — are invaluable aids, and there are many good resources. Ritual acts such as candle lighting and candle extinguishing can be given a new meaning in the setting of a memorial service for the six million through creative imagination: Extinguishing six out of eleven candles can demonstrate the proportion of European Jews murdered; lighting six candles in memory of each of the six million can accompany six readings or a recital of names of the major killing centers or the countries or origin; the lighting of a seventh candle for the State of Israel as a symbol of the new hope and new existence/resurrection of the Jewish people would be most appropriate. The wearing of a Star of David armband by all participants in the service may give an immediacy of relationship that can be most significant. Liturgical dance offers a new dimension of expression. The use of art and poetry produced by Jews during or after the Holocaust may help us to rediscover the inner meaning of some traditional imagery that Christianity has torn out of its original Jewish setting. Abraham

---

19. See *On the Holocaust: Liturgies,* 57.

Rattner's artistic renditions of Moses, Job, and Christ reveal the continuity of their anguish and their grasping for the truth. The poetry of Hermann Adler (quoted briefly earlier) links Jewish suffering in the Holocaust to the suffering of Jesus, as it also links the bereft mother of Jesus with a Christian heroine of the Shoah who is called "a new madonna."[20]

In a way that many find strange, and yet is not, Christian Holocaust services can deepen and enrich the life of a congregation in a most unique and significant way by wresting theology from dogma and opening it up to existential re-evaluation (a re-evaluation shared at certain levels with our Jewish friends), by making the faithful more aware of the necessity of examining moral decisions more fully than ever before, and by sensitizing the worshipers to the experiences and responses in the Holocaust of the people from whose midst their own faith initially sprang and onto whose roots their own community claims to be engrafted.

---

20. Barry Ulanov, "Abraham Rattner, Painter of Anguish," and Elisabeth Orsten, "Light in Darkness," in *The Bridge,* 388–98 and 377–79.

3

Harvest of Hate/Seeds of Love:
Remembering the Voices That Were Silenced
JEWISH-CHRISTIAN DIALOGUE GROUP OF CEDAR RAPIDS

In the presence of eyes
which witnessed the slaughter,
which saw the oppression
the heart could not bear,
and as witness the heart
that once taught compassion
until days came to pass
that crushed human feeling,
I have taken an oath: To remember it all,
to remember, not once to forget!
Forget not one thing to the last generation
when degradation shall cease,
to the last, to its ending,
when the rod of instruction
shall have come to conclusion.
An oath: Not in vain passed over
the night of terror.
An oath: No morning shall see
me at flesh pots again.
An oath: Lest from this we learned nothing.

—Abraham Shlonsky

(The original poem may be seen in the Yad Vashem Holocaust Memorial in Jerusalem.)

This service was organized and funded by the Jewish-Christian Dialogue Group of Cedar Rapids, Iowa, consisting of clergy, laity, and professors from Coe, Cornell, and Mt. Mercy Colleges.

ORDER OF SERVICE

Prelude

Greetings and Remarks . . . . Dr. Glenn Janus

Introit

Invocation . . . . The Rev. Carolyn Myers

Call to Worship

Leader:	Now in the presence of loved ones and friends,
People:	Before us the symbols and memories of loved ones lost,
Leader:	We gather for this sacred observance,
People:	The house of Israel and Christian sisters and brothers.
Leader:	For the sake of those who died,
People:	We are linking and bonding the past with the future.
Leader:	In coming together to remember the victims of the Holocaust, we say that all life is sacred.
People:	In lighting candles for six million Jews and five million others we preserve their memory.
Leader:	With every light we kindle this evening we pledge ourselves to remember, not once to forget.
People:	And we commit the victims and martyrs to your eternal care, O Lord,
Unison:	Remembering that whether we take the wings of the morning, or dwell in the uttermost parts of the sea, even there, Your hand will hold us, and your right hand will guide us.

Hymn

GOD OF OUR FATHERS

God of our fathers, whose almighty hand
Leads forth in beauty all the starry band
Of shining worlds in splendor through the skies,
Our grateful songs before Thy throne arise.

Thy love divine hath led us in the past,
In this free land by Thee our lot is cast;
Be Thou our ruler, guardian, guide, and stay,
Thy word our law, Thy paths our chosen way.

From war's alarm, from deadly pestilence,
Be Thy strong arm our ever sure defense;
Thy true religion in our hearts increase,
Thy bounteous goodness nourish us in peace.

Refresh Thy people on their toilsome way,
Lead us from night to never-ending day;
Fill all our lives with love and grace divine,
And glory, laud, and praise be ever Thine.

Amen.

HISTORICAL BACKGROUND AND LIGHTING OF THE CANDLES

RABBI EDWARD CHESMAN   DR. RICHARD THOMAS
DR. DAVID WEDDLE

The Memorial Candles for the Eleven Million:
Six Million Jews, Five Million Others

The Holocaust was the systematic, bureaucratic annihilation of six million Jews by the Nazis and their collaborators as a central act of state during the Second World War; as night descended, millions of other people were swept into this net of death. It was a crime unique in the annals of human history, different not only in the quantity of violence — the sheer numbers killed — but in its manner and purpose as a mass criminal enterprise organized by the state against defenseless civilian populations. The decision to kill every Jew everywhere in Europe: the definition of Jew as target for death transcended all boundaries....

Lighting of Memorial Candle: Auschwitz

Elie Wiesel, survivor of Auschwitz, stated: "We will accomplish a mission that the victims have assigned to us: to collect memories and tears, fragments of fire and sorrow, tales of despair and defiance, and names — above all — names."

What we all have in common is an obsession not to betray the dead we left behind or who left us behind. They were killed once. They must not be killed again through forgetfulness.

Response: O Lord, remember your martyred people, as we pledge to remember them. And may their memory be for us a challenge and an inspiration.

Lighting of Memorial Candle: Dachau

The Holocaust was not simply a throwback to medieval torture or archaic barbarism but a thoroughly modern expression of bureaucratic organization, industrial management, scientific achievement, and technological sophistication. The entire apparatus of the German bureaucracy was marshalled in the service of the extermination process....

Response: O Lord, remember your martyred people, as we pledge to remember them.
And may their memory be for us a challenge and an inspiration.

Lighting of Memorial Candle: Buchenwald

The following words were found scratched on the walls of a cellar in Cologne, Germany,
where Jews hid from Nazis who would take their lives:

> I believe in the sun,
> even when it is not shining.
> I believe in love
> even when I don't feel it.
> I believe in God,
> even when He is silent.

Response: O Lord, remember your martyred people, as we pledge to remember them.
And may their memory be for us a challenge and an inspiration.

Lighting of Memorial Candle: Treblinka

The Reverend Martin Niemoeller, a pastor in the German Confessing Church, spent seven
years in a concentration camp. He wrote the following words:

> First they came for the communists,
> and I did not speak out —
> because I was not a communist.
> Then they came for the socialists,
> and I did not speak out —
> because I was not a socialist.
> Then they came for the trade unionists,
> and I did not speak out —
> because I was not a trade unionist.
> Then they came for the Jews,
> and I did not speak out —
> because I was not a Jew.
> Then they came for me —
> and there was no one left
> to speak out for me.

Response: O Lord, remember your martyred people, as we pledge to remember them.
And may their memory be for us a challenge and an inspiration.

Lighting of Memorial Candle: Bergen-Belsen

The following words come from the book *Man's Search for Meaning,* written by Victor Frankl:

> We who lived in the concentration camps can remember the men who walked through the huts comforting others, giving away their last pieces of bread. They may have been few in number, but they offer a sufficient proof that everything can be taken from a man but one thing: the last of his freedoms — to choose one's attitude in any given set of circumstances, to choose one's own way to die.

> *Response:* O Lord, remember your martyred people, as we pledge to remember them. And may their memory be for us a challenge and an inspiration.

Lighting of Memorial Candle: Sobibor

The following words come from Anne Frank's diary. They are dated July 15, 1944:

> It's really a wonder that I haven't dropped all my ideals, because they seem so absurd and impossible to carry out. Yet I keep them, because in spite of everything I still believe that people are really good at heart. I simply can't build up my hopes on a foundation consisting of confusion, misery, and death.
>
> I can see the world gradually being turned into a wilderness, I hear the ever approaching thunder, which will destroy us too, I can feel the sufferings of millions — and yet, if I look into the heavens, I think that it will all come out right, that this cruelty too will end, and that peace and tranquillity will return again.
>
> In the meantime, I must uphold my ideals, for perhaps the time will come when I shall be able to carry them out.

> *Response:* O Lord, remember your martyred people, as we pledge to remember them. And may their memory be for us a challenge and an inspiration.

Lighting Memorial Candle: Theresienstadt

On April 12, 1945, General Dwight D. Eisenhower, Supreme Commander of the Allied Forces Europe, wrote the following words in a letter to George Marshall, his Chief of Staff — describing his first visit to one of the camps liberated by U.S. forces:

> The things I saw beggar description. . . . The visual evidence and the verbal testimony of starvation, cruelty, and bestiality were so overpowering as to leave me a bit sick.
>
> In one room, where there were piled up twenty or thirty naked men killed by starvation, George Patton would not even enter. He said he would get sick if he did so.
>
> I made the visit deliberately, in order to be in a position to give first-hand evidence of these things if ever, in the future, there develops a tendency to charge these allegations merely to "propaganda."

Response: O Lord, remember your martyred people, as we pledge to remember them.
And may their memory be for us a challenge and an inspiration.

Proclamation: Days of Remembrance . . . . BILL VAUGHN
Executive Director for Civil Rights of Cedar Rapids

Introduction of the Speaker . . . . DR. CHARLES VERNOFF

Address: A Christian Remembers the Holocaust . . . . FRANKLIN LITTELL

Anthem: "El Maleh Rachamim" . . . . sung by RICHARD HARMON

Responsive Reading . . . . FR. MICHAEL TAUKE

Leader: Lord, as we gather today,
We pray for courage, and for strength.

People: When we remember the evils in the past,
The innocents tortured, maimed, and murdered.

Leader: We are almost afraid to make ourselves remember.
But we are even more afraid to forget.

People: We ask for wisdom, that we might mourn,
And not be consumed by hatred.

Leader: That we might remember,
and yet not lose hope.

People: We must face evil —
And, so doing, reaffirm our faith in future good.

Leader: We cannot erase yesterday's pains,
But we can vow that they will not have been suffered in vain.

People: And so, we pray:
For those who were given death,
Let us choose life —
for us and for generations yet to come.

Leader: For those who found courage to stand against evil —
often at the cost of their lives
Let us vow to carry on their struggle.

People: We must teach ourselves, and our children:
To learn from hate that we must love,
To learn from evil to live for good.

Hymn: "O God Our Help in Ages Past"

O God, our help in ages past,
Our hope for years to come,
Our shelter from the stormy blast,
And our eternal home.

Under the shadow of Thy throne
Thy saints have dwelt secure,
Sufficient is their arm alone,
And our defense is sure.

Before the hills in order stood,
Or earth received her frame,
From everlasting Thou art God,
To endless years the same.

A thousand ages in Thy sight
Are like an evening gone,
Short as the watch that ends the night
Before the rising sun.

Time, like an ever-rolling stream,
Bears all its sons away,
They fly, forgotten, as a dream
Dies at the opening day.

O God, our help in ages past,
Our hope for years to come,
Be Thou our guide while life shall last,
And our eternal home.

                                        Amen.

Benediction .... JAMES DUNIGAN AND CATHERINE QUEHL-ENGEL

Benediction Response

Postlude: Recessional .... ERNEST BLOCH

Participants in the Service:

Rabbi Edward Chesman, Rabbi of Temple Judah
Mr. James Dunigan, St. Matthew Parish
Richard Harmon, Temple Judah
Dr. Glenn Janus, Coe College, All Saints Parish
The Rev. Carolyn Myers, First Lutheran Church
Ms. Catherine Quehl-Engel, Mt. Vernon
Sister Mary Sylvester, Sacred Heart Convent, Organist
Fr. Michael Tauke, Mt. Mercy College
Dr. Richard Thomas, Chaplain, Cornell College
Bill Vaughn, Executive Director of Civil Rights for Cedar Rapids
Dr. Charles Vernoff, Cornell College
Dr. David Weddle, Cornell College

Lighting the Memorial Candles:

Marianne Bern, Temple Judah
Marc Goldman, student, Cornell College
Davida Handler, Temple Judah
Jim Handler, Temple Judah
Naomi Magnus, student, Cornell College
Fred Rogers, Temple Judah
Muriel Rogers, Temple Judah

4

Art Amidst Death:
The Cultural Life of Theresienstadt
A Musical Remembrance
MADISON JEWISH COMMUNITY COUNCIL

Introduction

ROBERT SKLOOT

Sonata for Piano (1943) — Gideon Klein (1919–1945)
Allegro con fuoco
Adagio
Allegro vivace
Howard Karp, piano

"Säerspruch" (1943) — Viktor Ullmann (1898–1944)
Richard Bessman, baritone
Howard Karp, piano

"Wiegenlied" (1942) — Gideon Klein
Deborah Martin-Semrow, mezzo-soprano
Howard Karp, piano

Trio for violin, viola, and violoncello (1944) — Gideon Klein
Allegro
Variations on a Moravian Folk Song
Molto vivace
Jae-Kyung Kim, violin
Sally Chisholm, viola
Parry Karp, violoncello

Sponsored by the Madison (Wisconsin) Jewish Community Council, including representatives of Beth Israel Center, B'nai B'rith Hillel Foundation, and Temple Beth El.

About Gideon Klein: Born in Prerov, Czechoslovakia, on December 6, 1919, Gideon Klein studied at the Prague Conservatory and Charles University until the anti-Jewish laws of the 1930s forced him to suspend his studies. He performed under several pseudonyms to evade the ban on Jewish artists.

Klein's pre-imprisonment compositions were discovered only in 1990, including his *String Quartet, Op. 2,* written in August 1940. He was deported to Theresienstadt in December 1941, where he wrote choral works for the Jewish choral group and completed the *Fantasie and Fugue for String Quartet,* and *Piano Sonata* in October 1943. He completed his last work, the *String Trio* (in three movements) on October 9, 1944, nine days before he was transported to Auschwitz. In this last work, "the first and last movements contain the spirited flavor of lively Czech folk dance rhythms and melodies. In the second movement, Klein develops a set of variations on a Moravian folk song." He died in the Furstengrubbe Concentration Camp in January 1945.

Klein's musical colleague, the world famous conductor (and Theresienstadt/Auschwitz survivor) Karl Ancerl, wrote this about his close friend:

> The first time I met Gideon was in a loft in Terezin, where he tried to repair an old broken piano. The piano soon stood on stools that replaced legs. It was tuned and Gideon began practicing. He played his favorite Mozart, Brahms, and Janacek for us. He formed chamber ensembles and achieved so high a standard that we would not be ashamed even in Prague. He organized solo concerts and performed Bach as well as modern music, works by other composers living in Terezin, and his own compositions.... Shortly before the transport to Auschwitz he began to conduct.... Had he survived he could have been one of the best, and could have achieved the highest standard as a pianist, composer, and conductor.

About Viktor Ullmann: Viktor Ullmann, born in Teschen, Czechoslovakia, in 1898, was Klein's older contemporary who had established a considerable international reputation as a composer, conductor, and orchestrator by the time he was deported to Theresienstadt in September 1942. While there, he served as a music critic and reviewer, and the record of his writings attests to the musical vitality in the cultural life of the camp. He wrote twenty surviving musical compositions, including a string quartet, three piano sonatas, the opera *Der Kaiser von Atlantis,* and a number of songs. Together with his wife, Elizabeth, he was sent to Auschwitz on October 16, 1994, where he died.

[Taken, in part, from liner notes to *Chamber Music from Theresienstadt: 1941–1945,* Channel Classics CD #CCS 1691, 1991. Produced by the Terezin Chamber Music Foundation.]

About Howard Karp: Born in Chicago, Howard Karp is a graduate of the Oberlin Conservatory and the Juilliard School of Music. Additional studies were completed in Vienna and Italy.

Mr. Karp is Professor of Music at the University of Wisconsin–Madison School of Music. He has given solo recitals throughout the United States and won acclaim in Europe for concerts in Vienna, London, Brussels, Amsterdam, Budapest, among other cities. He is a frequent performer of chamber music, appearing in duo and duet recitals with his wife,

Frances, and sonata performances with his son and colleague, Parry, cellist of the Pro Arte Quartet.

Mr. Karp has taught at the Universities of Illinois and Kentucky and has been a Fulbright Scholar. His recording with the Pro Arte Quartet of the Piano Quintets Nos. 1 and 2 by Ernest Bloch has just been released on Laurel Record (LR 848-CD).

Members of the Pro Arte Quartet

Jae-Kyung Kim, violin: Born in South Korea, Miss Kim came to the United States at the age of thirteen. She holds a master's degree from the Peabody Conservatory in Baltimore. A prize-winning violinist, she has performed in the Spoleto Festival and the Aspen Music Festival, among others. In the summer of 1989, she joined the Monte Verde Quartet at the Rocky Ridge Music Center in Colorado. Miss Kim has been a member of the Pro Arte Quartet since 1988.

Sally Chisholm, viola: A philosophy graduate of the University of Oklahoma with a master's degree in viola from Indiana University, Chisholm was a founding member of the Thouvenal String Quartet. She has toured internationally and performed with the Kronos Quartet. She joined the Pro Arte Quartet and the faculty of the UW School of Music in 1991.

Parry Karp, violoncello: Mr. Karp was invited to join the Pro Arte Quartet in 1976 at the age of twenty-one. He is Associate Professor of Music and Director of the String Chamber Music Program at the UW. A graduate of the University of Illinois, he won the National String Artist Competition in 1977. A frequent solo recitalist throughout the United States and abroad, Mr. Karp is a recording artist currently completing the premiere recording of the three unaccompanied cello suites of Ernest Bloch.

Richard Bessman, baritone: Richard Bessman, a native Madisonian, has performed in religious services at Beth Israel Center and Temple Beth El as well as Sha'arei Shamayim, Madison's Reconstructionist congregation. He has entertained for the Jewish Social Services *Lechayim* and various theatrical productions in Madison. He is currently studying voice with Patricia Nelson in Milwaukee.

Deborah Martin-Semrow, mezzo-soprano: Deborah Martin-Semrow has sung professionally in many genres: opera, art song, oratorio, music theater. She obtained her formal training with a bachelor of music with honors from the New England Conservatory of Music and a master of music degree from Boston Conservatory. She has sung with such organizations as the Boston Symphony, Wolf Trap, Dayton Opera, St. Paul Chamber Orchestra and Cincinnati Opera. She is currently the Cantorial Soloist and Music Director at Temple Beth El.

Further Reading about Life and Art in Theresienstadt

Bondy, Ruth. *"Elder of the Jews": Jacob Edelstein of Theresienstadt.* New York, 1981.
Green, Gerald. *The Artists of Terezin.* New York, 1968.
Karas, Joza. *Music in Terezin.* New York, 1985.
Massachusetts College of Art. *Seeing through "Paradise": Artists and the Terezin Concentration Camp.* Boston, 1991.
Prague State Jewish Museum. *I Never Saw Another Butterfly: Children's Drawings and Poems from the Theresienstadt Concentration Camp, 1942–44.* New York, 1964.
Troller, Norbert. *Theresienstadt: Hitler's Gift to the Jews.* Chapel Hill, N.C., 1991.

[The sponsors of the event wish to acknowledge the invaluable assistance of Mark Ludwig of the Terezin Chamber Music Foundation, Boston, and of Jerry Borsuk.]

Madison Jewish Community Council
Yom HaShoah Committee
310 North Midvale Boulevard, Suite 325
Madison, Wisconsin 53705

Hannah Rosenthal, Chair
including representatives of
Beth Israel Center
B'nai B'rith Hillel Foundation
Temple Beth El

5

An Interfaith Holocaust Remembrance Service
Houston Education Center and Holocaust Museum

What Was the Holocaust?

The Holocaust was the planned, systematic attempt by the Nazis and their active supporters to annihilate every Jewish man, woman, and child in the world. Largely unopposed by the free world, it resulted in the murder of six million Jews. This calculated campaign of the destruction of Jewish life began in January 1933 in Europe and continued without respite for nearly twelve years.

Mass annihilation is not unique in the history of this century. The Nazis, however, stand alone in their utilization of state power and modern science and technology to destroy a people. While other people were swept into the Third Reich's net of death, the Nazis with cold calculation focused on destroying Jews, not because they were a political or economic threat, but simply because they were Jews.[1]

In nearly every country the Nazis occupied during the war, Jews were rounded up, isolated from the native population, brutally forced into detention camps, and ultimately deported to labor and death camps. Jews everywhere in Europe were unconditionally targeted for death; all were to share the same fate. An estimated 65 to 70 percent of all Jews in Europe, including virtually all German and Eastern European Jews, were killed.[2]

In addition to the six million Jewish men, women, and children who were murdered, at least five million non-Jews were victims of the Nazi regime. These victims included Poles, Slavs, Serbs, Czechs, Gypsies, Greeks, Italians, Russians, Spaniards, Jehovah's Witnesses, homosexuals, and physically and mentally handicapped people.

O God, Our Help in Ages Past

1. O God, our help in ages past,
   Our hope for years to come,
   Our shelter from the stormy blast,
   And our eternal home.

2. Under the shadow of your throne
   Your saints have dwelt secure;
   Sufficient is your arm alone,
   And our defense is sure.

---

1. Karen Shawn, "The End of Innocence: Anne Frank and the Holocaust," course study, 89.
2. Ibid.

3. Before the hills in order stood,
   Or earth received its frame,
   From everlasting you are God,
   To endless years the same.
4. A thousand ages in your sight
   Are like an evening gone,
   Short as the watch that ends the night
   Before the rising sun.

Choir will sing fifth verse solo
5. Time like an ever-rolling stream.
   Soon bears us all away
   We fly forgotten as a dream
   Dies at the op'ning day.
6. O God, our help in ages past,
   Our hope for years to come,
   Still be our guard while troubles last,
   And our eternal home.

The Memorial

O God, at this hour of memorial, we recall with loving reverence all of Your children who have perished through the cruelty of the oppressor: the aged and the young, the learned and the simple, driven in multitudes along the road of pain and pitiless death. Their very presence on earth was begrudged them, for they brought to mind the recollection of Your covenant of mercy and justice.

For no sin of theirs did they perish, but because they were a symbol of Your eternal teaching. They have died, as did the martyrs of bygone days, for the sanctification of Your name on earth.

We pray, Merciful God, that Your law, to which Your children have borne witness in life and death, shed now a renewed light in our hearts, and that all these martyrs, nameless to us but known to You, shall not have suffered in vain. May their memory be an enduring blessing to all Your children.

They lie in nameless graves. Their resting places in far-off forests and lonely fields are lost to the eyes of revering kin. Yet they shall not be forgotten. We take them into our hearts and give them a place beside the cherished memories of our beloved. They are now ours. Amen.

Candle Lighting

Tonight we light eleven candles in memory of the six million Jewish people killed in the Holocaust and the five million other victims of the Nazi regime. We light candles in memory of all the men, young and old, who perished in the camps — the elderly and infirm who were immediately sent to death, the young and healthy who were worked to their deaths, to all those who were executed.

We light candles in memory of all the women, young and old, who perished in the camps — mothers who witnessed the deaths of their children, women who risked all to bring new life into the death camps, mothers who had to choose the life of one child over another, or their life over their child's. We light candles in memory of the children — of young lives snuffed out before they had a chance to live, dreams never fully dreamt, let alone realized, childhoods cut short. We light candles in honor and memory of those who survived, who lived through the nightmare and began life anew, those who had the strength to reopen their wounds to share stories with later generations, and those for whom the memory was too painful to bear. We light candles in honor and memory of those righteous gentiles who risked their lives to save Jewish lives, who hid neighbor or stranger, who brought them food, who tended their wounds. We light candles to honor those who brought the only light to a gloomy world, who brought hope when all was dark....

The Reverend Martin Niemoeller, a pastor in the German Confessing Church, spent seven years in a concentration camp. He wrote the following words:

> First they came for the communists,
> and I did not speak out —
> because I was not a communist.
> Then they came for the socialists,
> and I did not speak out —
> because I was not a socialist.
> Then they came for the trade unionists
> and I did not speak out —
> because I was not a trade unionist.
> Then they came for the Jews,
> and I did not speak out —
> because I was not a Jew.
> Then they came for me —
> and there was no one left
> to speak out for me.

The following passage is an excerpt from Night *written by Elie Wiesel:*

Never shall I forget that night, the first night in camp, which has turned my life into one long night, seven times cursed and seven times sealed. Never shall I forget that smoke. Never shall I forget the little faces of the children, whose bodies I saw turned to wreaths of smoke beneath a silent blue sky. Never shall I forget those flames which consumed my faith forever.

Never shall I forget the nocturnal silence which deprived me, for all eternity, of the desire to live. Never shall I forget those moments which murdered my God and my soul and turned my dreams to dust. Never shall I forget these things, even if I am condemned to live as long as God himself. Never.

On April 12, 1945, General Dwight D. Eisenhower, Supreme Commander of the Allied Forces Europe, wrote the following words in a letter to George Marshall, his Chief of Staff — describing his first visit to one of the camps liberated by U.S. forces:

The things I saw beggar description.... The visual evidence and the verbal testimony of starvation, cruelty, and bestiality were so overpowering as to leave me a bit sick.

In one room, where there were piled up twenty or thirty naked men killed by starvation, George Patton would not even enter. He said he would get sick if he did so.

I made the visit deliberately, in order to be in a position to give first-hand evidence of these things if ever, in the future, there develops a tendency to charge these allegations merely to "propaganda."

The following words come from Anne Frank's diary. They are dated July 15, 1944:

It's really a wonder that I haven't dropped all my ideals, because they seem so absurd and impossible to carry out. Yet I keep them, because in spite of everything I still believe that people are really good at heart. I simply can't build up my hopes on a foundation consisting of confusion, misery, and death.

I can see the world gradually being turned into a wilderness, I hear the ever approaching thunder, which will destroy us too, I can feel the sufferings of millions — and yet, if I look into the heavens, I think that it will all come out right, that this cruelty too will end, and that peace and tranquility will return again.

In the meantime, I must uphold my ideals, for perhaps the time will come when I shall be able to carry them out.

Let now an Infinite Presence enter our souls, hearts, and minds, teaching us gentleness and melting our hardness, making us more sensitive to the needs of our neighbors and more responsive to their pleas for help.

Those whose faces we forget from one encounter to the next.
and those who never seem to find a resting place in the family of the secure
All whose minds are clouded or weak,
and those who bear the burden of broken bodies;
Those who are alone, unloved, with none to love,
the orphaned and widowed, deserted husbands, wives, and children;
All who are deprived of rights by the callousness of others,
and all who have been driven from their homes by wars they never made.
We sin against You when we sin against our fellow human beings,
For our sins of indifference, O God, we ask forgiveness;
For the sin of callousness in the face of human suffering and hunger;
For the sin of playing it safe when moral issues flame up in our communities
and in the world;
For the sin of cynicism and of patronizing the moral passion of the few
because they upset the careful arrangements of our lives;
For the sin of smirking at others, whether Jews who worship differently
or Christians who believe differently;
For the sin of feeling so comfortable that we are no longer bothered by the misery
of others;
For the sin of saying the words "covenant and mission and peace and justice"
but failing to carry them out;
For the sin of wrongdoing our neighbor, by wounding people with unkind words
or insulting epithets;
For the sin of slander, malice and spite;

For the sin of causeless hatreds: closing our hearts and our neighborhoods
to other races;
*For the sin we have committed by polluting our children's attitudes with our
prejudices;*
For the sins we have committed by not seeing God's image in every human being,
*For all these sins, O merciful God,
forgive us, pardon us, grant us atonement.*

PRAYER OF ST. FRANCIS

Lord, make us instruments of thy peace.
Where there is hatred, let us sow love;
Where there is injury, pardon;
Where discord, union;
Where there is doubt, sow faith;
Where despair and darkness, sow hope and light;
Where there is sadness, sow joy!
For thy mercy, and thy truth's sake, Amen.

—Prayer of St. Francis
Sebastian Temple, 1967

Speaker Presentation

BLESSED IS THE MATCH

Blessed is the match consumed in kindling flame.
Blessed is the flame that burns in the heart's secret places.
Blessed is the heart with strength to stop its beating for honor's sake.
Blessed is the match consumed in kindling flame.

In Memory of the Victims

אֵל מָלֵא רַחֲמִים שׁוֹכֵן בַּמְּרוֹמִים הַמְצֵא מְנוּחָה נְכוֹנָה תַּחַת
כַּנְפֵי הַשְּׁכִינָה בְּמַעֲלוֹת קְדוֹשִׁים וּטְהוֹרִים כְּזֹהַר הָרָקִיעַ מַזְהִירִים,
אֶת־נִשְׁמוֹת כָּל־אַחֵינוּ בְּנֵי יִשְׂרָאֵל, אֲנָשִׁים נָשִׁים וָטַף, שֶׁנֶּהֶרְגוּ
וְשֶׁנִּטְבְּחוּ וְשֶׁנִּשְׂרְפוּ וְשֶׁנֶּחְנְקוּ. בְּגַן עֵדֶן תְּהֵי מְנוּחָתָם. אָנָּא בַּעַל
הָרַחֲמִים, הַסְתִּירֵם בְּסֵתֶר כְּנָפֶיךָ לְעוֹלָמִים וּצְרֹר בִּצְרוֹר הַחַיִּים
אֶת־נִשְׁמוֹתֵיהֶם. יְיָ הוּא נַחֲלָתָם, וְיָנוּחוּ בְשָׁלוֹם עַל מִשְׁכְּבוֹתֵיהֶם.
וְנֹאמַר אָמֵן.

Exalted, compassionate God, grant perfect peace in Your sheltering Presence, among
the holy and the pure, to the souls of all our brethren, men, women, and children who
were slaughtered and burned. May their memory endure, inspiring truth and loyalty

in our lives. May their souls thus be bound up in the bond of life. May they rest in peace. And let us say: Amen.

God, the generations rise and pass away before You. You are the strength of those who labor; You are the rest of the blessed dead. We remember all who have lived in faith, all who have died, and especially those most dear to us who rest in eternal peace.... Give us in time our portion with those who have trusted in You and have striven to do Your holy will. To Your name, we ascribe all honor and glory, now and forever.

Mourner's Kaddish

קדיש יתום

יִתְגַּדַּל וְיִתְקַדַּשׁ שְׁמֵהּ רַבָּא בְּעָלְמָא דִּי־בְרָא כִרְעוּתֵהּ,
Yit·ga·dal ve·yit·ka·dash she·mei ra·ba be·al·ma di·ve·ra chi·re·u·tei,

וְיַמְלִיךְ מַלְכוּתֵהּ בְּחַיֵּיכוֹן וּבְיוֹמֵיכוֹן וּבְחַיֵּי דְכָל־בֵּית
ve·yam·lich mal·chu·tei be·cha·yei·chon u·ve·yo·mei·chon u·ve·cha·yei
de·chol beit

יִשְׂרָאֵל, בַּעֲגָלָא וּבִזְמַן קָרִיב, וְאִמְרוּ: אָמֵן.
Yis·ra·eil, ba·a·ga·la u·vi·ze·man ka·riv, ve·i·me·ru: a·mein.

יְהֵא שְׁמֵהּ רַבָּא מְבָרַךְ לְעָלַם וּלְעָלְמֵי עָלְמַיָּא.
Ye·hei she·mei ra·ba me·va·rach le·a·lam u·le·al·mei al·ma·ya.

יִתְבָּרַךְ וְיִשְׁתַּבַּח, וְיִתְפָּאַר וְיִתְרוֹמַם וְיִתְנַשֵּׂא, וְיִתְהַדָּר
Yit·ba·rach ve·yish·ta·bach, ve·yit·pa·ar ve·yit·ro·mam ve·yit·na·sei, ve·yit·ha·dar

וְיִתְעַלֶּה וְיִתְהַלָּל שְׁמֵהּ דְּקֻדְשָׁא, בְּרִיךְ הוּא, לְעֵלָּא מִן־כָּל־
ve·yit·a·leh ve·yit·ha·lal she·mei de·ku·de·sha, be·rich hu, le·ei·la min kol

בִּרְכָתָא וְשִׁירָתָא, תֻּשְׁבְּחָתָא וְנֶחֱמָתָא דַּאֲמִירָן בְּעָלְמָא,
bi·re·cha·ta ve·shi·ra·ta, tush·be·cha·ta ve·ne·che·ma·ta, da·a·mi·ran be·al·ma,

וְאִמְרוּ: אָמֵן.
ve·i·me·ru: a·mein.

יְהֵא שְׁלָמָא רַבָּא מִן־שְׁמַיָּא וְחַיִּים עָלֵינוּ וְעַל־כָּל־יִשְׂרָאֵל,
Ye·hei she·la·ma ra·ba min she·ma·ya ve·cha·yim a·lei·nu ve·al kol Yis·ra·eil,

וְאִמְרוּ: אָמֵן.
ve·i·me·ru: a·mein.

עֹשֶׂה שָׁלוֹם בִּמְרוֹמָיו, הוּא יַעֲשֶׂה שָׁלוֹם עָלֵינוּ וְעַל־כָּל־
O·seh sha·lom bi·me·ro·mav, hu ya·a·seh sha·lom a·lei·nu ve·al kol

יִשְׂרָאֵל, וְאִמְרוּ: אָמֵן.
Yis·ra·eil, ve·i·me·ru: a·mein.

Hallowed and enhanced may God be throughout the world which the Almighty created. May God's sovereignty soon be accepted, during our life and the life of all. And let us say: Amen.

May God be praised throughout all time.

Glorified and celebrated, lauded and praised, acclaimed and honored, extolled and exalted may the Holy One be, far beyond all song and psalm, beyond all tribute which can be uttered. And let us say: Amen.

Let there be abundant peace from Heaven, with life's goodness for us and for all peoples. And let us say: Amen.

God who brings peace to the universe will bring peace to us and to all. And let us say: Amen.

Lord, Give Us Strength

God, as we gather today,
We pray for courage, and for strength.
When we remember the evils in the past,
The innocents tortured, maimed, and murdered,
We are almost afraid to make ourselves remember.
But we are even more afraid to forget.
We ask for wisdom, that we might mourn,
And not be consumed by hatred.
That we might remember, and yet not lose hope.
We must face evil —
And, so doing, reaffirm our faith in future good.
We cannot erase yesterday's pains,
But we can vow that they will not have been suffered in vain.
And so, we pray:
For those who were given death,
Let us choose life —
For us and generations yet to come.
For those who found courage to stand against evil
— often at the cost of their lives —
Let us vow to carry on their struggle.
We must teach ourselves, and our children:
To learn from hate that we must love,
To learn from evil to live for good.

Praise to the Living God

We praise the Living God
Forever praise God's name
Who was and is and is to be
For e'er the same;
The one eternal God

Before our world appears,
And there can be no end of time
Beyond God's years.

You know our ev'ry thought,
Our birth and death ordain;
You understand our fervent dreams,
Our hopes and our pains.
Eternal life have You
Implanted in our soul,
We dedicate our life to You
Your way, our goal!

Benediction

– 6 –

From Death to Hope: A Catholic/Jewish Service

Eugene Fisher and Leon Klenicki

The service begins in silence and in darkness as the narrators, readers, and choir enter in procession. Slowly the lights are turned on.

The narrator stands on one side, a podium for readers on the other. The readers are seated near this podium. Readers can be chosen to light the candles, or others from the community can go up to light the candles at the appropriate time.

> *Narrator:* We begin our service in remembrance of the Holocaust in silence. Let us surround our worship, our community in prayer, with silence, silence in preparation for the Presence of God.

Silent Meditation

Silence does not just bring to a standstill words and noise. Silence is more than the temporary renunciation of speech. It is a door opening before prayer, toward the very realms of the spirit and the heart. Silence is the beginning of a reckoning of the soul, the prelude to an account of the past and the consideration of the present. May our shared silence lead us to awareness of a time of total evil that degraded our most precious values, the very meaning of religious existence, and life itself. Our silence is to be a committed accounting for other silences that accepted persecutions and were indifferent to debasement and crime.

> *Narrator:* And after silence let us stand and give expression personally and communally, to the proclamation of God's Name to the World:

> *Congregation stands.*

> *Reader:* Praise and proclaim God's Name, to whom all praise is due!

> *Congregation:* Praised and proclaimed be the Name of God, to whom all praise is due, now and forever!

First published in 1983; prepared by Dr. Eugene Fisher, Executive Secretary, National Conference of Catholic Bishops–Secretariat for Catholic-Jewish Relations, and Rabbi Leon Klenicki, Associate Director, Department of Interfaith Affairs of the Anti-Defamation League of B'nai Brith; Professor of Jewish Theology, Immaculate Conception Seminary, N.J.

Congregation be seated.

Narrator: Out of silence, and darkness, the creative Word of God was spoken. It first
took the form of wind, of *ruach,* God's spirit hovering over the waters
of chaos to control them, to hold them back and to make possible the
goodness of creation itself.

Reader (Genesis 1:1–5, 26–31; 2:1–3):
When God began to create the heaven and the earth the earth being un-
formed and void, with darkness over the surface of the deep and a wind
from God sweeping over the water — God said, "Let there be light"; and
there was light. God saw how good the light was, and God separated the
light from the darkness. God called the light Day, and the darkness He
called Night. And there was evening and there was morning, a first day.

Reader: And God said, "I will make man in My image, after My likeness. They
shall rule the fish of the sea, the birds of the sky, the cattle, the whole
earth, and all the creeping things that creep on earth." And God created
man in His image, in the image of God He created him; male and female
He created them. God blessed them and God said to them, "Be fertile and
increase, fill the earth and master it; and rule the fish of the sea, the birds
of the sky, and all the living things that creep on earth."

Reader: God said, "See, I give you every seed-bearing plant that is upon all the
earth, and every tree that has seed-bearing fruit; they shall be yours for
food. And to all the animals on land, to all the birds of the sky, and to
everything that creeps on earth, in which there is the breath of life, [I
give] all the green plants for food." And it was so. And God saw all that
He had made, and found it very good. And there was evening and there
was morning, the sixth day.

Congregation: The heaven and the earth were finished, and all their array. And on the
seventh day God finished the work which He had been doing, and He
ceased on the seventh day from all the work which He had done. And
God blessed the seventh day and declared it holy, because on it God ceased
from all the work of creation which He had done.

Narrator: But there can be another type of silence, and another kind of wind. At
a time of horror in the middle of the twentieth century, the silence of
the world made possible the monstrous crime of genocide, the attempted
murder of a whole people for no other reason than they were a particular
type of people, a people called by God "the Chosen People": the Jews.

Reader: In the heart of civilized Europe, aided by the silent acquiescence of so
many of the nations and peoples of the world, a wind of abomination
and racial hostility, a wind of evil whipped a continent into a frenzy of
senseless killing. In Hebrew, this destructive event, the Nazi murder of
two-thirds of European Jewry, is likened to the Shoah of the biblical text,

a devastating, diabolic wind that scours the earth of all life, leaving only chaos and death in its wake.

Reader: Six million Jewish men and women, one million children among them, were taken by other human beings to die in gas and fire, their very ashes spewed from the chimneys of Auschwitz to mingle with the soft breezes of the air and fall, nameless and graveless, spread over a continent that had itself become a graveyard.

Narrator: Not only did Jews die, caught in the eddies and swirls of the Holocaust; millions of Poles and Gypsies, Russians and other Europeans also ended their lives as victims of Nazism's diabolically efficient technology of death. But to be Jewish in Nazi Europe of itself meant alienation and death.

Reader: Martin Niemoeller, a pastor in the German Confessing Church, spent eight and a half years in a concentration camp. He wrote:

> First they came for the Communists
> and I did not speak out—
> because I was not a Communist.
>
> Then they came for the Socialists
> and I did not speak out—
> because I was not a Socialist.
>
> Then they came for the trade unionists
> and I did not speak out—
> because I was not a trade unionist.
>
> Then they came for the Jews
> and I did not speak out—
> because I was not a Jew.
>
> They they came for me
> and there was no one left
> to speak out for me.

Reader: Pope John Paul II, a Pole who knew well the heel of Nazi inhumanity, prayed during his pilgrimage to Auschwitz in 1979:

> I kneel before all the inscriptions that come one after another bearing the memory of the victims of Oswiecim.... In particular I pause with you, dear participants in this encounter, before the inscription in Hebrew. This inscription awakens the memory of the people whose sons and daughters were intended for total extermination. This people draws its origin from Abraham, our father in faith as was expressed by Paul of Tarsus. The very people who received from God the commandment "thou shalt not kill," itself experiences in a special measure what is meant by killing. It is not permissible for anyone to pass by this inscription with indifference.

The Lighting of the Memorial Candles

Narrator: We now light six candles in memory of the six million. As we light these
                candles, we commit ourselves to responsibility for one another, to build
                on this earth a world that has no room for hatred, no place for violence.
                Together, we pray for the strength to fulfill this vocation.

*Congregation stands. Representatives of the community light the candles.
While they are being lit, the community joins in praying Psalm 22.*

Psalm 22

Congregation: My God, my God,
                   why have you abandoned me;
                   why so far from delivering me
                   and from my anguished roaring?

Reader: My God,
                   I cry by day — You answer not;
                   by night, and have no respite.

Congregation: But You are the Holy One,
                   enthroned, the Praise of Israel.
                   In You our fathers trusted;
                   they trusted and You rescued them.
                   To you they cried out
                   and they escaped;
                   in You they trusted
                   and were not disappointed.

Congregation be seated.

Testimonies

Narrator: Jewish voices were heard in reciting prayers and biblical texts, on the
               trains to the concentration camps, at the doors of the gas chambers, in
               hiding, in fighting the enemy, manifesting grief, hope, despair, trust in
               God, faith.
                   One of those voices, Moshe Flinker, an adolescent hiding in Belgium,
               expressed his religious fervor and commitment in verse and prayer. One
               afternoon he wrote in his diary.

Reader: "I am sitting at the window and readying myself for the Minha prayer. I
               look out, and I see that all is red, and the whole horizon is red. The sky
               is covered with bloody clouds, and I am frightened when I see it. I say
               to myself: 'Where do these clouds come from? Bleeding clouds, where are

you from?' Suddenly everything is clear to me, everything is simple and easily understood. Don't you know? They come from the seas of blood. These seas have been brought about by millions of Jews who have been captured and who knows where they are? 'We are the bleeding clouds, and from the seas of blood have we come. We have come to you from the place where your brothers are, to bring greetings from your people. We are witnesses; we were sent by your people to show you their troubles. We have come from the seas of blood: we were brought into being by an inferno of suffering, and we are a sign of peace to you....'"

Young Moshe who died in Auschwitz was able to find hope in his faith in God, and in the continuity of Jewish peoplehood:

Narrator:	*Congregation:*
A Jew in thought	A Jew in deeds
A Jew in trouble	A Jew in joy
A Jew in speech	A Jew in silence
A Jew in arising	A Jew in sitting
A Jew in God	A Jew in people
A Jew in life	A Jew in death
A Jew you were born	A Jew you will die.

Congregation stands.

Hear, O Israel

Hear, O Israel, the Lord, our God, the Lord is one.
Hear, O Israel, the Lord, our God, the Lord is one.
Hear, O Israel, Hear, O Israel.

Congregation be seated.

Two thousand years have we been in exile.
Two thousand years have we been suffering.
Two thousand years have we been hoping for our long delayed salvation.
Two thousand years have we been wandering,
two thousand years have we been moving.
Two thousand years have we been yearning for our long delayed salvation,
and now we are standing here.

By Israel Gregory Norbet, O.S.B. © 1983 The Benedictine Foundation of the State of Vermont, Inc. Weston Priory, Weston, Vermont 05161. This song is dedicated to the memory of Abbot Leo Rudloff, O.S.B., of Weston Priory.

Verses:
1. Standing here we yearn for your help.
   O Lord, shall you help us?
   Yes, our Lord shall help us.

2. Yes, our redeemer, you shall redeem.
   You have forgotten, you shall remember.
   You have neglected and you shall return.

Narrator: Christian witness, in this time of degradation, was barely heard. While
                many were silent, some spoke with their deeds. Let us listen now to a few
                of their stories.

                One or more of the following selections may be chosen.

From Germany

Bernard Lichtenberg was a priest at the St. Hedwig Cathedral Church in Berlin. In August 1941, he declared in a sermon that he would include Jews in his daily prayers because "synagogues have been set afire and Jewish businesses have been destroyed."

One evening Monsignor Lichtenberg did not appear at his church. A brief announcement in the newspapers informed his followers that he had been arrested for "subversive activities." He was sent to prison and, after serving his term, sent to a concentration camp for "reeducation." A poor student, so far as the Nazis were concerned, the ailing old priest asked to be deported to the Jewish ghetto of Lodz. His plea was ignored. He died November 3, 1943, on the way to Dachau.

From Poland

Abraham H. Foxman was born in Poland in 1940, a few months after the Germans had occupied the country. His parents fled to Vilna in an effort to keep ahead of the Nazis. But in less than a year, the German armies occupied Vilna and rounded up all Jews in a ghetto, the first step toward shipping them to concentration camps. A maid, Bronislawa Kurpi, offered to hide the baby, and within a few months he had a new name and baptismal certificate. His mother and father were together in the Vilna ghetto for one year when his mother escaped, managed to get false papers, and moved in with the maid as her sister and the baby's aunt. His father, liberated in 1945, made his way back to Vilna and his family. The whole family was smuggled out of Poland to a displaced persons' camp in the American zone of Austria. They reached the United States in 1950 when Abe was ten years old.

From Denmark

Dr. Aage Bertelsen was a pedagogue. Principal of Aarhus Cathedral College and an outstanding biblical scholar, he had shunned politics before the outbreak of the war. With his wife, Gerda, and several friends, Bertelsen formed a rescue organization that eventually numbered sixty people. Known as the Lyngby Group, after the town in which it operated, these modern Vikings, who struck only at night, smuggled twelve hundred Jews past a flotilla of German warships depositing them safely on Swedish shores. Eventually the Germans learned of Bertelsen's operations and surrounded his home. But Bertelsen successfully eluded the Gestapo noose, slipped out of town, and continued to direct the rescue operations from hiding places. Finally he was forced to escape to Sweden. The Germans arrested his wife, Gerda, but she refused to divulge any of the group's secrets. In reply to the bludgeoning Gestapo official who pressed her to confess that she had participated in the smuggling of Jews to Sweden, the gallant woman asserted: *"All* decent people do!"

From Belgium

In May, 1943, Mme. Marthe De Smet of Dilbeek, in the countryside near Brussels, received a telephone call from Sr. Claire, a nun at the Convent des Soeurs du Très St. Sauveur in the city. Was she willing to hide another Jewish child, the caller asked.

The situation was desperate. The nuns had hidden fifteen little Jewish girls until their hiding place was betrayed to the Gestapo. Just hours before the Gestapo's truck arrived to take the children to their death, the nuns had somehow gotten word to the underground. The children had been hastily moved under cover of darkness and then placed in safe but temporary homes. Now, it was essential to find a permanent hiding place for each of them.

St. Claire knew that the De Smets — Georges, his wife, Marthe, and their children, Marie-Paule, Andre, Eliane, and Francis — were already hiding a Jewish child, three-year-old Regine Monk. Nonetheless, she was confident that Mme. De Smet would not turn her down. She was right. A few days later, three-year-old Yvette Lerner came into the De Smet household, to be safely sheltered there until the liberation of Brussels in September 1944. Shortly after her arrival, the De Smets took a third child, then an infant, Liliane Klein.

At the risk of their own lives and those of their children, the De Smets embarked on a course of active opposition to the Nazis' plan for the extermination of all Jews. In this, they were motivated by deep religious conviction and by a strong love of children.

After the war, the De Smets refused all remuneration and asked only for the continued friendship of the families to whom they had given so much.

From France

Important rescue work was carried on by a Catholic missionary organization, the Fathers of our Our Lady of Zion.... At the head of this group was the Reverend Father Superior Charles Devaux, who is credited with saving 443 Jewish children and 500 adults. At the end of 1942, Father Devaux organized a temporary shelter for his wards on Rue Notre Dame de Champs. From here he sent the children to many parts of the country, where they found temporary homes with workmen's families, among peasants, in convents and monasteries. The expenses were provided for by the group. When the relief work grew beyond their modest means, they solicited and received money from individuals, Jews and non-Jews alike, and from various organizations. The Gestapo were irked by the clergyman's ceaseless activities on behalf of the Jews. They summoned Father Devaux and cited a long list of his offenses. Theodore Dannecker, an SS officer noted as a hangman of French Jews, personally dealt with Devaux. He slapped the priest's face as an initial warning and cautioned him to cease helping Jews or accept the consequences. Father Devaux returned to his rescue work. In 1945, the brave priest was interviewed by a Jewish journalist who asked him whether he had not been aware of the great danger involved in his rescue activities. Father Devaux's answer was simple: "Of course I knew it, but this knowledge could not stop me from doing what I considered to be my duty as a Christian and a human being."

From Italy

The City of Assisi, home of St. Francis, turned itself into a place of clandestine refuge for Jews. Organized by a priest of peasant stock, Padre Rufino Niccacci, hundreds of Jews were hidden in the town's ancient monasteries and convents and provided with fake identity papers. The Germans raided the religious houses searching for the Jewish refugees, who were dressed in religious habits, given rosaries, and temporarily transformed into monks and nuns piously saying their prayers. A small printing press in the town's pharmacy at night cranked out false documents, which were then smuggled to Jewish survivors throughout Italy. In all, thirty-two thousand Italian Jews, representing 80 percent of Italian Jewry, and thousands of foreign Jews were hidden successfully by Christians, many in religious houses.

From Holland

After the Nazi invasion of Holland, a farm that trained Jewish youths in agriculture prior to sending them to Palestine formed a youth underground to smuggle Jewish children across the Pyrenees to Spain and from there to Palestine. But the Jews needed help and appealed to the Dutch Socialist underground. Among those who offered their assistance was a man named Joop Westerville, a principal in a Lundsrecht high school. Son of a pastor, Westerville was a noted educator, the father of three children, a fourth on the way — he was eager for his first journey across the many borders bristling with Nazi bayonets.

Early in 1943, Shushu Simon, the leader of the Jewish underground, was captured by the Gestapo. Joop Westerville was thrust into the position of leadership. It was now his job to lead the Jewish children across the Low Countries and mountainous peaks of France and Spain. This became part of his everyday existence, and he dedicated himself to it fully. At the foot of the Pyrenees, where he usually took leave of the young Zionist pioneers, Westerville enjoined them not to forget their non-Jewish comrades and reminded them that they were all bound to humanity.

> *Narrator:*   A popular Yiddish song expressed the Jewish people's determination to stand up in the struggle against the oppressor and to affirm and reaffirm Judaism's covenant with God. *Zog nit keyn mol* is an example of human affirmation that can inspire us today. Let us read together the English translation.

Narrator and Congregation:

> So never say you now go on your last way,
> Though darkened skies may now conceal the blue of day,
> Because the hour for which we've hungered is so near,
> Beneath our feet the earth shall thunder, "We are here!"

Congregation Sings:

> Zog nit keyn mol as du geyst dem letstn veg
> Khotsh himlen blayene farshteln bloye teg.
> Kumen vet nokh undzer oysgebenkte sho,
> S'vet a poyk ton undzer trot — MIR ZAINEN DO!

זאָג ניט קיין מאָל, אַז דו גייסט דעם לעצטן וועג,
כאָטש הימלען בלײַענע פֿאַרשטעלן בלויע טעג.
קומען וועט נאָך אונדזער אויסגעבענקטע שעה,
עס וועט אַ פּויק טאָן אונדזער טראָט — מיר זײַנען דאָ !

Narrator: We remember the six million by reciting the *Kaddish,* the traditional Jewish prayer for the dead.

This prayer is not a funeral hymn but an affirmation of God's everlasting Presence and dominion, praising God's existence and creative love. It is in this spirit that we pray the *Kaddish,* remembering the victims of the Holocaust. We also pray for the survivors, whose faith in life enabled them to rebuild in other countries their shattered lives, their destroyed worlds. Joining together they brought about new life; they raised new families in new lands, in defiance of absolute terror and despair, an invincible hope. Exalted by that spirit of lifegiving and faith we pray today.

The narrator or a reader familiar with Hebrew says or chants the Kaddish.

Congregation stands.

קדיש יתום

יִתְגַּדַּל וְיִתְקַדַּשׁ שְׁמֵהּ רַבָּא בְּעָלְמָא דִּי־בְרָא כִרְעוּתֵהּ,
Yit·ga·dal ve·yit·ka·dash she·mei ra·ba be·al·ma di·ve·ra chi·re·u·tei,

וְיַמְלִיךְ מַלְכוּתֵהּ בְּחַיֵּיכוֹן וּבְיוֹמֵיכוֹן וּבְחַיֵּי דְכָל־בֵּית
ve·yam·lich mal·chu·tei be·cha·yei·chon u·ve·yo·mei·chon u·ve·cha·yei de·chol beit

יִשְׂרָאֵל, בַּעֲגָלָא וּבִזְמַן קָרִיב, וְאִמְרוּ: אָמֵן.
Yis·ra·eil, ba·a·ga·la u·vi·ze·man ka·riv, ve·i·me·ru: a·mein.

יְהֵא שְׁמֵהּ רַבָּא מְבָרַךְ לְעָלַם וּלְעָלְמֵי עָלְמַיָּא.
Ye·hei she·mei ra·ba me·va·rach le·a·lam u·le·al·mei al·ma·ya.

יִתְבָּרַךְ וְיִשְׁתַּבַּח, וְיִתְפָּאַר וְיִתְרוֹמַם וְיִתְנַשֵּׂא, וְיִתְהַדָּר
Yit·ba·rach ve·yish·ta·bach, ve·yit·pa·ar ve·yit·ro·mam ve·yit·na·sei, ve·yit·ha·dar

וְיִתְעַלֶּה וְיִתְהַלָּל שְׁמֵהּ דְּקֻדְשָׁא, בְּרִיךְ הוּא, לְעֵלָּא מִן־כָּל־
ve·yit·a·leh ve·yit·ha·lal she·mei de·ku·de·sha, be·rich hu, le·ei·la min kol

בִּרְכָתָא וְשִׁירָתָא, תֻּשְׁבְּחָתָא וְנֶחֱמָתָא דַּאֲמִירָן בְּעָלְמָא,
bi·re·cha·ta ve·shi·ra·ta, tush·be·cha·ta ve·ne·che·ma·ta, da·a·mi·ran be·al·ma,

וְאִמְרוּ: אָמֵן.

ve·i·me·ru: a·mein.

יְהֵא שְׁלָמָא רַבָּא מִן שְׁמַיָּא וְחַיִּים עָלֵינוּ וְעַל־כָּל־יִשְׂרָאֵל,

Ye·hei she·la·ma ra·ba min she·ma·ya ve·cha·yim a·lei·nu ve·al kol Yis·ra·eil,

וְאִמְרוּ: אָמֵן.

ve·i·me·ru: a·mein.

עֹשֶׂה שָׁלוֹם בִּמְרוֹמָיו, הוּא יַעֲשֶׂה שָׁלוֹם עָלֵינוּ וְעַל־כָּל־

O·seh sha·lom bi·me·ro·mav, hu ya·a·seh sha·lom a·lei·nu ve·al kol

יִשְׂרָאֵל, וְאִמְרוּ: אָמֵן.

Yis·ra·eil, ve·i·me·ru: a·mein.

Reader: Hallowed and enhanced may God be throughout the world. May God's sovereignty soon be accepted, during our life and the life of all Israel. And let us say: Amen.

Congregation: May God be praised throughout all time.

Reader: Glorified and celebrated, lauded and praised, acclaimed and honored, extolled and exalted may the Holy one be, far beyond all song and psalm, beyond all tributes which humanity can utter. And let us say: Amen.

Congregation: Let there be abundant peace from Heaven, with life's goodness for us and for all the people Israel. And let us say: Amen.

Reader: God who brings peace to the universe will bring peace to us, to humanity, and to Israel. And let us say: Amen.

Congregation: Exalted, compassionate God, grant perfect peace in your sheltering Presence, among the holy and the pure, to the soul of all the men, women and children of the house of Israel, to the Righteous Gentiles, to the millions who died defending the right to be different, at a time of madness and terror.

May their memory endure, may it inspire truth and loyalty in our lives, in our religious commitment and tasks. May their memory be a blessing and sign of peace for all humanity. And let us say all together: Amen.

Congregation be seated.

Narrator: We end our worship by reciting together the words found on the walls of a cellar in Cologne, Germany, where Jews hid from the Nazis:

Narrator and Congregation:

> I believe,
> I believe in the sun
> even when it is not shining.
> I believe in love
> even when feeling it not.
> I believe in God
> even when God is silent.

A short period of silence.

Narrator: We have proclaimed together our faith in the One God, Ground and Nurturer of us all. Before we go our separate ways again, let us extend to one another a sign of reconciliation expressing our hope for peace.

Congregation stands.

Please turn to those around you, share the blessing of peace, wholeness, and life, and wish them Shalom!

Congregation: Shalom!

7

A Christian Service
in Memory of the Holocaust

BLOOR STREET UNITED CHURCH, TORONTO

Organist: Douglas Bodle
Cantor: Ben Maissner

CONVOCATION

DR. CLIFFORD ELLIOTT
Minister of Bloor Street United Church

We are gathered here this evening as Christians in remembrance, in repentance, and in resistance.

We are gathered here to remember our six million Jewish brothers and sisters who were the victims of the Holocaust. We are invited tonight to listen to the words and to the silence of the suffering of these people.

With them, we are called by the Spirit to the edges of our hearts and minds, to that borderline between doubt and faith, between despair and hope.

We are called to face the darkness within ourselves, within our churches, and within our Christian tradition which continues to make the Holocaust a dark night of faith for Jews and Christians alike.

We are summoned to a response forged in the fires of Auschwitz. We are summoned to a Job-like faith, to a stronger covenant with humanity, and to an active resistance against the powers of darkness in our times.

In our remembrance, in our repentance, and in our resistance let us become more truly Christian.

An event sponsored by Diocese of Toronto of the Anglican Church of Canada; Roman Catholic Archdiocese of Toronto; Toronto Area Presbytery of the United Church of Canada; Toronto West Presbytery of the United Church of Canada; The Ukrainian Catholic Eparchy of Toronto; Toronto Presbytery of the Presbyterian Church of Canada; The Society of Friends (Quakers); The Canadian Council of Christians and Jews; The Holocaust Remembrance Committee; the Christian-Jewish Dialogue of Toronto.

LITURGY OF WORD AND SILENCE:
THE DARKNESS

A Reading from *Night* by Elie Wiesel: . . . . read by Steven Yermus,
"Never Shall I Forget That Night" age eleven

Never shall I forget that night, the first night in camp, which has turned my life into one long night, seven times cursed and seven times sealed. Never shall I forget that smoke. Never shall I forget the little faces of the children, whose bodies I saw turned to wreaths of smoke beneath a silent blue sky.

Never shall I forget those flames which consumed my faith forever.

Never shall I forget the nocturnal silence which deprived me, for all eternity, of the desire to live. Never shall I forget those moments which murdered my God and my soul and turned my dreams to dust. Never shall I forget these things, even if I am condemned to live as long as God Himself. Never.

The Song of the Children: . . . . presented by The Children's Choir
"I Never Saw Another Butterfly" of Leo Baeck Day School, Toronto

The last, the very last
so richly, brightly, dazzlingly yellow.
Perhaps if the sun's tears would sing
against a white stone . . .

Such, such a yellow
Is carried lightly 'way up high
It went away I'm sure because it wished
to kiss the world goodbye.

For seven weeks I've lived in here,
Penned up inside this ghetto
But I have found my people here,
The dandelions call to me
And the white chestnut candles in the court,
Only I never saw another butterfly.

That butterfly was the last one.
Butterflies don't live in here,
In the ghetto.

—poem written in camp by Pavel Friedmann,
age eleven

A Psalm of Suffering: Psalm 88 . . . . led by REV. CLIFF ELLIOTT

Leader: Lord, my God, I call for help all day.
I weep to You all night;
may my prayer reach You,
hear my cries for help.

Congregation: For my soul is troubled,
my life is on the brink of Sheol;
I am numbered among those who go down to the pit,
a person bereft of strength.

Leader: A person alone, down among the dead,
among the slaughtered in their graves,
among those You have forgotten,
those deprived of Your protecting hand.

Congregation: You have plunged me to the bottom of the pit,
to its darkest, deepest place,
weighted down by Your anger,
drowned beneath your waves.

Leader: You have turned my friends against me
and made me repulsive to them;
in prison and unable to escape
my eyes are worn out with suffering.

Congregation: Lord, I invoke You all day
I stretch out my hands to You:
are Your marvels meant for the dead,
can ghosts rise up to praise You?

Leader: Who talks of Your love in the grave,
or Your faithfulness in the place of perdition?

Congregation: Do they hear about Your marvels in the dark,
and Your righteousness in the land of oblivion?
But I am here, calling for Your help,
praying to You every morning:
Why do You reject me?
Why do You hide Your face from me?

All: Wretched, slowly dying since my youth,
I bore Your terrors — now I am exhausted.
Your anger overwhelmed me,
You destroyed me with Your terrors
which, like a flood, were round me all day long,
altogether closing in on me.
You have turned my friends and neighbors against me.
Now darkness is my one friend left.

A Reading from *The Last of the Just* . . . . Read by RABBI MARK SHAPIRO,
by André Schwarz-Bart: representing the Holocaust Remembrance
'Why Do Christians Hate Us?" Committee of Toronto

(Ernie and Golda are two young Jews who meet in Paris during the "Nazi Occupation")

"Oh, Ernie," Golda said, "you know them. Tell me why, why do the Christians hate us the way they do? They seem so nice when I can look at them without my star."

Ernie put his arm around her shoulders solemnly. "It's very mysterious," he murmured in Yiddish. "They don't know exactly why themselves. I've been in their churches and I've read their gospel. Do you know who the Christ was? A simple Jew like your father. A kind of Hasid."

Golda smiled gently. "You're kidding me."

"No, no, believe me, and I'll bet they'd have got along fine the two of them, because he was really a good Jew you know, sort of like the Baal Sham Tov — a merciful man, and gentle. The Christians say they love him, but I think they hate him without knowing it. So they take the cross by the other end and make a sword out of it and strike us with it! You understand, Golda," he cried suddenly, strangely excited, "they take the cross and they turn it around, they turn it around, my God. . . ."

"Sh, quiet," Golda said. "They'll hear you." And stroking the scars on Ernie's forehead, as she often liked to do, she smiled. "And you promised you wouldn't think all afternoon. . . ."

Ernie kissed the hand that had caressed his forehead and went on stubbornly, "Poor Jesus, if he came back to earth and saw that the pagans had made a sword out of him and used it against his sisters and brothers, he'd be sad, he'd grieve forever. And maybe he does see it. They say that some of the Just Men remain outside the gates of Paradise, that they don't want to forget humanity, that they too await the Messiah. Yes, maybe he sees it. Who knows? You understand, Goldeleh, he was a little old-fashioned Jew, a real Just Man, you know, no more nor less than . . . all our Just Men. And it's true, he and your father would have got along together. I can see them so well together, you know. "Now," your father would say, "now my good rabbi, doesn't it break your heart to see all that?"

(Within a few months, both Ernie and Golda were dead in a gas chamber.)

The Cry of the Children: "Es Brent" . . . . Sung by THE CHILDREN'S CHOIR
OF LEO BAECK DAY SCHOOL, Toronto

> It burns, brothers, it burns.
> The time of anguish now churns
> When the village and you in one blow
> Turn to ashes, to flames all aglow.
> Nothing will remain at all —
> Just a blackened wall . . .

CALL TO REPENTANCE

Rev. Kenneth Purden
representing the Toronto Area Presbytery
of the United Church of Canada

Leader: For the sin which we committed before You
and before them by closing our ears

All: Lord have mercy

Leader: And for the sin which we committed before You
and before them by not using our power

All: Lord have mercy

Leader: For the sin which we committed before You
and before them by being overcautious

All: Lord have mercy

Leader: And for the sin which we committed before You
and before them by hesitating

All: Lord have mercy

Leader: For the sin which we committed before You
and before them by treachery toward sisters and brothers

All: Lord have mercy

Leader: And for the sin which we committed before You
and before them by being content with those times

All: Lord have mercy

Leader: For the sin which we committed before You
and before them by fearing the powerful

All: Lord have mercy

Leader: And for the sin which we committed before You
and before them by bowing to their will

All: Lord have mercy

Leader: For the sin which we committed before You
and before them by continued frivolity

All: Lord have mercy

Leader: And for the sin which we committed before You
and before them by rationalization

All: Lord have mercy

    Leader: For the sin which we committed before You
                  and before them by our silence

      All: Lord have mercy

    Leader: And for the sin which we committed before You
                  and before them by our words of prejudice

      All: Lord have mercy

    Leader: For the sin we committed against You
                  and before them by making your cross a sign of hatred
                  rather than a sign of love

      All: Lord have mercy.

           For all these sins, O God of forgiveness.
           Forgive us, pardon us, and grant us
           strength to say "Never Again"

THE SUMMONS TO REMEMBER

The Summons . . . . led by FR. MASSEO LOMBARDI
representing the Roman Catholic Archdiocese of Toronto

We gather together tonight to light six candles in memory of the six million Jews — men, women, and children — who were systematically murdered in the heart of our civilized, Christian world.

Our remembrance is a profound form of resistance and a radical act of solidarity. We resist the forces of forgetfulness which would deny the infinite value of their lives and the absolute meaninglessness of their annihilation.

In remembering our Jewish brothers and sisters, we keep alive within ourselves the spark of our own humanity, we rekindle the flame of human solidarity, and we affirm the light of our faith in one another.

Let us remember in sorrow and in solidarity.

The Lighting of the Memorial Candles

The first candle is lit by a Jewish child, Steven Yermus. The next five candles are lit by representatives of the various Christian denominations: Fr. M. Lombardi (for the Roman Catholics), Ursula Franklin (for the Quakers), Rev. Thomas Little (for the Anglicans), Rev. Peter Gilbert (for the Presbyterians) and Rev. Kenneth Purden (for the United Church).

In Sorrow and in Solidarity: . . . . sung by CANTOR BEN MAISSNER
The Mourner's Kaddish and El Maleh Rachamim

The Mourner's Kaddish:

> Let the glory of God be extolled, let His great name be hallowed, in a world whose creation He willed. May His kingdom soon prevail, in our own day, our own lives, and the life of all Israel, and let us say: Amen.

> Let His great name be blessed for ever and ever.

> Let the name of the Holy One, blessed is He, be glorified, exalted, and honored, though He is beyond all the praises, songs, and adorations that we can utter, and let us say: Amen.

> For us and for all Israel, may the blessing for peace and the promise of life come true, and let us say: Amen.

> May He who causes peace to reign in the high heavens, let peace descend on us, on all Israel, and all the world, and let us say: Amen.

El Maleh Rachamim:

> O God full of compassion, Eternal Spirit of the Universe, grant perfect rest under the wings of Your Presence to our loved ones who have entered eternity. Master of Mercy, let them find refuge for ever in the shadow of Your wings, and let their souls be bound up in the bond of eternal life. The Eternal God is their inheritance. May they rest in peace, and let us say: Amen.

REFLECTIONS . . . . Sr. MAUREENA FRITZ (SION)
Professor of Theology, St. Michael's College,
University of Toronto

LIGHT WITHIN THE DARKNESS

A Reading from *Lest Innocent Blood Be Shed* . . . . . . read by DR. URSULA FRANKLIN
by Philip Hallie   representing the Society of Friends

. . . I saw more clearly than ever the images that had made me weep. I saw the two clumsy khaki-colored buses of the Vichy French police pull into the village square. I saw the police captain facing the pastor of the village and warning him that if he did not give up the names of the Jews they had been sheltering in the village, he and his fellow pastor, as well as the families who had been caring for the Jews, would be arrested. I saw the pastor refuse to give up these people who had been strangers in his village, even at the risk of his own destruction.

Then I saw the only Jew the police could find, sitting in an otherwise empty bus. I saw a thirteen-year-old boy, the son of the pastor, pass a piece of his precious chocolate through the window to the prisoner, while twenty gendarmes who were guarding the lone prisoner watched. And then I saw the villagers passing their little gifts through the window until there were gifts all around him — most of them food in those hungry days during the German occupation of France.

...The people of Le Chambon whom Pastor André Trocmé led into a quiet struggle against Vichy and the Nazis were not fighting for the liberation of their country or their village. They felt little loyalty to governments. Their actions did not serve the self-interest of the little commune of Le Chambon-sur-Lignon in the department of Haute-Loire, southern France. On the contrary, those actions flew in the face of that self-interest: by resisting a power far greater than their own they put their village in grave danger of massacre, especially in the last two years of the Occupation, when the Germans were growing desperate. Under the guidance of a spiritual leader they were trying to act in accord with their consciences in the very middle of a bloody, hate-filled war.

And what this meant for them was nonviolence. Following their consciences meant refusing to hate or kill any human being. And in this lies their deepest difference from the other aspects of World War II. Human life was too precious to them to be taken for any reason, glorious and vast though that reason might be. Their consciences told them to save as many lives as they could, even if doing this meant endangering the lives of all the villagers; and they obeyed their consciences.

A Reading from the *Diary of Anne Frank:* . . . . read by KRISTIN COLLE, "Goodness Will Prevail" age ten

Interpreted through dance and music by Ginny Macevicius and Kyle Kutasewich

It's really a wonder that I haven't dropped all my ideals, because they seem so absurd and impossible to carry out. Yet I keep them because in spite of everything I still believe that people are really good at heart. I simply can't build my hopes on a foundation of confusion, misery and death. I see the world gradually being turned into a wilderness. I hear the approaching thunder, I can feel the suffering of millions, and yet, if I look up into the heavens, I think that it will all come right one of these days, that this cruelty will end, and that peace and tranquility will return again. In the meantime, I must hold on to my ideals for perhaps the day will come when I shall be able to carry them out.

A Reading from the Gospel of Matthew 28:31–46 . . . . REV. PETER GILBERT
representing the Toronto Presbytery
of the Presbyterian Church of Canada

Prayer . . . . led by REV. THOMAS LITTLE,
representing the Diocese of Toronto
of the Anglican Church of Canada

Leader: Lord make us instruments of peace on earth.
Where there is hatred, let us sow love.
Where there is injury, pardon.
Where there is discord, unity.

Where there is doubt, faith.
Where there is error, truth.
Where there is despair, hope.
Where there is sadness, joy.
Where there is darkness, light.

All: O Divine Master, grant that we may not so much seek
To be consoled, as to console.
To be understood, as to understand.
To be loved, as to love. Amen.

A COMMITMENT TO THE LIGHT
led by Rev. Cliff Elliott

In memory of our Jewish brothers and sisters, let us light our candles of human solidarity. Let us light our candles of life and stand together against the dark powers of hatred and fear within ourselves, within our churches, and within our world.

Six Christians who are members of the Holocaust Remembrance Committee take the light from the memorial candles and pass it on to those assembled: Ruth Mechanicus, Michael Colle, Joanna Wilson, Anna Moynihan, Carol Payne and Edith Land.

While the tapers are being lit, the Cantor sings Ani Maamin:

I believe with perfect faith in the Messiah's coming. And even if he be delayed, I will await him.

The Challenge to Mercy and Justice . . . . Rev. Cliff Elliott

There were some Christians, the righteous gentiles, who stood as flickering flames of humanity in the darkest of times. At the risk of their own lives, they sheltered and saved their Jewish brothers and sisters. Were it not for them, the light of our own faith would grow dim. In their mercy, these gentiles saved some Jews — but these few could not save all. Never again must our Jewish brothers and sisters remain dependent on the good will of only a few people.

And so tonight we commit ourselves to the light, to justice. We commit ourselves to a world in which the Jews, and all peoples, will have a political and social guarantee of their human rights. We commit ourselves to a world of justice.

Lord God, strengthen us in our commitment to the light of Your mercy and Your justice. O God of Abraham, of Moses, of the prophets, of Job and of Jesus bless us all and be with us. Amen.

RECESSIONAL
"FOR THE HEALING OF THE NATIONS"
led by FR. RON SCOTT

For the healing of the nations, Lord, we pray with one accord
for a just and equal sharing of the things that earth affords
To a life of love in action helps us rise and pledge our word.

Lead us, Father, into freedom,
from despair your world release;
that redeemed from war and hatred,
we may come and go in peace.
Show us how through care and goodness
fear will die and hope increase.

All that kills abundant living,
let it from the earth he banned:
pride of status, race, or schooling,
dogmas keeping each from each.
In our common quest for justice
may we hallow life's brief span.

You, creator-God, have written
your great name on all the world
for our growing in your likeness
bring the life of Christ to mind
that, by our response and service
earth its destiny may find.

—Frederick Herman Kaan (1929–)

8

A Holocaust Commemoration
for Days of Remembrance

For Communities, Churches, Centers, and for Home Use

HARRY JAMES CARGAS

Narrator: We come together for this memorial service to remember. Re-member means to bring certain events of the past together again, to make them whole in order that they may not be forgotten. We must make efforts not to let the great tragedy of the Holocaust slip from the mind of the world or to slip from our minds individually. For if the Holocaust is forgotten, the way will be paved for another, perhaps a final destruction of all of humanity. The massacre of six million Jews must not be a prelude to a future disaster. Our attitude toward the Holocaust may well determine that of our children and of our children's children. What we do today (this evening), now, is of extreme importance.

We pay homage to the dead in what must be seen as momentous Christian tragedy. If Dr. Martin Luther King, Jr., was right when he insisted that racism is really a white people's problem, then we are correct in witnessing to the Holocaust as a Christian problem. It was in traditionally Christian nations that the murders took place. Many Christians died at the death camps of Auschwitz, Dora, Bergen-Belsen, and the rest, and we gather today to re-member these non-Jewish dead as well. Yet many non-Jews were able to save themselves by espousing the Nazi cause. No Jew was allowed to do so. While Poles and Germans and French and others were victims of Hitler's policies, only the Jews were victims of victims; that is, only Jews were singled out for killing *by* Poles and Germans and French and others.

Think of it! How many people does it take to kill six million Jews and perhaps an equal number of non-Jews as well. Who even thought of the plan of trying to rid the world of every Jewish woman, man, and child? Who thought of ovens for human beings while living in nations committed to Jesus Christ, called the Prince of Peace? Who designed the ovens and the gas chambers? Who engineered them, bribed high government officials

---

Dr. Harry James Cargas is a Professor of Literature and Religion at Webster University.

to gain the murderous contracts? Who operated the demonic facilities, repaired them when they broke down, studied their operations to make them more efficient? When Nazi troops conquered countries and did not know which people were Jews and which were not, who pointed out the Jews to the invaders?

The question remains: How many people does it take to cooperate in such a large scale slaughter?

And who among us can be certain that if we were in the wrong place at the wrong time, we too might cooperate with the forces of evil? Are we, in some way, doing exactly that by our subtle racism, our lack of interest in war-torn nations around the world, our deliberate ignorance of genocide through starvation that some people are experiencing as we sit here, this very moment?

Let us beg the Lord God for forgiveness and make a firm purpose of amendment.

Thirty-second meditation.

First Reader (a woman):

Written in Pencil in the Sealed Railway-Car
    here in this carload
    i am eve
    with abel my son
    if you see my other son
    cain son of man
    tell him i

                — Dan Pagis (translated from the Hebrew
                      by Stephen Mitchell)

Narrator: The mother speaking in this poem did not have time to complete her thought. Death was too eager to take her. She went to her end like so many mothers and children without having a chance at life.

Second Reader (a child):

These words were written by a young Jewish girl, imprisoned in a ghetto:

THE GARDEN

A little garden,
Fragrant and full of roses.
The path is narrow
And a little boy walks along it.

A little boy, a sweet boy,
Like that growing blossom.
When the blossom comes to bloom,
The little boy will be no more.

                      — Franta Bass

Narrator: Over one million Jewish children under the age of twelve lost their lives in the Holocaust.

Third Reader (a man):

And so a long line is formed in the front of the orphanage on Sliska Street. A long procession, children, small, tiny, rather precocious, emaciated, weak, shriveled, and shrunk. They carry shabby packages, some have schoolbooks, notebooks under their arms. No one is crying.

Slowly they go down the steps, line up in rows, in perfect order and discipline, as usual. Their little eyes are turned toward the doctor. They are strangely calm; they feel almost well. The doctor is going with them, so what do they have to be afraid of? They are not alone, they are not abandoned.

Dr. Janusz Korczak busies himself with the children with a sober earnestness. He buttons the coat of one child, ties up a package of another, or straightens the cap of a third. Then he wipes off a tear which is rolling down the thin little face of a child....

Then the procession starts out. It is starting out for a trip from which — everybody feels it — one never comes back. All these young, budding lives.... And all this is marching quietly and orderly to the place of their untimely doom.

The children are calm, but inwardly they must feel it, they must sense it intuitively. Otherwise how could you explain the deadly seriousness on their pale little faces? But they are marching quietly in orderly rows, calm and earnest, and at the head of them is Janusz Korczak.

All in Unison (or Narrator and congregation alternate stanzas):

PSALM 79

God, the pagans have invaded your heritage,
they have desecrated your holy Temple;
they have left the corpses of your servants
to the birds of the air for food,
and the flesh of your devout to the beasts of the earth.

They have shed blood like water
throughout Jerusalem, not a gravedigger left!
we are now insulted by our neighbors,
butt and laughing-stock of all those around us.
How much longer will you be angry, Yahweh? For ever?
Is your jealousy to go on smoldering like a fire?

Pour out your anger on the pagans, who do not acknowledge you,
and on those kingdoms that do not call on your name,
for they have devoured Jacob and reduced his home to desolation.

Do not hold our ancestors' crimes against us,
in tenderness quickly intervene,

we can hardly be crushed lower;
help us, God our savior,
for the honor of your name;
Yahweh, blot out our sins,
rescue us for the sake of your name.

Why should the pagans ask, "Where is their God?"
May we soon see the pagans learning what vengeance
you exact for your servants' blood shed here!
May the groans of the captive reach you;
by your mighty arm rescue those doomed to die!

Pay our neighbors sevenfold, strike to the heart
for the monstrous insult preferred to you, Lord!
And we your people, the flock that you pasture,
giving you everlasting thanks,
will recite your praises for ever and ever.

Fourth Reader (a woman):

O THE CHIMNEYS

O the chimneys
On the ingeniously devised habitations of death
When Israel's body drifted as smoke
Through the air —
Was welcomed by a star, a chimney sweep,
A star that turned black
Or was it a ray of sun?

Oh the Chimneys!
Freedomway for Jeremiah and Job's dust —
Who devised you and laid stone upon stone
The road for refugees of smoke?

O the habitations of death,
Invitingly appointed
For the host who used to be a guest —
O you fingers
Laying the threshold
Like a knife between life and death —

O you chimneys,
O you fingers
And Israel's body as smoke through the air!

—Nelly Sachs from *In the Habitations of Death*

Fifth Reader (a man):

As it began to grow light, the fire was lit in two of the pits in which about twenty-five hundred dead bodies lay piled one on top of the other. Two hours later all that could be discerned in the white-hot flames were countless charred and scorched shapes, the blackish-phosphorescent hue a sign that they were in an advanced stage of cremation. At this point the fire had to be kept going from outside because the pyre which at first protruded about half a meter above the edge of the pit had, in the meantime, gone below this level. While in the crematorium ovens, once the corpses were thoroughly alight, it was possible to maintain a lasting red heat with the help of fans, in the pits the fire would burn only as long as the air could circulate freely in between the bodies. As the heap of bodies settled, no air was able to get in from outside. This meant that we stokers had constantly to pour oil or wood alcohol on the burning corpses, in addition to human fat, large quantities of which had collected and was boiling in the two collecting pans on either side of the pit. The sizzling fat was scooped out with buckets on a long curved rod and poured all over the pit causing flames to leap up amid much crackling and hissing. Dense smoke and fumes rose incessantly. The air reeked of oil, fat, benzole, and burnt flesh.

—Filip Muller, *Eyewitness Auschwitz*

Narrator: Master of the universe, help us to bear in mind always our potential for evil. And strengthen us, our God, so that we may fulfill our potential for good instead.

Sixth Reader (a man):

One day when we came back from work, we saw three gallows rearing up in the assembly place, three black crows. Roll call. SS all around us, machine guns trained: the traditional ceremony. Three victims in chains — and one of them, the little servant, the sad-eyed angel.

The SS seemed more preoccupied, more disturbed than usual. To hang a young body in front of thousands of spectators was no light matter. The head of the camp read the verdict. All eyes were on the child. He was lividly pale, almost calm, biting his lips. The gallows threw its shadow over him.

This time the Lagerkapo refused to act as executioner. Three SS replaced him.

The three necks were placed at the same moment within the nooses.

"Long live liberty!" cried the two adults.

But the child was silent.

"Where is God? Where is He?" someone behind me asked.

At a sign from the head of the camp, the three chairs tipped over.

Total silence through the camp. On the horizon, the sun was setting.

"Bare your heads!" yelled the head of the camp. His voice was raucous. We were weeping.

"Cover your heads!"

Then the march past began. The two adults were no longer alive. Their tongues hung swollen, blue-tinged. But the third rope was still moving; being so light, the child was still alive....

For more than half an hour he stayed there, struggling between life and death, dying in slow agony under our eyes. And we had to look him full in the face. He was still alive when I passed in front of him. His tongue was still red, his eyes were not yet glazed. Behind me, I heard the same man asking: "Where is God now?"

And I heard a voice within me answer him:

"Where is He? Here He is — He is hanging here on this gallows..."
That night the soup tasted of corpses.

—Elie Wiesel, *Night*

Seventh Reader (a woman):

If as Christians we thought that Church and Synagogue no longer affected one another, everything would be lost. And where this separation between the community and the Jewish nation has been made complete, it is the Christian community which has suffered. The whole reality of the revelation of God is then secretly denied....

For in the person of the Jew there stands a witness before our eyes, the witness of God's covenant with Abraham, Isaac and Jacob and in that way with us all. Even one who does not understand Holy Scripture can see this reminder.

And don't you see, the remarkable theological importance, the extraordinary spiritual and sacred significance of the National Socialism that now lies behind us is that right from its roots it was antisemitic, that in this movement it was realized with a simply demonic clarity, that *the* enemy is *the Jew*. Yes, the enemy in this matter had to be a Jew. In this Jewish nation there really lives to this day the extraordinariness of the revelation of God....

When the Christian Church confesses Jesus Christ as Savior and the Servant of God for us, for all men, also for the mighty majority of those who have no direct connection with the People Israel, then it does not confess Him *although* He was a Jew....

No, we must strictly consider that Jesus Christ, in whom we believe, whom we Christians out of the heathen call our Savior and praise as the consummator of God's work on our behalf — He was *of necessity a Jew*. We cannot be blind to this fact; it belongs to the concrete reality of God's work and of his revelation.

The problem of Israel is, since the problem of Christ is inseparable from it, the problem of existence as such. The man who is ashamed of Israel is ashamed of Jesus Christ and therefore of his own existence.

The attack on Judah means the attack on the rock of the work and revelation of God, beside which work and which revelation there is no other.

—Karl Barth, *Dogmatics in Outline*

Homily

A brief homily by a pastor is in order here. Perhaps two short talks would be appropriate, one by a Christian minister, one by a rabbi.

Narrator: Holocaust survivor and author Elie Wiesel has said this:

✓

> If someone suffers and he keeps silent, it can be a good silence. If someone suffers and I keep silent, then it's a destructive silence. If we envisage literature and human destiny as endeavors by man to redeem himself, then we must admit the obsession, the overall dominating theme of responsibility, that we are responsible for one another. I am responsible for his or her suffering, for his or her destiny. If not, we are condemned by our solitude forever and it has no meaning. This solitude is a negative, destructive solitude, a self-destructive solitude.
>
> —from *Harry James Cargas in Conversation with Elie Wiesel*

Eighth Reader:

Indeed we may not remain silent in view of the horror of the Holocaust. And yet we must choose our words carefully. We must not oversentimentalize the tragedy, we must not treat it with irreverence. How, then, are we to speak out? Rabbi Irving Greenberg has given us this guide: "Let us offer, then, as a working principle the following: No statement, theological or otherwise, should be made that would not be credible in the presence of burning children."

Narrator: There are times, also, for silence in the face of the awesome proportions of the tragedy of the Holocaust. We arrive at such a time now, as we ask six Holocaust survivors from our community [*or, if this is not possible, six diverse members of the community*] to each light a candle, one candle to represent one million Jewish dead, the totality, when lit, to symbolize all those who died in the Holocaust.

When the candles are lit, the overhead lights will be extinguished for two minutes while we each offer our own prayers. When the electric lights are turned back on, you may, of course, continue to pray, but when you do begin to leave, please do so quietly.

Lighting of the Candles

Lowering of the Lights (two minutes)

Lights Back On

Dismissal

9

Yom HaShoah V'Hagvurah

Fiftieth Anniversary of the Warsaw Ghetto Uprising

JEWISH COMMUNITY OF GREATER TORONTO

---

27 Nisan 5703   April 18, 1993

Due to the character of this special Observance and the decorum expected, the following rules are to be observed:

1. There is to be NO APPLAUSE at any time during the program.

2. During the recitation of *El Maleh Rachamim* and the *Kaddish* all will stand.

3. All present are requested to rise and join in the singing of "O Canada," "Ani Mamin," "Partizaner Song," and "Hatikvah."

Miriam Gelbloom   Robert Weiss
CO-CHAIRMEN
YOM HASHOAH 1993 COMMITTEE

PROGRAM COORDINATORS
Cantor Benjamin Z. Maissner
Musical Director

YIDDISH READINGS
Aron Fainer
Simcha Simchovitch

ENGLISH READINGS
Haia Hason
Rosie Parnass

CHOIRS

HOLY BLOSSOM TEMPLE SINGERS
Nadegda Adler
Accompanist

BIALIK SCHOOL CHAMBER CHOIR
Judith Peleg
Accompanist

Doron Ophir
Musical Director

CANTORS
Louis Danto   Benjamin Z. Maissner

ZACHOR...WE REMEMBER...

Reading of Names

O Canada . . . . BIALIK SCHOOL CHAMBER CHOIR

> O Canada! Our home and native land!
> True patriot love in all thy sons' command.
> With glowing hearts we see thee rise,
> The True North strong and free!
> From far and wide, O Canada,
> We stand on guard for thee.
> God keep our land glorious and free!
> O Canada, we stand on guard for thee.
> O Canada, we stand on guard for thee.

Unter Dayne Vayse Stern . . . . BIALIK SCHOOL CHAMBER CHOIR
(Under Your White Starry Heaven)
  Words: Abraham Sutskever
  Music: Abraham Brodne

Written in the Ghetto at the beginning of 1943 by Yiddish writer and partisan Abraham Sutskever, now living in Israel. The composer, one of Vilna's young Jewish musicians, perished in the Kluga concentration camp (Estonia) in 1944.

> *Translation:*
>
> Under your white starry heaven
> Offer me your pale white hand.
> All my words are flowing teardrops,
> I would place them in your hand.
> Gone the luster from their brightness,
> Seen through morbid cellar view —
> And I no longer have my own space
> To reflect them back to you.

Opening Remarks . . . . MIRIAM GELBLOOM
                                                                    Co-Chairman
                                                                    Yom HaShoah 1993

                                                                    ROBERT WEISS
                                                                    Co-Chairman
                                                                    Yom HaShoah 1993

Greetings . . . . Jack Chisvin
President
Jewish Federation of Greater Toronto

Gabriel Nachman
President, B'nai Brith Canada

Greetings from the State of Israel . . . . Dror Zeigerman
Consul General

Call to Remember . . . . Dr. Joel Dimitry
Chairman
Canadian Society for Yad Vashem

Shiviti . . . . Holy Blossom Temple Singers
Lyrics: S. Sulzer
Music: L. Lewandowski

KEYNOTE ADDRESSES

Survivor . . . . Rabbi Dow Marmur
Liberator . . . . Rabbi David Monson
Second Generation . . . . Rabbi Avraham Rothman

Es Brent . . . . Cantor Louis Danto
Cantor Benjamin Z. Maissner

Lyrics: M. Gebirtig
Arrangement: Lazar Weiner

Life in the Ghetto . . . . Nadine Rabinovitch

Churban Warshe . . . . Holy Blossom Temple Singers
Lyrics: W. Kelman
Music: Adolph Mann

Zing . . . . Allen Farkas

Translation:

Scream from every sand dune,
from under every stone,
Scream from the dust and fire and smoke —
It is your blood, your sap, the marrow of your bones,
It is your flesh and blood! Scream, scream aloud!

Do not scream to heaven that is as deaf as the dunghill earth.
Do not scream to the sun, nor talk to that lamp.... If I could only
Extinguish it like a lamp in this bleak murderers' cave!
My people, you were radiant more than the sun,
a purer, brighter light!

Show yourself, my people. Emerge, reach out
From the miles-long, dense, deep ditches,
Covered with lime and burned, layer upon layer,
Rise up! up! from the deepest, bottommost layer!

Come, you dried, ground, crushed Jewish bones.
Come, form a big circle around me, one great ring —
Grandfathers, grandmothers, fathers, mothers carrying babies.
Come, Jewish bones, out of powder and soap.

Warshe . . . . CANTOR BENJAMIN Z. MAISSNER
  Lyrics: S. Katcherginski
  Music: Michael Gelbart

Everyone Has a Name . . . . ISRAEL DAVID
  Lyrics: Zelda

Each and every one has a name
Bestowed on him by G-d
And given him by his parents.
Everyone has a name
accorded him by his stature and type of smile
and style of dress.
Everyone has a name
conferred by the mountains and his home
Everyone has a name
granted him by Fortune
or that by which his neighbors call,
Everyone has a name
assigned him by his failings
or contributed by his yearnings.
Everyone has a name
given him by his enemies
or by his loved one.
Everyone has a name
derived from his celebrations
and his occupation.

Everyone has a name
presented him by the seasons
and his blindness.
Everyone has a name
he receives from the sea
and that, given him, by his death.

My Bar Mitzvah . . . . .JOSH GROSSMAN
Lyrics: Howard Kahn

In Varshever Geto Iz Itst Khoydesh Nisn . . . . ETHEL COOPER
(In Warsaw Ghetto the Month Is Now Nissan)
Lyrics: Binem Heller
Translation: Fagel Gartner Krolitsky

It is Passover in the Warsaw Ghetto.
The story of the Exodus from Egypt is told anew.
But, now, behind dark curtained windows
The table is set with crude matzos and wine.
The seder is observed, but with a difference —
The Passover dishes are empty
And the crying of hungry children
Together with the sobbing of the aged and blind
Make it hard to distinguish truth from falsehood.
Past miracles from present horrors.

Elijah's cup stands filled and ready.
But who has interrupted this Seder night?
The angel of death has come to drink instead.
They have come with their coarse commands
To lead people to their slaughter.
But no! No more will the ghetto listen
To the insults of Nazis
No more will they allow themselves to be baited and dragged off.

The word is passed on from neighbor to neighbor
As long as a Jew will remain alive in the ghetto.
German blood shall not cease to flow!
For them let your eyes show no meekness — no tears.
Just hatred and great satisfaction
Of rising up against them, of being able to defend oneself . . .
Hear, how death marches on bloody tracks.
Hear, how history is now being recorded
With heroism in holocaust.
On a night of salvation and freedom.

The Battle . . . . Josh Grossman
                                                        Nadine Rabinovitch

Excerpts from: *The Declaration of Revolt by the Jewish Fighter Organization*

Every threshold in the Ghetto has been and will remain a fortress. . . . At the cost of our lives, we shall not surrender. Along with you, we aim to punish our common foe for all the crimes. . . . This is a struggle for our common freedom, for common human and social dignity and honor! . . . We shall avenge the crimes committed in Auschwitz, Treblinka, Belzhetz, and Maidanek! . . . Long live liberty. . . . Long live the mortal struggle against the occupier!

Excerpts from: *The last letter of Mordecai Anielewicz, commander of the Warsaw Ghetto Uprising*

It is now clear to me that what took place exceeded all expectations. In our opposition to the Nazis we did more than our strength allowed — but now our forces are waning. We are on the brink of extinction. We forced the Nazis to retreat twice — but they returned stronger than before. . . . The last wish of my life has been fulfilled. Jewish self-defense has become a fact. Jewish resistance and revenge have become actualities. I am happy to have been one of the first Jewish fighters in the Ghetto. . . . Where will rescue come from?

Excerpts from: *The Diaries of Mark Edelman*

On May 10, 1943, this period of our bloody history, the history of the Warsaw Jews came to an end. The site where the buildings of the Ghetto had once stood became a ragged heap of rubble reaching three stories high. . . . Those who were killed in action had done their duty to the end, to the last drop of blood that soaked into the pavements of the Warsaw Ghetto. . . . We, who did not perish, leave it to you to keep their memory alive — forever.

In Memory of the Six Million . . . . Cantor Benjamin Z. Maissner
    Arrangement: Lazar Weiner

Ani Mamin . . . . Cantor Benjamin Z. Maissner
    Arrangement: Max Hellman

Jews in Warsaw, Lublin, Lodz, and Bialystock, the first victims of the Nazis, sang this Hebrew song, on their way to their death.

Ani mamin, ani mamin.
Ani mamin —
Beemuno shleymo
Bevias hamoshiakh
Bevias hamoshiakh ani mamin.
Veaf al pi sheyismameya
im kol-ze ani mamin.

Ani-mamin. Ani-mamin, I believe,
I believe.
I believe with reassuring faith.
He will come, he will come.
I believe Messiah, he will come.
I believe although he may delay,
I believe he'll come. Ani-mamin.

אני מאמין

אֲנִי מַאֲמִין בֶּאֱמוּנָה שְׁלֵמָה
בְּבִיאַת הַמָּשִׁיחַ.
וְאַף עַל פִּי שֶׁיִּתְמַהְמֵהַּ,
עִם כָּל זֶה אֲנִי מַאֲמִין,
עִם כָּל זֶה אֲחַכֶּה לוֹ
בְּכָל יוֹם שֶׁיָּבוֹא.

CANDLE LIGHTING IN MEMORY OF THE SIX MILLION

First Candle by Survivors . . . . ALEX EISEN
ALA & MICHAEL FINKELSTEIN
MARILYN & ISSIE LIGHT
JUDY & GEORGE LYSY
PAULETTE & TED SCHWARTZ

Second Candle by Second Generation . . . . LOUIS GREENBAUM
LEON HOCHGLAUBE
ARNOLD KRAVETZ

Third Candle by Third Generation
"March of the Living" Participants . . . . AVI POLLACK
LEIGH SALSBERG

Fourth Candle by Partizans . . . . PETER SILVERMAN
DAVID SMUSCHKOWITZ
PETER SMUSZKOWICZ
EVA & CHARLES WITTENBERG

Fifth Candle by Righteous among the Nations . . . . TIBOR ALMASSY
JOOP & JOHN VAN DER BOOM

Sixth Candle by War Veterans of Canada . . . . SAM PASTERNACK
SAM ROMBERG

A Seventh Candle Is Lit in Memory of Those
"Righteous among the Nations" Who Died for Rescuing Jews,
by a Former Hidden Child . . . . SUSAN PASTERNAK

El Maleh Rachamim . . . . CANTOR LOUIS DANTO
by Ephraim Oyerbakh

Translation:
Exalted, compassionate God,
grant perfect peace in Your sheltering Presence among the holy and the pure,
to the souls of all our brethren,
men, women, and children of the House of Israel
who were slaughtered and suffocated and burned to ashes.
May their memory endure, inspiring truth and loyalty in our lives.
May their souls thus be bound up in the bond of life.
May they rest in peace. And let us say: Amen.

אֵל מָלֵא רַחֲמִים שׁוֹכֵן בַּמְּרוֹמִים הַמְצֵא מְנוּחָה נְכוֹנָה תַּחַת
כַּנְפֵי הַשְּׁכִינָה בְּמַעֲלוֹת קְדוֹשִׁים וּטְהוֹרִים כְּזֹהַר הָרָקִיעַ מַזְהִירִים,
אֶת־נִשְׁמוֹת כָּל־אַחֵינוּ בְּנֵי יִשְׂרָאֵל, אֲנָשִׁים נָשִׁים וָטַף, שֶׁנֶּהֶרְגוּ
וְשֶׁנִּטְבְּחוּ וְשֶׁנִּשְׂרְפוּ וְשֶׁנֶּחְנְקוּ. בְּגַן עֵדֶן תְּהִי מְנוּחָתָם. אָנָּא בַּעַל
הָרַחֲמִים, הַסְתִּירֵם בְּסֵתֶר כְּנָפֶיךָ לְעוֹלָמִים וּצְרֹר בִּצְרוֹר הַחַיִּים
אֶת־נִשְׁמוֹתֵיהֶם. יְיָ הוּא נַחֲלָתָם, וְיָנוּחוּ בְּשָׁלוֹם עַל מִשְׁכְּבוֹתֵיהֶם.
וְנֹאמַר אָמֵן.

Kaddish . . . . RABBI DOW MARMUR
                                             RABBI DAVID MONSON
                                     RABBI AVRAHAM ROTHMAN

קדיש יתום

יִתְגַּדַּל וְיִתְקַדַּשׁ שְׁמֵהּ רַבָּא בְּעָלְמָא דִּי־בְרָא כִרְעוּתֵהּ,
Yit·ga·dal ve·yit·ka·dash she·mei ra·ba be·al·ma di·ve·ra chi·re·u·tei,

וְיַמְלִיךְ מַלְכוּתֵהּ בְּחַיֵּיכוֹן וּבְיוֹמֵיכוֹן וּבְחַיֵּי דְכָל־בֵּית
ve·yam·lich mal·chu·tei be·cha·yei·chon u·ve·yo·mei·chon u·ve·cha·yei
        de·chol beit

יִשְׂרָאֵל, בַּעֲגָלָא וּבִזְמַן קָרִיב, וְאִמְרוּ: אָמֵן.
Yis·ra·eil, ba·a·ga·la u·vi·ze·man ka·riv, ve·i·me·ru: a·mein.

יְהֵא שְׁמֵהּ רַבָּא מְבָרַךְ לְעָלַם וּלְעָלְמֵי עָלְמַיָּא.
Ye·hei she·mei ra·ba me·va·rach le·a·lam u·le·al·mei al·ma·ya.

יִתְבָּרַךְ וְיִשְׁתַּבַּח, וְיִתְפָּאַר וְיִתְרוֹמַם וְיִתְנַשֵּׂא, וְיִתְהַדָּר

Yit·ba·rach ve·yish·ta·bach, ve·yit·pa·ar ve·yit·ro·mam ve·yit·na·sei, ve·yit·ha·dar

וְיִתְעַלֶּה וְיִתְהַלָּל שְׁמֵהּ דְּקֻדְשָׁא, בְּרִיךְ הוּא, לְעֵלָּא מִן־כָּל־

ve·yit·a·leh ve·yit·ha·lal she·mei de·ku·de·sha, be·rich hu, le·ei·la min kol

בִּרְכָתָא וְשִׁירָתָא, תֻּשְׁבְּחָתָא וְנֶחֱמָתָא דַּאֲמִירָן בְּעָלְמָא,

bi·re·cha·ta ve·shi·ra·ta, tush·be·cha·ta ve·ne·che·ma·ta, da·a·mi·ran be·al·ma,

וְאִמְרוּ: אָמֵן.

ve·i·me·ru: a·mein.

יְהֵא שְׁלָמָא רַבָּא מִן שְׁמַיָּא וְחַיִּים עָלֵינוּ וְעַל־כָּל־יִשְׂרָאֵל,

Ye·hei she·la·ma ra·ba min she·ma·ya ve·cha·yim a·lei·nu ve·al kol Yis·ra·eil,

וְאִמְרוּ: אָמֵן.

ve·i·me·ru: a·mein.

עֹשֶׂה שָׁלוֹם בִּמְרוֹמָיו, הוּא יַעֲשֶׂה שָׁלוֹם עָלֵינוּ וְעַל־כָּל־

O·seh sha·lom bi·me·ro·mav, hu ya·a·seh sha·lom a·lei·nu ve·al kol

יִשְׂרָאֵל, וְאִמְרוּ: אָמֵן.

Yis·ra·eil, ve·i·me·ru: a·mein.

Zog Nit Keinmol . . . . Cantor Benjamin Z. Maissner
Partizaner Song

Lyrics: Hirsh Glick   *Music:* D. Pokras
English Version: Aron Cremer

Hirsh Glick was born in Vilna in 1920 and fought as a partisan in the Vilna Woods. He was killed in battle in 1944. Subsequently his partisan song became a recognized anthem of the Jewish partisans, a symbol of the fighting spirit in the ghetto.

Zog nit keyn mol, az du geyst dem letsn veg,
Khotsh himlen blayene farshtein bloye teg —
Kumen vet nokh undzer oysgebenkte sho,
S'vet a poyk ton undzer trot-mir zaynen do!

Fun grinem palmenland biz vaysn land fun shney,
Mir keumen on mit undzer payn, mit undzer vey;
Un vu gefain iz a shprits fun undzer blut,
Shprotsn vet don undzer gvure, undzer mut!

S'vet di morgnzun bagildn undz dem haynt,
Un der nektn vet farshvindn mit dem faynt;
Nor oyb farzamen vet di zun un der kayor,
Vi a parol zol geyn dos lid fun dot tsu dot!

Dos lid geshribn iz mit blut, un nit mit blay,
S'iz nit keyn lidl fun a foygl oyf der flay, —

Dos hot a folk tsvishn faindike vent
Dos lid gezungen mit naganes in di hent! ...

To zog nit keyn mol, az du geyst dem letstn veg,
Khotsh himlen blayene farshetln bloye teg;
Kumen vet nokh undzer oysgebenkte sho —
Es vet a poyk ton undzer trot: mir zaynen do!

זאָג ניט קיין מאָל, אַז דו גייסט דעם לעצטן וועג.
כאָטש הימלען בלײַענע פֿאַרשטעלן בלויע טעג.
קומען וועט נאָך אונדזער אײַנגעבענקטע שעה.
עס וועט אַ פויק טאָן אונדזער טראָט — מיר זײַנען דאָ!

Never say that there is only death for you
Though leaden clouds may be concealing skies of blue —
Because the hour that we have hungered for is near;
Beneath our tread the earth shall tremble: We are here!

From land of palm-tree to the far-off land of snow
We shall be coming with our torment and our woe,
And everywhere our blood has sunk into the earth
Shall our bravery, our vigor blossom forth!

We'll have the morning sun to set our day aglow,
And all our yesterdays shall vanish with the foe,
And if the time is long before the sun appears,
Then let this song go like a signal through the years.

This song was written with our blood and not with lead;
It's not a song that birds sing overhead.
It was a people, among toppling barricades,
That sang this song of ours with pistols and grenades.

So never say that there is only death for you
For leaden clouds may be concealing skies of blue —
And yet the hour that we have hungered for is near;
Beneath our tread the earth shall tremble: We are here!

Lo Isa Goi (Isaiah 2:4) . . . . BIALIK SCHOOL CHAMBER CHOIR
Music: Doron Levinson

They shall beat their swords into ploughshares
And their spears into pruning hooks
Nation shall no longer raise up arms against nation
Neither shall they learn war anymore.

Hatikvah . . . . BIALIK SCHOOL CHAMBER CHOIR

Kol od ba-lei-vav pe-ni-ma,   As long as deep in the heart
Ne-fesh Ye-hu-di ho-mi-ya.   The soul of a Jew yearns
U-le-fa-a-tei miz-rach ka-di-ma,   And towards the East
A-yin le-tsi-yon tso-fi-ya.   An eye looks to Zion.

Od lo av-da tik-va-tei-nu,   Our hope is not yet lost
Ha-tik-va she-not al-pa-yim,   The hope of two thousands years
Li-yot am chof-shi be-ar-tsei-nu,   To be a free people in our land
Be-e-rets tsi-yon Ye-ru-sha-la-yim. The land of Zion and Jerusalem.

הַתִּקְוָה

כָּל עוֹד בַּלֵּבָב פְּנִימָה

נֶפֶשׁ יְהוּדִי הוֹמִיָּה,

וּלְפַאֲתֵי מִזְרָח קָדִימָה

עַיִן לְצִיּוֹן צוֹפִיָּה.

עוֹד לֹא אָבְדָה תִקְוָתֵנוּ,

הַתִּקְוָה שְׁנוֹת אַלְפַּיִם,

לִהְיוֹת עַם חָפְשִׁי בְּאַרְצֵנוּ,

בְּאֶרֶץ צִיּוֹן וִירוּשָׁלָיִם.

ZACHOR . . . WE REMEMBER . . .

Reading of Names

Message from the President of the Yad Vashem Executive . . . . YITZHAK ARAD
for Holocaust Martyrs and Heroes Commemoration Day,
April 18, 1993

This year we commemorate the Fiftieth Anniversary of the revolt in the ghettos of War-saw, Vilna, and Bialystock, in the extermination camps of Treblinka and Sobibor, as well as other ghettos and camps.

1943 was a year in which thousands of young Jewish men left the ghettos for the forests in the hope of joining the partisan struggle against the Nazi assassins. The countless acts of resistance which took place in all parts of occupied Europe during the Holocaust have been recorded — from France in the West, Yugoslavia in the South, and vast areas under Nazi occupation in the East.

Today we remember all these acts of heroism, especially the revolt in the Warsaw Ghetto, which has come to symbolize the foremost act of struggle and bravery in the history of the Jewish people.

The Jewish opposition, which grew in resistance to the Nazi main aim — the extermina-tion of the Jewish people — took on many facets, the most important of which was armed combat. The revolts in the ghettos and in the camps were doomed from the outset: they had no chance of success against the great Nazi German war machine, which had conquered the majority of the European continent.

The Jewish heroism of the ghetto fighters, those in the camps, and the partisans encapsulate the obligatory values for the education of new generations, and the crucial message that even in the most difficult moments, one must not lose hope.

In his last letter, Mordecai Anielewicz, the commander of the revolt, wrote: "I have seen the dream of my life accomplished. The self-defense of the ghetto is a reality. I was a witness to an extraordinary struggle filled with heroism on the part of the Jewish fighters."

The ghetto and camp fighters in the context of the difficult and tragic realities of the Holocaust unknowingly wrote the heroic pages of the history of the Jewish people.

This year, through the commemoration of the Holocaust and Jewish heroism, we, from Israel and all the Jewish communities around the world, will eternalize the heroic acts of our Jewish fighters.

10

Yom HaShoah:
Holocaust Remembrance Day
FIRST UNITED METHODIST CHURCH, SANTA MONICA

Never Shall I Forget That Night

(*As Elie Wiesel, then age fourteen, remembers his first night in Auschwitz:*)

Never shall I forget that night, the first night in camp, which has turned my life into one long night, seven times cursed and seven times sealed. Never shall I forget that smoke. Never shall I forget the little faces of the children, whose bodies I saw turned to wreaths of smoke beneath a silent blue sky.

Never shall I forget those flames which consumed my faith forever.

Never shall I forget the nocturnal silence which deprived me, for all eternity, of the desire to live. Never shall I forget these things, even if I am condemned to live as long as God Himself. Never.

—Elie Wiesel, *Night*

Processional of the Six Million and the Five Million

ANI MA'AMIN	I BELIEVE
A-ni ma-a-min be-e-mu-na she-lei-ma be-vi-at ha-ma-shi-ach Ve-af al pi she-yit-ma-he-mei-a, im kol zeh a-ni ma-a-min, im kol zeh a-cha-keh lo be-chol yom she-ya-vo	אֲנִי מַאֲמִין בֶּאֱמוּנָה שְׁלֵמָה בְּבִיאַת הַמָּשִׁחַ. וְאַף עַל פִּי שֶׁיִּתְמַהְמֵהַּ. עִם כָּל זֶה אֲנִי מַאֲמִין. עִם כָּל זֶה אֲחַכֶּה לוֹ בְּכָל יוֹם שֶׁיָּבוֹא.

I believe with perfect faith in the coming of the messiah. And even though the messiah tarry, still will I believe.

It was this song that the Jews sang as they marched together to their deaths.

A service of remembrance at First United Methodist Church in Santa Monica, California. Co-sponsored by the Santa Monica Bay Area Chapter of the National Conference of Christians and Jews and the Westside Ecumenical Conference.

Reader: Count by ones to six million, a number each second, you will be here until August...not even naming names, each person a number.

"Do not despise justice...take care not to pervert it, for by doing so, you shall shake the world." (Deuteronomy Rabbah 5:1)

THE WORLD WAS SHAKEN. Six million Jews and five million other children of God — the handicapped, the unwanted, other "minorities," and those few who dared to speak out against the madness — were led to the gas chambers and the crematoria. We are here today to remember them.

Congregation: Yet, in spite of the emptiness and horror we experience every time we recall the Holocaust and the deaths of the Six Million and the Five Million, we are here today to affirm LIFE.

Reader: During this season the Passover and Paschal Candles burn as reminders that freedom and death are not in vain. Today we also light eleven candles in memory of those who died in the death camps. By our dedication to righteousness and justice, may our freedom, and their deaths not be in vain.

Reader: Light is the symbol of the divine.

Congregation: *The Lord is my light and my salvation.*

Reader: Light is the symbol of the divine in men and women.

Congregation: *The Spirit of humanity is the light of the Lord.*

Reader: Light is the symbol of divine law.

Congregation: *For the commandment is a lamp and the law is a light.*

Reader: Light is the symbol of our mission. I the Lord have set thee for a covenant people, for a light unto the nations.

Congregation: *Not to curse the darkness, but to light the flame, and to light it as an act of faith this day of all days.*

All: *Hear, O Israel: the Lord our God the Lord is one. Praised be His name whose glorious kingdom is forever and forever.*

Reader: At this sacred hour we pause to remember a time when night was obscured by darkness, when the faces of evil were arrayed against our brothers and sisters.

Their memory must remain forever etched in the conscience of humanity.

Thus do we kindle these lamps to penetrate the moral blackness and chaos of the Holocaust.

A Litany for God's People

All:	*Almighty God, we gather here as your children in this community to affirm our love for you and for each other.*
Reader:	Lord God of Abraham and Sarah, call us to move into a fuller relationship with our neighbors and with you.
Congregation:	*Show us how to be faithful, and obedient to Your will.*
Reader:	God of Moses and Aaron and Miriam, lead us, your people, on our journey to full freedom.
Congregation:	*Keep us aware of your presence with us, by night and by day.*
Reader:	O God of the judges, of Deborah and Gideon, judge us and call us back when we wander from your way.
Congregation:	*Give us of your strength, that we may stand firm against oppression and evil.*
Reader:	God of the prophets, of Isaiah and Jeremiah and Amos, speak your word to us, that we may hear your message for this day.
Congregation:	*Keep us ever ready to speak the truth, to call for justice, and to serve you.*
Reader:	We pray to you, God of Judas Maccabeus and of Judith, and of all brave souls who dare, in the name of the Lord.
Congregation:	*Make us brave, and able to strengthen others in faithfulness to you.*
Reader:	Hear our prayers, God of John in the wilderness, calling the way and of Jesus, and of Mary and Martha.
Congregation:	*May we come to know You in our hearts, and thereby draw closer to You and to each other.*
Reader:	O God of Paul and Priscilla and Aquila, put your love into our hearts, that we may grow in your image.
Congregation:	*Give us faith and hope and love, a gift from you too share with our brothers and sisters, all Your children.*
Reader:	God of Albert Schweitzer and Anne Frank and Martin Buber, give us insight and willingness to learn.
Congregation:	*May we never forget the sacredness of every human life.*
Reader:	God of Martin Luther and Sister Kenny, of Dietrich Bonhoeffer, Pope John, and Martin Luther King, give us vision, that we may seek the truth and dare to dream in your name.
Congregation:	*Expand our limited view and lift us to new levels of understanding.*

All: *For we are Your sons and daughters, brought together in this community of faith. Jew, Protestant, Catholic, we worship You, O great God, for we are all Your children. Amen.*

Inscription on the walls of a cellar in Cologne, where Jews hid from Nazis:

Reader: I believe in the sun even when it is not shining; I believe in love when feeling it not; I believe in God even when God is silent.

And now, we rise as we praise You, O God:

Borchu et Adonai ha-m'vorach.

Praise the Lord, to whom our praise is due!

Baruch Adonai ha-m'vorach l'olam va-ed.

Praised be the Lord, to whom our praise is due, now and forever!

Congregation: The Universe is unfinished: humankind must strive toward its perfection. We must realize that only by our own hand can we achieve victory. The good suffer and the best suffer most, because it is the just and the true and the righteous that take upon themselves the task of bringing justice and truth into the world. When we have achieved our task, only then will a new heaven and a new earth appear together, and only then God shall be One and God's name shall be One.

Reader: Together we say the watchword of the Jewish faith:

Sh'ma yisrael Adonai eloheinu Adonai echad.

Hear, O Israel: The Lord is our God, the Lord is One.

Baruch sheim K'vod malchuto l'olam va-ed.
Praised be God's name whose glorious kingdom is forever and ever.

שְׁמַע יִשְׂרָאֵל יְהֹוָה אֱלֹהֵינוּ יְהֹוָה ׀ אֶחָד׃

בָּרוּךְ שֵׁם כְּבוֹד מַלְכוּתוֹ לְעוֹלָם וָעֶד.

וְאָהַבְתָּ אֵת יְהֹוָה אֱלֹהֶיךָ בְּכָל־לְבָבְךָ וּבְכָל־נַפְשְׁךָ וּבְכָל־מְאֹדֶךָ: וְהָיוּ הַדְּבָרִים הָאֵלֶּה אֲשֶׁר אָנֹכִי מְצַוְּךָ הַיּוֹם עַל־לְבָבֶךָ: וְשִׁנַּנְתָּם לְבָנֶיךָ וְדִבַּרְתָּ בָּם בְּשִׁבְתְּךָ בְּבֵיתֶךָ וּבְלֶכְתְּךָ בַדֶּרֶךְ וּבְשָׁכְבְּךָ וּבְקוּמֶךָ: וּקְשַׁרְתָּם לְאוֹת עַל־יָדֶךָ וְהָיוּ לְטֹטָפֹת בֵּין עֵינֶיךָ: וּכְתַבְתָּם עַל־מְזֻזוֹת בֵּיתֶךָ וּבִשְׁעָרֶיךָ:

Congregation is seated.

Congregation: You shall love the Lord your God with all your mind, with all your strength, with all your being.

Set these words, which I command you this day, upon your heart. Teach them faithfully to your children: speak of them in your home and on your way, when you lie down and when you rise up.

Bind them as a sign upon your hand: let them be a symbol before your eyes: inscribe them on the doorposts of your house, and on your gates.

Reader: And you shall take two onyx stones, and grave on them the names of the children of Israel: six of their names on one stone and the names of the six that remain on the other stone. And you shall put the two stones upon the shoulderpieces of the ephod, to be stones of memorial for the children of Israel; and Aaron shall bear their names before the Lord upon his two shoulders for a memorial. And these are the names of the twelve tribes that crossed the desert with Moses: the tribe of Poland, the tribe of Russia, the tribe of Lithuania, the tribe of Rumania, the tribe of Czechoslovakia, the tribe of Latvia, the tribe of Yugoslavia, the tribe of Hungary, the tribe of Germany, the tribe of France, the tribe of Holland, and the tribe of Greece.

And the Lord spoke to Moses, saying: Speak to the children of Israel, and tell them to make a yellow star upon their garments throughout their generations, one star over their heart and one on their back, of equal size and proportion: and it shall be for you a sign, that you may look upon it, and remember all the commandments of the Lord, and do them.

Congregation: Do not follow your own heart and your own eyes, by which you are seduced: but remember and do all my commandments and be holy to your God. I am the Lord your God, who brought you out of the land of Egypt, to be your God.

Ani Adonai eloheichem, asher hotseti etchem m'eretz
Mitsrayim, l'hiyot lachem l'elohim, Ani Adonai eloheichem.

Ashrei Hagafrur (Poem by Hannah Senesh)

Cantor: Blessed is the match consumed in kindling flame.
Blessed is the flame that burns in the heart's secret places.
Blessed is the heart with strength to stop its beating for honor's sake.
Blessed is the match consumed in kindling flame.

Reader: Today the ghetto knows a different fear,
Close in its grip, Death wields an icy scythe.
An evil sickness spreads a terror in its wake.
The victims of its shadow weep and writhe,
Today a father's heartbeat tells his fright
And mothers bend their heads into their hands,
Now children choke and die with typhus here,

A bitter tax is taken from their bands.
My heart still beats inside my breast
While friends depart for other worlds.
Perhaps it's better — who can say? —
Than watching this, to die today?

No, no, my God, we want to live!
Not watch our numbers melt away.
We want to have a better world,
We want to work — we must not die!

— Eva Pickova, twelve years old

Congregation: God our Creator, teach us to love freedom as we love life. Make us understand that only when all are free can we be free. Let none be masters and none be slaves. Then shall we sing as our people did when they were freed from Pharaoh's grip:

Mi cha-mo-cha ba-ei-lim, A-do-nai?
Mi ka-mo-cha, ne-dar ba-ko-desh.
no-ra te-hi-lot, o-sei fe-leh?

Mal-chu-te-cha ra-u va-ne-cha,
bo-kei-a yam li-fe-nei Mo-sheh;
"Zeh Ei-li a-nu ve-a-me-ru.
"A-do-nai yim-loch le-o-lam va-ed."

Who is like You. Eternal One, among the gods that are worshiped?
Who is like You, majestic in holiness, awesome in splendor, doing wonders?
In their escape from the sea, Your children saw Your sovereign might displayed.
    "This is my God!" they cried. "The Eternal will reign for ever and ever!"

All rise.

A Protest — A Prayer

Dear God, so much innocent bloodshed!
We are supposed to be created in your image
but, oh, how we have distorted it.

Must cruelty always be?
Must inhumanity ever be the signature of man?
No! No! We refuse to accept that!
We refuse to give hatred the last word
Because we know the power of love.

We refuse to believe that cruelty will prevail
because we have felt the strength of kindness.
We refuse to award the ultimate victory to evil
because we believe in You too much.

So help us God to live by our faith.
Where there is hatred, may we bring love.
Where there is pain, may we bring healing.
Where there is darkness, may we bring light.
Where there is despair, may we bring hope.
Where there is discord, may we bring peace.
Make this a better world and begin with us.

Amen.

Congregation: Blessed are You, O God, God of our ancestors, Who, in spite of all our suffering, has confirmed Your faithfulness to those who sleep in the dust by the lives that have come after them and remember them. You are holy, Your name is holy. We have taken time this day — time to pause and take account of what we still must do to perfect the world. May we ever be worthy of Your gifts — our life, our land, our love. O God, we give thanks to You forever.

Congregation is seated.

Silent Prayer

Dear God, so much innocent bloodshed!
We are supposed to be created in your image
but, oh, how we have distorted it.

Must cruelty always be?
Must inhumanity ever be the signature of man?

No! No! We refuse to accept that!
We refuse to give hatred the last word
Because we know the power of love.

We refuse to believe that cruelty will prevail
because we have felt the strength of kindness.
We refuse to award the ultimate victory to evil
because we believe in You too much.

So help us God to live by our faith.
Where there is hatred, may we bring love.
Where there is pain, may we bring healing.
Where there is darkness, may we bring light.
Where there is despair, may we bring hope.
Where there is discord, may we bring peace.
Make this a better world and begin with us.

Amen.

Music

May the words of my mouth, and the meditations of my heart, be acceptable to You, O lord, my Rock and my Redeemer.

Speakers . . . . Joseph Freeman
Irene Op Dyke

From Tomorrow On (by Motele)

> *Reader:*   From tomorrow on, I shall be sad —
> From tomorrow on!
> Today I will be gay.
> What is the use of sadness — tell me that?
> Because these evil winds begin to blow?
> Why should I grieve for tomorrow — today?
> Tomorrow may be so good, so sunny.
> Tomorrow the sun may shine for us again;
> We shall no longer need to be sad —
> From tomorrow on!
> Not today; no! Today I will be glad.
> And every day, no matter how bitter it be,
> I will say:
> From tomorrow on, I shall be sad,
> Not today!

Zog Nit Keinmol (Hymn of the Partisans)

> *Zog nit keinmol az du geist dem letztn veg.*
> *Ven himlen blaiene farshtaln bloie teg.*
> *Kumen vet noch unzer oisgebenkte sho,*
> *S'vet apoik ton unzer trot mir zainen do.*

> Never say that you are walking your last miles,
> When blackened skies conceal the heaven's bluer smiles,
> The hour will come because we've paid a price so dear,
> When hearts will beat and marching feet will roar we're here.

> From verdant palm tree lands to lands of bitter snow,
> We're marching onward with our heartbreak and our woe,
> And where our drops of blood have fallen to the ground,
> There our strength and courage fearlessly will sound.

> Today our load is lightened by tomorrow's sun,
> The past will vanish when our foe's been overcome,
> And if our sun's delayed as dawn withholds its wife,
> This hymn will trumpet land to land its song of life.

This song was written down in blood and not with lead,
It's not a song proclaiming summer birds have fled,
A people trapped within collapsing, bombed out lands,
We sang this song of hope with rifles in our hands.

So never say that you are walking your last miles,
When blackened skies conceal the heaven's bluer smiles,
The hour will come because we've paid a price so dear,
Our hearts will beat and marching feet will roar we're here.

—English adaptation by Leslie Aisenman

Please rise.

Adoration

Let us adore the ever-living God, and render praise unto God
Who spread out the heavens and established the earth.
Whose glory is revealed in the heavens above,
And Whose greatness is manifest throughout the world.
You are our God; there is none else.

Va-a-nach-nu ko-re-im
u-mish-ta-cha-vim u-mo-dim
li-fe-nei me-lech ma-le-chei ha-me-la-chim,
ha-ka-dosh ba-ruch Hu.

We therefore bow in awe and thanksgiving before the One Who is Sovereign over all, the Holy One, blessed be God.

Please be seated.

Reader: There are times when God's presence in history is eclipsed — but only eclipsed. For somehow we know, from the unexplainable events in our people's history, from the unexplainable turns in our lives, the mystery was, the mystery is, the mystery will be.

Congregation: Thus we are commanded by all that was to survive, lest we all perish: to remember the victims of the Holocaust, lest their memory perish. We are commanded never to despair of God lest we perish.

Reader: Holding fast to our history and destiny, our challenge and hope is to journey toward the Divine, as we struggle to conquer evil and establish God's kingdom on earth.

Congregation: On that day God shall be One and God's name shall be One.
Bayom hahu y'hyeh Adonai echad u'shmo echad.

Kaddish

In gratitude for all the blessings our loved ones, friends, teachers, and the martyrs of our people have brought to us, to our people, and to humanity we dedicate ourselves anew to the sacred faith for which they have lived and died, and to the tasks they have bequeathed to us. O God, let them be remembered for blessing, together with the righteous of all peoples, and let us say: Amen.

Yahrzeit — for the victims of the Holocaust

We remember those who died at

Auschwitz, Buchenwald, Belzec, Bergen-Belsen, Bojunavo, Chelmno, Dachau, Dora, Flossenberg, Gross-Rosen, Janow, Lida, Lichtenberg, Lvov, Mauthausen, Maidanek, Natzweiler, Neuengamme, Oranienberg, Ponar, Pustkow, Potulice, Ravensbruck, Sobibor, Skarzhysko, Sachsenhausen, Stargard, Treblinka, Travniki, Theresienstadt, Vilna, Warsaw, Wolzhek...

We rise as one congregation to praise God's name:

קדיש יתום

יִתְגַּדַּל וְיִתְקַדַּשׁ שְׁמֵהּ רַבָּא בְּעָלְמָא דִּי־בְרָא כִרְעוּתֵהּ,
Yit·ga·dal ve·yit·ka·dash she·mei ra·ba be·al·ma di·ve·ra chi·re·u·tei,

וְיַמְלִיךְ מַלְכוּתֵהּ בְּחַיֵּיכוֹן וּבְיוֹמֵיכוֹן וּבְחַיֵּי דְכָל־בֵּית
ve·yam·lich mal·chu·tei be·cha·yei·chon u·ve·yo·mei·chon u·ve·cha·yei
de·chol beit

יִשְׂרָאֵל, בַּעֲגָלָא וּבִזְמַן קָרִיב, וְאִמְרוּ: אָמֵן.
Yis·ra·eil, ba·a·ga·la u·vi·ze·man ka·riv, ve·i·me·ru: a·mein.

יְהֵא שְׁמֵהּ רַבָּא מְבָרַךְ לְעָלַם וּלְעָלְמֵי עָלְמַיָּא.
Ye·hei she·mei ra·ba me·va·rach le·a·lam u·le·al·mei al·ma·ya.

יִתְבָּרַךְ וְיִשְׁתַּבַּח, וְיִתְפָּאַר וְיִתְרוֹמַם וְיִתְנַשֵּׂא, וְיִתְהַדָּר
Yit·ba·rach ve·yish·ta·bach, ve·yit·pa·ar ve·yit·ro·mam ve·yit·na·sei, ve·yit·ha·dar

וְיִתְעַלֶּה וְיִתְהַלָּל שְׁמֵהּ דְּקוּדְשָׁא, בְּרִיךְ הוּא, לְעֵלָּא מִן־כָּל־
ve·yit·a·leh ve·yit·ha·lal she·mei de·ku·de·sha, be·rich hu, le·ei·la min kol

בִּרְכָתָא וְשִׁירָתָא, תֻּשְׁבְּחָתָא וְנֶחֱמָתָא דַּאֲמִירָן בְּעָלְמָא,
bi·re·cha·ta ve·shi·ra·ta, tush·be·cha·ta ve·ne·che·ma·ta, da·a·mi·ran be·al·ma,

וְאִמְרוּ: אָמֵן.
ve·i·me·ru: a·mein.

יְהֵא שְׁלָמָא רַבָּא מִן שְׁמַיָּא וְחַיִּים עָלֵינוּ וְעַל־כָּל־יִשְׂרָאֵל,
Ye·hei she·la·ma ra·ba min she·ma·ya ve·cha·yim a·lei·nu ve·al kol Yis·ra·eil,

וְאִמְרוּ: אָמֵן.

ve·i·me·ru: a·mein.

עֹשֶׂה שָׁלוֹם בִּמְרוֹמָיו, הוּא יַעֲשֶׂה שָׁלוֹם עָלֵינוּ וְעַל־כָּל־

O·seh sha·lom bi·me·ro·mav, hu ya·a·seh sha·lom a·lei·nu ve·al kol

יִשְׂרָאֵל, וְאִמְרוּ: אָמֵן.

Yis·ra·eil, ve·i·me·ru: a·mein.

Let the glory of God be extolled, let God's great name be hallowed in the world whose creation God willed.

May God's kingdom soon prevail, in our own day, our own lives, and the life of all Israel, and let us say: Amen.

Let God's great name be blessed forever and ever.

Let the name of the Holy One, blessed is God, be glorified, exalted, and honored, though God is beyond all the praises, songs, and adorations that we can utter, and let us say: Amen.

For us and for all Israel, may the blessing of peace and the promise of life come true, and let us say: Amen.

May the One Who causes peace to reign in the high heavens, let peace descend on us, on all Israel, and all the world, and let us say: Amen.

May the Source of peace send peace to all who mourn, and comfort to all who are bereaved, Amen.

Closing Song: "Eili, Eili"

Poem: Hannah Senesh
Music: David Zahavi

O Lord, my God,	Eili, Eili
I pray that these things never end:	she-lo yi-ga-meir le-ol-am
The sand and the sea.	ha-chol ve-ha-yam,
The rush of the waters,	rish-rush shel ha-ma-yim,
The crash of the heavens,	be-rak ha-sha-ma-yim,
The prayer of the heart.	te-fi-lat ha-a-dam.

Benediction

Reader: And who among us can be certain that if we were in the wrong place at the wrong time, we would not cooperate with the forces of evil? Are we not, in some way, doing exactly that by our subtle racism, our lack of interest in war-torn nations around the world, our deliberate ignorance of genocide through starvation that some people are experiencing as we sit here, this very moment?

               Master of the universe, help us to bear in mind always our potential for evil. And strengthen us, our God, so that we may fulfill our potential for good instead.

11

Yom HaShoah

Community-wide Observance

Beth Shalom Synagogue, Pittsburgh

Introduction
THE ANNE FRANK WE REMEMBER
by Alvin H. Rosenfeld*

Have we lost sight of the little girl?

Anne Frank's diary is the most widely read book of World War II. First published in Dutch
in 1947, it has since been translated into more than fifty languages and circulated in some
18 million copies. It has also been successfully adapted for stage and screen, so that millions of people who may never have read Anne Frank's book know of the girl from the
popular play and film that tell her story. Several different countries have issued commemorative stamps and coins bearing the image of Anne Frank; sculptors have cast her in bronze;
songwriters have written songs to her; poets dedicated poems to her; memoirists recorded
their impressions of her. As a result of these and numerous other acts of tribute and commemoration, the name and face of Anne Frank are instantly recognizable to large numbers
of people throughout the world. She is, in sum, one of the most famous children of the
twentieth century.

Her fame was purchased at an exceedingly high price. People know of Anne Frank and
respond to her as they do because her story is intimately bound up with a horrifying fate:
the mass destruction of European Jewry. To many, Anne Frank is the symbol of that fate,
a child victim of a genocidal war that victimized millions. She is remembered as a bright,
intelligent, vivacious girl, who was guilty of no crime but the "crime," as her enemies defined it, of her Jewish birth. For that reason and that reason alone, she fled into hiding with
her family until she was finally hunted down and dispatched to Nazi murder camps. Before
then, during her twenty-five-month period of confinement in her Amsterdam hideaway, she
wrote a remarkable book. It survived her and, over the past four decades, has been taken up
as vivid testimony of her courage, hope, and faith in humanity. This came at a time when

---

At Beth Shalom Synagogue, Pittsburgh, Pennsylvania, under the auspices of the Holocaust Center of the United
Jewish Federation.
*From *ADL Dimensions Magazine* 5, no. 1. Alvin H. Rosenfeld, Professor of English and Director of Jewish
Studies at Indiana University, is the author of *Imagining Hitler* and *A Double Dying: Reflections on Holocaust
Literature*.

"humanity" was a concept that was rapidly losing its meaning. If we continue to read Anne Frank and ponder her ordeal, no doubt we do so because we remain haunted by the failure a generation ago of those very forces of culture in which this bright young girl seemed to place such ardent belief.

Candle Lighting Procession

Third generation members will recall the names of some of the Concentration Camps:

Auschwitz	Flossenberg
Babi Yar	Mauthausen
Bergen-Belsen	Ravensbruck
Buchenwald	Sobibor
Chelmno	Terezin
Dachau	Treblinka

THIRD GENERATION	SECOND GENERATION	SURVIVORS
Allison & David Brown	Stephanie & Peter Brown	Elizabeth & Paul Brown
Ronna Greenberg	Vera & Lesley Greenberg	Irene & Maz Weinberger
Orit Greenberg	Alexandra & Jacob Greenberg	Anna & Harry Delowsky
Cari Kornblit	Anita & Morris Kornblit	Dora & David Kornblit
Jeffrey Margolis	Gladys & Alan Margolis	Frances & Harry Spiegel
Jennifer & Todd Neufeld	Toby & Ronald Neufeld	Helen & David Heringer
Elana Rosenberg	Cynthia & Paul Rosenberg	Irene & Herman Stanger
Jennifer Schwartz	Marcy & Howard Schwartz	Irene & Israel Samuel

Candle for the Righteous Gentile . . . . STEVE ZUPCIC

Steve Zupcic, a member of the Holocaust Commission, is a Community Liaison with the University of Pittsburgh. After participating in the 1988 Yad Vashem course in Jerusalem on teaching the Holocaust he has become active in presenting Holocaust materials to multiethnic and multireligious audiences. He has also actively applied Holocaust and survivor materials to his work with Pittsburgh Action Against Rape, Pittsburgh AIDS Task Force, Human Rights Campaign Fund, Pittsburgh Men's Collective, and Center for Victims of Violent Crime.

Opening Prayer . . . . RABBI STEPHEN E. STEINDEL

Responsive Reading: . . . . ISABEL ALCOFF AND ABE KOHANE
We Remember The Holocaust
Presidents of Legacy and Survivors Organizations

Reader: We recall with bitter grief the catastrophe which overwhelmed our people in Europe, adding an unprecedented chapter to our history of suffering.

All: We mourn for six million of our people, brutally destroyed by "civilized people" behaving like savages. The cruelties of Pharaoh, Haman,

Nebuchadnezzar, and Titus cannot be compared with the diabolical schemes of the modern tyrants in their design to exterminate an entire people.

Reader: The blood of the innocent who perished in the gas chambers of Auschwitz, Bergen-Belsen, Buchenwald, Dachau, Treblinka, and Theresienstadt cries out to God and humanity.

All: We will never forget the burning of synagogues and houses of study, the destruction of holy books and scrolls of Torah, the sadistic torment and murder of scholars, sages, and teachers.

Reader: They tortured the flesh of our brothers and sisters; but they could not crush their spirit, their faith, their love.

All: We recall our brothers and sisters in the Warsaw Ghetto and in other hellish places who valiantly rose up and defied the monstrous adversaries.

Reader: We recall the heroism of those who, in the face of unprecedented and overwhelming force, maintained Jewish life and culture and asserted Jewish values in the very midst of enslavement and degradation.

All: Even as we mourn, we recall those precious few compassionate men and women of other faiths and nationalities who, at the peril of their lives, saved some of our people. Truly, "The righteous of all nations have a share in the world to come."

Reader: O Lord, remember Your martyred children. Remember all who have given their lives for the sanctification of Your name.

Welcome . . . . JAMES RUDOLPH
Chairman, Soviet Resettlement Committee

Ani Maamin (I Believe) . . . . VERA GREENBERG
Hebrew text sung by ALAN POLANSKY

Jews in Warsaw, Lublin, Lodz, Bialystock, the first victims of the Germans, sang this Hebrew song, which subsequently became popular among all Jews.

Narrator: I believe that the light will shine, even if I do not live to see the end of the night.

All: Ani Maamin!

Narrator: I believe in love, even though hatred surrounds me.

All: Ani Maamin!

Narrator: I believe in the Jewish people united like the fingers of one hand: a hand that can clench in strength, yet reaches out for peace.

All: Ani Maamin!

Narrator: I believe that I am my brother's keeper, that all Jews are responsible for one another.

All: Ani Maamin!

Narrator: I believe that, despite the fury and wrath of those who rise up in every generation to destroy us... the people of Israel lives.

All: Ani Maamin!

Narrator: "Now we are a nation like other nations: Masters of our destiny for the first time in twenty centuries...." (Haim Hefer)

"The dream came true, too late to save those who perished in the Holocaust, but *not* too late for the generation to come." (Golda Meir)

All: I believe that the land, the book and the people are one: not only today, but always.

Narrator: I believe...

All: We are one... Ani Maamin!

Narrator: Now, in memory of those who perished before us... and in pledge to those who will live after us... repeat after me the words of Isaiah's vow:

Narrator: "For Jerusalem's sake I will not be still...."

All: "For Jerusalem's sake I will not be still."

Narrator: Remember: Do not forget.
"And for Zion's sake I will not be silent...."

All: "And for Zion's sake I will not be silent...."

Narrator: Remember: Do not forget. "Till her victory emerges resplendent...."

All: "Till her victory emerges resplendent."

Narrator: Remember: Do not forget. "And her triumph like a flaming torch...."

All: "And her triumph like a flaming torch."

Narrator: Remember: Do not forget.

All: Ani Maamin!

Ani Ma-Amin

אני מאמין

אֲנִי מַאֲמִין בֶּאֱמוּנָה שְׁלֵמָה
בְּבִיאַת הַמָּשִׁיחַ.
וְאַף עַל פִּי שֶׁיִּתְמַהְמַהּ,
עִם כָּל זֶה אֲנִי מַאֲמִין,
עִם כָּל זֶה אֲחַכֶּה לוֹ
בְּכָל יוֹם שֶׁיָּבוֹא.

Ani ma-amin be-emuna sh'leyma b'vi-at ha-mashiah,
V'af al pi sh'yitma-mey-ha, im kol ze ani ma-amin.

I believe in the coming of the Messiah, although he may tarry.

All rise.

El Maleh Rachamin .... CANTOR MARK SHULMAN
Beth El Synagogue, South Hills

Memorial Prayer for the Departed

In memory of the six million:

שְׁמַע יִשְׂרָאֵל יְהֹוָה אֱלֹהֵינוּ יְהֹוָה | אֶחָד:

בָּרוּךְ שֵׁם כְּבוֹד מַלְכוּתוֹ לְעוֹלָם וָעֶד.

וְאָהַבְתָּ אֵת יְהֹוָה אֱלֹהֶיךָ בְּכָל־לְבָבְךָ וּבְכָל־נַפְשְׁךָ וּבְכָל־
מְאֹדֶךָ: וְהָיוּ הַדְּבָרִים הָאֵלֶּה אֲשֶׁר אָנֹכִי מְצַוְּךָ הַיּוֹם עַל־לְבָבֶךָ:
וְשִׁנַּנְתָּם לְבָנֶיךָ וְדִבַּרְתָּ בָּם בְּשִׁבְתְּךָ בְּבֵיתֶךָ וּבְלֶכְתְּךָ בַדֶּרֶךְ
וּבְשָׁכְבְּךָ וּבְקוּמֶךָ: וּקְשַׁרְתָּם לְאוֹת עַל־יָדֶךָ וְהָיוּ לְטֹטָפֹת בֵּין
עֵינֶיךָ: וּכְתַבְתָּם עַל־מְזֻזוֹת בֵּיתֶךָ וּבִשְׁעָרֶיךָ:

Exalted, compassionate God, grant perfect peace in Your sheltering Presence, among the holy and the pure, to the souls of all our brethren, men, women, and children of the House of Israel who were slaughtered and suffocated and burned to ashes. May their memory endure, inspiring truth and loyalty in our lives. May their souls thus be bound up in the bond of life. May they rest in peace. And let us say: Amen.

All sit.

Excerpts from *Anne Frank: The Diary of a Young Girl* .... ORIT GREENBERG

At My Bar Mitzvah — and His

Dedicated to the memory of a thirteen-year-old hero of the Resistance.

When I was thirteen, I became Bar Mitzvah.
When he was thirteen, he became Bar Mitzvah.

When I was thirteen, my teachers taught me — to put *Tefillin* on my arm.
When he was thirteen, his teachers taught him — to throw a hand grenade with his arm.

When I was thirteen, I studied the pathways of the Bible and roadways of the Talmud.
When he was thirteen, he studied the canals of Warsaw and the sewers of the Ghetto.

At my Bar Mitzvah, I took an oath to live as a Jew.
At his Bar Mitzvah, he took an oath to die as a Jew.

At my Bar Mitzvah, I blessed God.
At his Bar Mitzvah, he questioned God.

At my Bar Mitzvah, I lifted my voice and sang.
At his Bar Mitzvah, he lifted his fists and fought.

At my Bar Mitzvah, I read from the Scroll of the Torah.
At his Bar Mitzvah, he wrote a Scroll of Fire.

At my Bar Mitzvah, I wore a new *Tallit* over a new suit.
At his Bar Mitzvah, he wore a rifle and bullets over a suit of rags.

At my Bar Mitzvah, I started my road of life.
At his Bar Mitzvah, he began his road to martyrdom.

At my Bar Mitzvah, family and friends came to say *l'chayim.*
At his Bar Mitzvah, Rabbi Akiba and Trumpeldor, Hannah and her seven sons came — to escort him to Heaven.

At my Bar Mitzvah, they praised my voice, my song, my melody.
At his Bar Mitzvah, they praised his strength, his courage, his fearlessness.

When I was thirteen, I was called up to the Torah — I went to the *Bimah.*
When he was thirteen, his body went up in smoke — his soul rose to God.

When I was thirteen, I became Bar Mitzvah — and lived.
When he was thirteen, he became Bar Mitzvah — and lives now within each of us.

All rise.

Mourner's Kaddish . . . . Rabbi Mordecai Glatstein
Riverview Center for Jewish Seniors

קדיש יתום

יִתְגַּדַּל וְיִתְקַדַּשׁ שְׁמֵהּ רַבָּא בְּעָלְמָא דִּי־בְרָא כִרְעוּתַהּ,
Yit-ga-dal ve-yit-ka-dash she-mei ra-ba be-al-ma di-ve-ra chi-re-u-tei,

וְיַמְלִיךְ מַלְכוּתֵהּ בְּחַיֵּיכוֹן וּבְיוֹמֵיכוֹן וּבְחַיֵּי דְכָל־בֵּית
ve-yam-lich mal-chu-tei be-cha-yei-chon u-ve-yo-mei-chon u-ve-cha-yei
de-chol beit

יִשְׂרָאֵל, בַּעֲגָלָא וּבִזְמַן קָרִיב, וְאִמְרוּ: אָמֵן.
Yis-ra-eil, ba-a-ga-la u-vi-ze-man ka-riv, ve-i-me-ru: a-mein.

יְהֵא שְׁמֵהּ רַבָּא מְבָרַךְ לְעָלַם וּלְעָלְמֵי עָלְמַיָּא.
Ye-hei she-mei ra-ba me-va-rach le-a-lam u-le-al-mei al-ma-ya.

יִתְבָּרַךְ וְיִשְׁתַּבַּח, וְיִתְפָּאַר וְיִתְרוֹמַם וְיִתְנַשֵּׂא, וְיִתְהַדָּר
Yit-ba-rach ve-yish-ta-bach, ve-yit-pa-ar ve-yit-ro-mam ve-yit-na-sei, ve-yit-ha-dar

וְיִתְעַלֶּה וְיִתְהַלָּל שְׁמֵהּ דְּקֻדְשָׁא, בְּרִיךְ הוּא, לְעֵלָּא מִן־כָּל־
ve-yit-a-leh ve-yit-ha-lal she-mei de-ku-de-sha, be-rich hu, le-ei-la min kol

בִּרְכָתָא וְשִׁירָתָא, תֻּשְׁבְּחָתָא וְנֶחֱמָתָא דַּאֲמִירָן בְּעָלְמָא,
bi-re-cha-ta ve-shi-ra-ta, tush-be-cha-ta ve-ne-che-ma-ta, da-a-mi-ran be-al-ma,

וְאִמְרוּ: אָמֵן.
ve-i-me-ru: a-mein.

יְהֵא שְׁלָמָא רַבָּא מִן שְׁמַיָּא וְחַיִּים עָלֵינוּ וְעַל־כָּל־יִשְׂרָאֵל,
Ye-hei she-la-ma ra-ba min she-ma-ya ve-cha-yim a-lei-nu ve-al kol Yis-ra-eil,

וְאִמְרוּ: אָמֵן.
ve-i-me-ru: a-mein.

עֹשֶׂה שָׁלוֹם בִּמְרוֹמָיו, הוּא יַעֲשֶׂה שָׁלוֹם עָלֵינוּ וְעַל־כָּל־
O-seh sha-lom bi-me-ro-mav, hu ya-a-seh sha-lom a-lei-nu ve-al kol

יִשְׂרָאֵל, וְאִמְרוּ: אָמֵן.
Yis-ra-eil, ve-i-me-ru: a-mein.

All sit.

Yiddish Remarks . . . . Rabbi Baruch A. Poupko

Keynote Address: "Innocence, Dignity, and Life" . . . . Ze'ev Mankowitz
Director of Jerusalem Fellows and lecturer on
Holocaust Studies and Education at Hebrew University

Closing . . . . JACK GORDON
Chair, Holocaust Commission

Zog Nit Keynmol . . . . SUSAN BUSCHO
(Song of the Partisans)   Second Generation
by Hirsh Glick

Hirsh Glick was born in Vilna in 1920 and fought as a partisan in the Vilna Woods. He was killed in battle in 1944. Subsequently his partisan song became the recognized anthem of the Jewish partisans, a symbol of the fighting spirit in the ghetto.

Responsive Reading

Reader: Never say that you have reached your journey's end:
That dark and heavy clouds conceal the light of day.
Upon us yet will dawn the day for which we yearn.
Our tramping feet will then proclaim that we are here.

All: From lands so green with palms to lands all white with snow.
We shall be coming with our anguish and our woe,
And where a spurt of our blood fell upon the earth,
There our courage and our spirit have rebirth.

Reader: The morning sun again will gild our day.
The past will with enemy fade away.
Yet should the sun delay and spring be late,
The song for generations will reverberate.

All: This song is written not with ink, but blood,
It is not a song of a free bird in the wood.
This song a people sang between collapsing walls.
This song to future generation calls.

Reader: So never say this is the last road we have gone.
This the last time that the sun has shone.
The day will dawn, the sun will reappear.
Our tread will fall like thunder — we are here.

All rise.

Hatikvah . . . . Cantor Mark Shulman

In unison:

הַתִּקְוָה

כָּל עוֹד בַּלֵּבָב פְּנִימָה
נֶפֶשׁ יְהוּדִי הוֹמִיָּה,
וּלְפַאֲתֵי מִזְרָח קָדִימָה
עַיִן לְצִיּוֹן צוֹפִיָּה.

עוֹד לֹא אָבְדָה תִקְוָתֵנוּ,
הַתִּקְוָה שְׁנוֹת אַלְפַּיִם,
לִהְיוֹת עַם חָפְשִׁי בְּאַרְצֵנוּ,
בְּאֶרֶץ צִיּוֹן וִירוּשָׁלָיִם.

Transliteration:	*Translation:*
Kol od ba-lei-vav pe-ni-ma,	As long as deep in the heart
Ne-fesh Ye-hu-di ho-mi-ya.	The soul of a Jew yearns
U-le-fa-a-tei miz-rach ka-di-ma,	And towards the East
A-yin te-tsi-yon tso-fi-ya.	An eye looks to Zion.
Od lo av-da tik-va-tei-nu,	Our hope is not yet lost
Ha-tik-va she-not al-pa-yim,	The hope of two thousand years
Li-yot am chof-shi be-ar-tsei-nu,	To be a free people in our land
Be-e-rets tsi-yon Ye-ru-sha-la-yim.	The land of Zion and Jerusalem.

Days of Remembrance:
Yom HaShoah

United States Holocaust Memorial Council

April 20, 1982
Capitol Rotunda
Washington, D.C.
12:00 Noon

Processional Music . . . . Atlanta Boy Choir

COUNCIL ENTRANCE

Invocation . . . . The Honorable Franklin Littell
Council Member
United States Holocaust Memorial Council

Introduction . . . . The Honorable Mark Talisman
Vice Chairman
United States Holocaust Memorial Council

Remarks . . . . The Honorable Sigmund Strochlitz
Chairman, Days of Remembrance Committee
United States Holocaust Memorial Council

Remarks . . . . The Honorable Thomas P. O'Neill, Jr.
Speaker of the House

Remarks . . . . The Honorable Ted Stevens
Majority Whip of the Senate

Candle Lighting: Participating Survivors

SIGMUND STROCHLITZ

HADASSAH ROSENSALT

MILES LERMAN

ELI ZBOROWSKI

SIGGI WILZIG

KALMAN SULTANIK

BENJAMIN MEED

Commemorative Address . . . . THE HONORABLE ELIE WIESEL
Chairman
United States Holocaust Memorial Council

El Maleh Rachamim . . . . CANTOR JOSEPH MALOVANY
Fifth Avenue Synagogue, New York City

Kaddish . . . . MR. ROBERT E. AGUS
Acting Director
United States Holocaust Memorial Council

Benediction . . . . THE HONORABLE ALFRED GOTTSCHALK
Council Member
United States Holocaust Memorial Council

COUNCIL EXIT

Recessional Music . . . . ATLANTA BOY CHOIR

Audience will please remain in place until the conclusion of the Recessional Music.

THE ATLANTA BOY CHOIR

The Atlanta Boy Choir, under the direction of Fletcher Wolfe, enjoys an international reputation for musical excellence. In the twenty-five years of its existence, the choir has been acclaimed, both in the United States and abroad, as one of the finest groups in the world. As ambassadors of good will and song, the choir has toured extensively, performing in major halls, cathedrals, churches, and music festivals of Europe, Africa, South America and the United States.

In the summer of 1981, the choir gave a command performance for President Pertini of Italy. The "Commendatore al Merito," Italy's highest medal of honor, was presented to Mr. Wolfe for his cultural and musical achievements in that country.

PROCESSIONAL NO. 1

BIRDSONG

He doesn't know the world at all
who stays in his nest and doesn't go out
He doesn't know what the birds know best
nor what I want to sing about,
that the world is full of loveliness.

When dew drops sparkle in the grass,
and Earth's aflood with morning light,
a blackbird sings upon a bush,
to greet the dawning after night.
Then I know how fine it is to be alive.

Hey, try to open up your heart to beauty,
go to the woods some day
and weave a wreath of memory there.

Then if tears obscure your way
you'll know how wonderful
it is to be alive, to be alive,
Sh'ma Yisrael

Hear, O Israel, the Lord is our God,
the Lord is One.

—Anonymous, 1941

PROCESSIONAL NO. 2

THE BUTTERFLY

Only I never saw another butterfly.
The last, the very last,
so richly, brightly, dazz'lingly yellow.

Perhaps if the sun's tears
would sing against a white stone,
such a yellow is carried lightly
way up high.
It went away, it went away I'm sure,
because it looked to kiss the world goodbye.

For seven weeks I've lived in here,
penned up inside this ghetto,
but I have found my people here,
the dandelions care for me
and the white chestnut candles in the court.
Only I never saw another butterfly.

—Pavel Friedmann, 1942

CANDLE LIGHTING

Ani Mamin
(I Believe)

Ani mamin
Beemuno shleima
Bevias hamoshiach, Ani mamin
Veaf al pi sheitmahmeiha
Im Kol zeh, Ani Mamin

RECESSIONAL

Zog Nit Keynmol
(Jewish Partisan Song)

Zog Nit Keyn Mol Az Du Geyst Dem Letztn Veg.
Himfen Blaiene Farshtelln Bloie Teg.
Kumen Vet Noch Unser Oisgebenkte Sho,
Es Vet A Poik Ton Unzer Trot; Mir Zainen Do!

Oh, never say that you have reached the very end.
Though leaden skies a better future may portend
Because the hour for which we yearned will yet arrive
And our marching steps will thunder: We Survive!

13

Days of Remembrance

UNITED STATES ARMY HOLOCAUST COMMEMORATION SERVICE

Hunter Garrison Chapel
Hunter Army Airfield, Georgia

ORDER OF WORSHIP

Prelude . . . . MRS. JUDY BULLEN

Welcoming Remarks . . . . LTC CLARENCE P. WHITAKER

Presentation of Colors . . . . 260 QM BN DETAIL/DRUMMER: SSG CARL WESLEY

National Anthem . . . . CONGREGATION

Seven Candles Lit for Six Million Jews and Others . . . . HOLOCAUST SURVIVORS

Meditation and Invocation . . . . CH MARVIN K. VICKERS

Historical Background . . . . COL WILLIAM A. IZZARD

Remarks by Jewish War Veterans . . . . COMMANDER MARTIN JACKEL

Old Testament Reading: The Twenty-third Psalm . . . . LTC WAYNE C. KABAT

Responsive Reading . . . . CH WILLIAM C. SHELNUTT

Holocaust Reading . . . . RABBI RAPHAEL GOLD

Special Music . . . . MRS. ANNITA HOMANSKY

Christian Commemoration Address .... CH PAUL R. WESSELHÖFT

Introduction of Guest Speaker .... COL IAN W. LARSON

Jewish Commemoration Address .... RABBI AVIGDOR SLATUS

Special Music.................................. MRS. ANNITA HOMANSKY

Prayer .... CH KENNETH A. SEIFRIED

One Minute of Silence .... CONGREGATION

Memorial Prayer Chant .... RABBI DAVID E. OSTRICH

Taps and Flag Lowered to Half Mast....... SFC JOHN MURPHY/SP4 BRYANT CADE

Retirement of Colors........... 260 QM BN DETAIL/DRUMMER: SSG CARL WESLEY

Postlude .... MRS. JUDY BULLEN

The result of this war will be the complete annihilation of the Jews.
— ADOLF HITLER, 1942

Not all victims were Jews,
But all Jews were victims.
— ELIE WIESEL
(SURVIVOR)

Though I walk through the valley
of the Shadow of Death,
I will fear no evil.
— DAVID

Responsive Reading: "Lord, Give Us Strength"

Chaplain: Lord, as we gather today,
We pray for courage and for strength

Congregation: *When we remember the evils in the past,*
The innocents tortured, maimed, and murdered,

Chaplain: We are almost afraid to make ourselves remember.
But we are even more afraid to forget.

Congregation: *We ask for wisdom, that we might mourn,*
And not be consumed by hatred.

Chaplain: That we might remember, and yet not lose hope.

Congregation: *We must face evil —*
                   And, so doing, reaffirm our faith in future good.

Chaplain: We cannot erase yesterday's pains, but we can vow that
                   they will not have been suffered in vain.

Congregation: *And so, we pray:*
                   For those who were given death,
                   Let us choose life —
                   for us and for generations yet to come.

Chaplain: For those who found courage to stand against evil —
                   often at the cost of their lives —
                   Let us vow to carry on their struggle.

Congregation: *We must teach ourselves, and our children:*
                   To learn from hate that we must love,
                   To learn from evil to live for good.

Memorial Prayer Chant: El Maleh Rachamim

O God, full of compassion, Thou who dwellest on high! Grant perfect rest unto the souls which have departed from this world. Lord of mercy, bring them into Thy presence and let their souls be bound up in the bond of eternal life. Be Thou their possession and may their repose be peace. Amen.

The Kaddish

May the Great Name be glorified and sanctified in the world created by God's will, and may the great kingdom soon prevail, in your lifetime, in your days, and in the days of the whole House of Israel — may it be very soon. And let us say Amen.

May the Great Name be praised forever and ever and ever.

May the Name of the Holy One be praised and honored and admired and uplifted and exalted and glorified and raised up and blessed — even though It is above all the blessings and songs and honors and glorious words that are spoken in the whole world. And let us say Amen.

May there be great peace and life for us and for all Israel, and let us say Amen.

May the Source of peace in the heavens make peace for us and for all Israel, and let us say Amen.

14

Days of Remembrance

National Civic Holocaust Commemoration Ceremony

DAYS OF REMEMBRANCE

The United States Congress unanimously created the United States Holocaust Memorial Council on October 7, 1980, in Public Law 96-388. In that legislation, the Congress directed the Council to sponsor an annual national civic commemoration of the Holocaust. Accordingly, the Council designated April 26–May 3, 1981, as the first annual Days of Remembrance.

Acting upon the Council's request, many governors and mayors of major cities issued proclamations and held ceremonies commemorating the Days of Remembrance in state capitals and city halls. Services and prayers were held in churches and synagogues, and special programs on the Holocaust were convened at community centers, on the campuses of universities and colleges, and in public schools across the country. Throughout the nation, public libraries posted a selected bibliography of Holocaust-related literature, and participating public broadcasting stations showed special films throughout the week.

The occasion was also observed in the nation's capital by two commemoration ceremonies, the first in the East Room of The White House, attended by President Ronald Reagan, and the second in the Rayburn House Office Building. In addition, the United States Congress convened a Special Order Session in recognition and memory of the victims of the Holocaust, and many government and congressional office buildings had exhibits on the events agencies of the Holocaust in their main lobbies. Also, the American Film Institute at the John F. Kennedy Center for the Performing Arts sponsored a special "Evening of Remembrance — Films of the Holocaust."

At the White House ceremony, President Reagan vividly and movingly recalled his experience as a soldier in the American Army, when he viewed unedited film footage taken by Army photographers upon entering the concentration camps.

Ceremonies held at The White House and Rayburn Office Building, House of Representatives, Washington, D.C. Organized by the Days of Remembrance Committee of the United States Holocaust Memorial Council.

UNITED STATES HOLOCAUST MEMORIAL COUNCIL

DAYS OF REMEMBRANCE

Yom HaShoah
April 30, 1981
East Room
The White House

Welcoming Remarks . . . . THE HONORABLE JACOB STEIN
Special Advisor to the White House

Remarks . . . . THE HONORABLE JOHN C. DANFORTH*
United States Senator (Missouri)

Entrance of the President of the United States

Address . . . . THE HONORABLE ELIE WIESEL
Chairman,
United States Holocaust Memorial Council

Mr. President, distinguished members of the House, of the Senate, and of the diplomatic corps, honored guests, friends. About sadness later; first some words of gratitude. We thank you, Mr. President, for joining us and for participating in this solemn assembly of remembrance. Your presence here today, Mr. President, so soon after the senseless attack upon your person, is a tribute to your understanding and concern for human values and is especially meaningful to us. We all know that your being here, Mr. President, is not a ceremonial gesture, but an expression of your sense of history and your dream of a future with hope and dignity for the American nation and for all humankind.

So, we thank you, Mr. President, and we thank our Father in heaven for having spared you. And now with your permission, Mr. President, I would like to read to you or rather to share with you some lines written first by an old Jewish poet and then by a young Jewish poet. The old Jewish poet was named Leivick, and he wrote in Yiddish, which was the language of the martyrs — the language of those who were killed in those days.

•

The other poem was written by a young boy in Theresienstadt named Mottele, and he wrote in that ghetto in those days of the awe and fear and sadness; he wrote a poem that reflects more than his own moods, more than his own fate, and I quote,

> From tomorrow on I shall be sad.
> From tomorrow on, not today.
> What is the use of sadness, tell me?
> Because these evil winds begin to blow?
> Why should I grieve for tomorrow today?
> Tomorrow may be good.

---

*The Honorable Rudy Boschwitz, Senator from Minnesota, graciously spoke for Senator John C. Danforth, who was unable to attend the ceremony.

Tomorrow the sun may shine for us again.
We shall no longer need to be sad.
From tomorrow on I shall be sad.
From tomorrow on, not today.
No, today I will be glad.
And every day, no matter how bitter it may be,
I will say from tomorrow on I shall be sad, not today.

Mr. President, how does one commemorate the million Motteles and Shloimeles and Leahles and Soreles? How does one commemorate six million victims, all descendents of Abraham and Isaac and Jacob? What words does one use? What metaphors does one invoke to describe the brutal and unprecedented extinctions of a world — thousands and thousands of flourishing Jewish communities survived the fury of the Crusades, the hatred of pogroms, the afflictions of wars and the misery, the shame, the despair of religious and social oppressions only to be swept away by the Holocaust? In all their chronicles and testaments, memoirs and prayers, litanies and poems, the victims stressed one single theme over and over again — remember, remember the horror, remember. Bear witness. And that is their legacy to us, the living.

Of course, there may be some who'll be asked, "Why remember at all? Why not allow the dead to bury the dead? Is it not in man's nature to push aside memories that hurt and disturb?" The more cruel the wound, the greater the effort to cover it. The more horrifying the nightmare, the more powerful the desire to exorcise it. Why then would anyone choose to cling to unbearable recollections of emaciated corpses or violations of every human law? Maybe we have not yet learned to cope with the events, intellectually, socially, philosophically, theologically. Perhaps we never will. The more we know, the less we understand. All we can do is remember. But how does one remember? How does one remember and communicate an event filled with so much fear and darkness and mystery that it negates language and imagination? Auschwitz, Mr. President, history marks it with the burning seal. Our century, Mr. President, may well be remembered not only for the monuments it erected, or for the astonishing technological advances it made, but most of all for Treblinka and Majdanek, Belsen and Ponar, Auschwitz and Buchenwald. How is one to explain what happened? It could have been stopped or at least slowed down at various stages. One word, one statement, one move — it was not stopped. Why not?

I'm a teacher, Mr. President. And my students, young, fervent, compassionate American students, often express their puzzlement in my classroom — why the complacency? Why the tacit acquiescence? Why weren't the Hungarian Jews, for example, warned about their fate? When they arrived in Auschwitz at midnight they mistook it for a peaceful village. Why weren't the railways to Birkenau bombed by either the Allies or the Russians? And the Russians were so close.

The calculated viciousness of the executioner, the helplessness of the doomed, the passivity of the bystander, — all these lie beyond our comprehension — the killers' fascination with death, the victims with hope, the survivors' testimony. A new vocabulary needs to be invented to describe the event. Can you imagine the silence preceding a selection in a death count? The feel of a man who suddenly understands that he is the last of his family — the last of the line? Imagine? No, no one can imagine that kingdom. Only those who were there know what it meant to be there — theirs was the kingdom that will forever remain forbidden and forbidding.

And yet, and yet, we must tell the tale, we must bear witness. Not to do so would mean to render meaningless the years and the lives that we, those of us who survived, received as a gift, as an offering to be shared and redeemed.

We must tell the tale, Mr. President, and we want to tell it not to divide people but, on the contrary, to bring them together, not to inflict more suffering but, on the contrary, to diminish it, not to humiliate anyone but, on the contrary, to teach others to humiliate no one. This is why we bear witness, Mr. President and friends, not for the sake of the dead. It is too late for the dead. Not even for our own sake. It may be too late for us as well.

We speak for mankind. The universality of the Jewish tragedy lies in its uniqueness. Only the memory of what was done to the Jewish people and through it to others can save the world from indifference to the ultimate dangers that threaten its very existence.

Mr. President, that the survivors have not lost their sanity, their faith in God, or in man, that they decided to build on ruins in Israel or in the United States of America, that they decided to choose generosity instead of anger, hope instead of despair, is a mystery even to us. They had every reason to give up on life and its promise. They did not. Still at times, Mr. President, they are overcome by doubt and fear. The world has not learned its lesson. Antisemitic groups spring up more and more and some shamelessly, viciously, deny that the Holocaust ever occurred. In our lifetime fascist groups increase their memberships and parade in the streets. Intolerance, bigotry, fanaticism, mass executions in some places, mass starvation in others, religious wars, quasi-mediaeval upheavals, and, of course, ultimately, the nuclear menace and our indifference to it. What is to be done?

Though Jewish, profoundly Jewish in nature, the Holocaust has universal implications, and I believe, we believe that the memory of what was done may shield us in the future.

Naturally, other nations were persecuted and even decimated by the Nazis and their allies and their collaborators, and we honor their memory. But the Jewish people represented a different target. For the first time in history being became a crime. Jews were destined for annihilation not because of what they said or proclaimed or did or possessed or created or destroyed, but because of who they were.

Is that why we survivors, we Jews, we human beings, are so concerned? And is that why we are so attached to a land where so many survivors have found a haven, pride and refuge and hope? Please understand us, Mr. President. We believe that the subject of the Holocaust must remain separate from politics, but if we plead so passionately for Israel's right not only to be secure but also to feel secure, it is because of Israel's nightmares which are also our nightmares.

Israel is threatened by a holy war, which means total war, which means total annihilation. Mr. President, some may say that these are words, words — yes, words. But we are a generation traumatized by experience. We take words seriously. The very idea of another Jewish catastrophe anywhere in our lifetime is quite simply unbearable to us.

Israel must never feel abandoned. Israel must never feel alone. Israel must never feel expendable, Mr. President. We plead with you because it is the dream of our dreams. It is perhaps the pain of our pain but the hope of our hopes. It is an ancient nation of four thousand years that should not be judged in categories of one day or one incident. Only in its totality can we understand and perceive and love Israel.

We must believe so because there were times, forty years ago, when Jewish communities felt abandoned and betrayed. In 1943 on April 16th the gallant, young commander in chief of the Warsaw Ghetto Uprising, Mordecai Anielewicz, wrote to a friend, and I quote, "We are fighting. We shall not surrender. But as our last days are approaching, remember that we have been betrayed." That is what he felt. That is what we all felt. That is what we all felt. They were betrayed then. To forget them now would mean to betray them again, and we must not allow this to happen.

In the Jewish tradition, Mr. President, when a person dies we appoint him or her as our emissary in heaven to intercede in our behalf. Could it be that they, the six million Jews, were messengers? But then, then, Mr. President and friends, whose messengers are we?

Thank you.

Address . . . . PRESIDENT RONALD REAGAN

I feel a little unnecessary because I don't know that anyone could say anything that would add to those words we just heard [from Elie Wiesel]. It is a particular pleasure for me to be here with you today. This meeting, this ceremony has meaning not only for people of the Jewish faith, those who have been persecuted, but for all who want to prevent another Holocaust.

Jeremiah wrote of the days when the Jews were carried off to Babylon and Jerusalem was destroyed. He said, "Jerusalem weeps in the night and tears run down her cheeks." Today, yes, we remember the suffering and the death of Jews and all those others who were persecuted in World War II. We try to recapture the horror of millions sent to gas chambers and crematoria. And we commemorate the days of April in 1945 when American and Allied troops liberated the Nazi death camps. The tragedy that ended thirty-six years ago is still raw in our memories because it took place, as we've been told, in our lifetime. We share the wounds of the survivors. We recall the pain only because we must never permit it to come again. And, yet, today, in spite of that experience, as an entire generation has grown to adulthood, who never knew the days of World War II, and we remember ourselves, when we were younger, how distant history seemed, anything that came before our time — and so the signs do exist, the ugly graffiti, the act of violence, the act of terrorism here and there, scattered throughout the world and not quite large enough in dimension for us to rally as we once did in that war.

I'm horrified today when I know that there are actually people now trying to say that the Holocaust was invented, that it never happened, that there weren't six million people whose lives were taken cruelly and needlessly in that event, that all of this is propaganda. Well, it's the old cliché that a picture is worth a thousand words. In World War II, not only do we have the survivors today to tell us firsthand, but in World War II, I was in the military and assigned to a post where every week we obtained from every branch of the service all over the world the combat film that was taken by every branch. And we edited this into a secret report for the general staff. We had access to and saw that secret report. And I remember April '45. I remember seeing the first film that came in when the war was still on, but our troops had come upon the first camps and had entered those camps. And you saw, unretouched — and no way that it could have ever been rehearsed — what they saw — the horror they saw.

And that film still, I know, must exist in the military, and there it is, living motion pictures, for anyone to see, and I won't go into the horrible scenes that we saw. But, it remains with me as confirmation of our right to rekindle these memories, because we need always to guard against that kind of tyranny and inhumanity. Our spirit is strengthened by remembering and our hope is in our strength. There is an American poem that says humanity, with all its fears and all its hopes, depends on us.

I think that that was a trust given to us that we should never betray. It is this responsibility as free people that we face today. It's this commitment among free people that we celebrate.

The hope of a ceremony such as this is that even a tortured past holds promise if we learn its lessons. According to Isaiah, there will be a new heaven and a new earth and the voice of weeping will be heard no more. Together, with the help of God, we can bear the burden of our nightmare. It is up to us to ensure that we never live it again.

Theodore Roosevelt said that the presidency was a bully pulpit. Well, I, for one, intend that this bully pulpit shall be used on every occasion, where it is appropriate, to point a finger of shame at even the ugliness of graffiti, and certainly wherever it takes place in the world, the act of violence or terrorism, and that even at the negotiating table, never shall it be forgotten for a moment that wherever it is taking place in the world, the persecution of people, for whatever reason — persecution of people for their religious belief — that is a matter to be on that negotiating table or the United States does not belong at that table.

Candle Lighting Ceremony . . . . The Honorable Sidney R. Yates
United States Congressman (Illinois)

Participating Survivors

Sigmund Strochlitz
Sol Goldstein
Miles Lerman
Benjamin Meed
Hadassah Rosensalt
Siggi Wilzig
Eli Zborowski

El Maleh Rachamim . . . . The Honorable Isaac Goodfriend
Cantor, Ahavath Achim Congregation
Atlanta, Georgia

Kaddish . . . . The Honorable Alfred Gottschalk
President, Hebrew Union College
Cincinnati, Ohio

Concluding Remarks . . . . The Honorable Monroe H. Freedman
Director,
United States Holocaust Memorial Council

DAYS OF REMEMBRANCE

Yom HaShoah
Rayburn House Office Building
Capitol Hill

Invocation . . . . THE HONORABLE JOHN T. PAWLIKOWSKI
Council Member

Opening Remarks . . . . THE HONORABLE MONROE H. FREEDMAN
Director,
United States Holocaust Memorial Council

Remarks . . . . THE HONORABLE SIGMUND STROCHLITZ
Chairman,
Days of Remembrance Committee
United States Holocaust Memorial Council

The Chairman of the United States Holocaust Memorial Council, Elie Wiesel, has said that "remembering the Holocaust is an act of generosity aimed at saving men and women from apathy and evil, if not from evil itself."

I do remember. I remember Bendzin, Poland, my birthplace, in September 1939, when the Nazis surrounded the Jewish quarters, set fire to the synagogue and the houses adjacent to it, and shot any Jew who tried to escape. I remember day after day soldiers arrogantly and noisily storming into Jewish homes and businesses, evicting everybody and confiscating everything. We were ordered to wear the yellow Star of David and herded into a ghetto. Day followed day and the days became weeks, months and years . . . years of hunger, poverty, sorrow, sadness, and suffering.

And then I remember, came September of 1943. It was a bright Sunday morning, tense and worrisome. On that afternoon I became a prisoner on the planet of Auschwitz. I saw the flames coming out of the crematoria and still did not believe it. I touched the air contaminated with the smell of burning human flesh. I still did not believe. I walked on the ashes of people who were alive in the morning, and did not feel it. I was already orphaned and didn't cry. I was told I was dead and did not want to believe. Yes, I do remember.

Finally, I remember I was liberated on April 15, 1945, from Bergen-Belsen. Colonel Taylor, the commander of an anti-tank regiment who entered the camp, wrote later in the restrained language of his official report:

As we walked down the main roadway of the camp we were cheered by the inmates and for the first time ever, I saw their condition. A great number were little more than living skeletons. There were men and women lying in heaps on both sides of the track. Others were walking slowly and aimlessly about, vacant expressions on their starved faces. There were at least ten thousand unburied bodies, many in an advanced stage of decomposition.

I do remember. Remember with me.

Remarks . . . . The Honorable Benjamin Meed
Co-Chairman,
Days of Remembrance Committee
United States Holocaust Memorial Council

"Remember us . . . they wrote in blood, in their last minutes before death scratched into the stones and walls of the ghetto. . . . Remember, you who had eyes but you refused to see millions of innocent people being murdered. . . . Remember, you had ears but were deaf to our brothers' and sisters' pleas for help."

Nowadays, historians and "Holocaust specialists" seem to focus on the nature of Jewish resistance. . . . They make it seem as if one form of resistance was more important than another. As if, somehow, the firing of a gun counted for more than the mother who went hungry so that she could feed her dying child, as if a grenade was more important than a clandestine school to teach the ghetto children of their heritage. . . .

Today our lives are not free of the horror of those poisoned roots that grew out of Auschwitz and Treblinka. In other countries around the world, and even here at home, there are new Nazis raising their sick heads and proclaiming the well-known Nazi symbols and theories. . . . We have learned from what has happened to our six million Jews and countless others that the unbelievable can come to pass, that the impossible is indeed possible — if we do not stop it in time. . . .

Can we betray those who perished? We must preserve their memory, so that the world is never allowed to forget their courage, their suffering, and, most important, their fierce determination for survival.

Music of the Holocaust . . . . Workmen's Circle Chorus
Zalmen Mlotek, Director
New York, New York

Remarks . . . . The Honorable Mark Talisman
Vice Chairman,
United States Holocaust Memorial Council

It was Joel who said, "Tell your children of it and let your children tell their children, and their children, and other generations." We gather again in this season of rebirth, this springtime in our Nation's capital, to remember the victims of the Holocaust. Remembrance is a flood of perceptions, recollections, pain, and sorrow. We are at the same time at this moment again afforded the time to project into the future from this painful past. Our children and the Nation must be sustained and nourished through this remembrance and the work upon which all our activity embarked. Human beings destroyed discriminately in the Holocaust must be honored through our search to assure that the meaning of this terrible collective death will assure the justice of the systems of governance on this troubled earth never to repeat these horrors of the Holocaust. We cannot be assured yet. We are beginning.

It is Isaiah who has taught us that if thou draw out thy soul to the hungry and satisfy the afflicted soul, then shall thy light rise in darkness and thy gloom be as the noonday. The Lord will guide thee continually and satisfy thy soul in drought and make strong thy bones. Thou shalt be like a watered garden, like a spring of water whose waters fail not.

And they that shall be of thee shall build the old waste places. Thou shalt raise up the foundations of many generations and thou shalt be called repairer of the breach and restorer of the paths to dwell in.

Music of the Holocaust . . . . Workmen's Circle Chorus

Kaddish . . . . The Honorable Bernard Raskas
Council Member

Recessional . . . . Workmen's Circle Chorus

WORKMEN'S CIRCLE CHORUS
Rayburn House Office Building
Program

Conductor: Zalmen Mlotek
Pianist: Laura Leon Cohen

"Es Brent" ("It Burns")	Chorus with Soloist Mary Feinsinger
"Dremlen Feygl" ("Drowsing Birds")	Chorus
"Am Ma-Amin" ("I Believe")	Chorus
"Babi Yar"	Chorus with Soloist Miriam Goldberg
"Zog Nit Keyn Mol" ("Never Say")	Chorus

The Workmen's Circle Chorus is the oldest chorus with a Yiddish repertoire functioning today. It was founded in 1918 by the Education Department of the Workmen's Circle, a Jewish fraternal organization that has as one of its primary aims the perpetuation of East European culture. Ten thousand Holocaust survivors are members of the Workmen's Circle and some of them are currently singing in the chorus.

Program Notes: Stuart Schear

"Es Brent" ("It Burns")
Mordecai Gebirtig
Arrangement: Lazar Weiner

Mordecai Gebirtig, one of the most popular twentieth-century Yiddish song writers, composed "Es Brent" ("It Burns") in 1938. "Es Brent" envisions future events in a frightfully accurate manner. Deeply disturbed by a series of pogroms in western Poland, Gebirtig expresses his fears concerning the future of European Jewry and beseeches other Jews to act on their own behalf. "Es Brent," sung by Jews in the ghettos and camps, still haunts us today because of its visionary power.

In 1942, Gebirtig, his wife, and their three daughters were killed by the Nazis in the Cracow ghetto.

> It burns, brothers, it burns
> our poor shtetl pitifully burns
> angry wind with rage and curses
> tears and shatters and disperses
> wild flames leap, they twist and turn
> everything now burns!
>
> And you stand there looking on
> hands folded, palms upturned
> and you stand there looking on
> our shtetl burns!
>
> It burns, brothers, it burns
> help can only come if you return
> love which shtetl once inspired
> take up arms put out the fire
> douse it with your blood — be true
> show what you can do!
>
> Don't just stand there looking on
> hands folded, palms upturned
> don't just stand, put out the fire
> our shtetl burns!

(Translation by Roslyn Bresnick Perry)

"ZOG NIT KEYN MOL" ("NEVER SAY")
(Hymn of the Partisans)
Words: Hirsh Glick
Music: D. Pokras

After hearing news of the Warsaw Ghetto Uprising, Hirsh Glick, a twenty-year-old poet and partisan living in the Vilna ghetto, wrote "Zog Nit Keyn Mol" ("Never Say"). Glick's poem, set to music by Soviet composer Dimitri Pokras, quickly became the hymn of Jewish resistance in Eastern Europe and assumed international importance after its subsequent translation into several languages. Today, "Zog Nit Keyn Mol" is the song most frequently associated with Jewish resistance.

Resistance to the Nazis assumed many forms. Partisan sabotage activity and armed rebellions in the ghettos and camps were accompanied by widespread acts of cultural and spiritual resistance. Under the most adverse and dangerous circumstances, Jews defied the efforts of their oppressors to dehumanize them. They studied and prayed, they recorded their experiences with determination, they perpetuated organizations and political parties, they planned concerts and plays, they ran underground schools, health facilities, and food kitchens. Countless individuals smuggled food, worked as couriers, and hid endangered friends and relatives.

> Never say that you are going your last way,
> Though lead-filled skies above blot out the blue of day,
> The hour for which we long will certainly appear,
> The earth shall thunder 'neath our tread that we are here!
>
> From lands of green palm trees to lands all white with snow,
> We are coming with our pain and with our woe,
> And where'er a spurt of our blood did drop,
> Our courage will again sprout from that spot.
>
> For us the morning sun will radiate the day,
> And the enemy and past will fade away,
> But should the dawn delay or sunrise wait too long,
> Then let all future generations sing this song.
>
> This song was written with our blood and not with lead,
> This is no song of free birds flying overhead,
> But a people amid crumbling walls did stand,
> They stood and sang this song with rifles held in hand.

(Translation by Elliot Palevsky)

15

Holocaust Commemoration

THE STATE OF CONNECTICUT

State Senate Chamber
Hartford, Connecticut

PROGRAM

Presiding . . . . JOSEPH I. LIEBERMAN
Senate Majority Leader

Invocation . . . . REV. MARK ROHRBAUGH
General Secretary, Christian Conference of Connecticut

Lighting of Yahrzeit Candle . . . . RABBI HANS BODENHEIMER
Tikvoh Chadoshoh Congregation

Remarks . . . . DR. MICHAEL BERENBAUM
United States Holocaust Memorial Council

Response . . . . GOVERNOR

Musical Selections . . . . CHORALE

Sleven Natelson   Marilyn Haskel
Conductor   *Pianist*

Martha Banzhaf   Gary Greden
Lynne Carter   David Katz
Michele Debrot   Doug Shambo
Andres Zimmerman

- Song of Faith — I believe in a perfect faith, and the coming of the Messiah
- Es Brent, Briderlech, Es Brent — It is burning, Brothers, it is aflame
- Zog Nit Keynmol — Don't ever say it — Hirsh Glick, born in 1920 in Vilna. When the ghetto was liquidated he was sent to a concentration camp in Estonia. He escaped, joined the Partisans, and died while fighting. His Partisan song, "Zog Nit Keynmol," became the hymn of the Underground.

Benediction . . . . Monsignor John Wodarski
Holy Cross Church, New Britain

Chairman
Joseph I. Lieberman

Honorary Chairmen
Governor
Rev. Mark Rohrbaugh
Monsignor John Wodarski

Committee

Rev. Daniel Anderson	Frank Logue
David Baram	Laughlin McLean
Paula Bradley	Joseph Miller
Nancy Carr	Jeffrey M. Mines
Henry Cohn	Gary Motin
Fr. Joseph Devine	Louis Orenstein
Eugene. F. Elander	Hon. Henry Parker
Louise Etklnd	Lai Patel
Sen. Joseph Fauliso	Gloria Polis
Arthur W. Feinstein	Rev. Charles Sardeson
Robert Fishman	Arnold Scribner
Dr. M. Delott	Garber Jack Spiegel
Martin Gold	Sigmund Strochlitz
Rep. Patricia Hendel	Hon. Judge Jerry Wagner
Rabbi Stanley Kessler	Avy Weberman
Simon Konover	Malcolm Webber
Joseph Korzenik	Harriet Dobin Woolf
Lewis Lehrer	

Sponsored by

- United States Holocaust Memorial Council

- State of Connecticut

- Anti-Defamation League of B'nai Brith

- Connecticut Jewish Community Relations-Council

- The Jewish Federations of Greater Hartford, New Haven, Stamford, Danbury, New London, Waterbury, Bridgeport, and Norwalk

- Committee for Holocaust Awareness — Univ. of Hartford

Program made possible by a special grant from the Connecticut Bank and Trust Co.

16

Civic Commemoration of the Holocaust

The Commonwealth of Pennsylvania

The Commonwealth of Pennsylvania,
The Capitol Rotunda, Harrisburg, Pennsylvania

PROGRAM

Introduction . . . . Rabbi Jeffrey A. Wohlberg
Beth El Temple
Harrisburg, Pennsylvania

Opening Prayer . . . . Reverend William Harter
Presbyterian Church of Falling Spring
Chambersburg, Pennsylvania

Proclamation and Remarks . . . . Governor Dick Thornburgh

Song of the Ghettos and Camps . . . . Messiah College Choir
   The Butterfly   Director, Dr. Ronald Miller
   Ani Maamin

Address . . . . Dr. Irving Greenberg
Director, National Jewish Resource Center

Candle Lighting Ceremony . . . . Dalck Feith
Elkins Park, Pennsylvania

Rabbi Mordecai Glatstein   Tibor Gross
Pittsburgh, Pennsylvania   Kingston, Pennsylvania

Martin Rosenschein   Goldie Mayers
Harrisburg, Pennsylvania   Erie, Pennsylvania

Representative Russell Kowalyshyn
Northampton, Pennsylvania

Scriptural Reading. . . . . J. Bishop Maximos
Greek Orthodox Diocese of Pittsburgh
Pittsburgh, Pennsylvania

Holocaust Memorial Prayer . . . . Cantor Charles Davidson
El Maleh Rachamim   Congregation Adath Jeshurun
Elkins Park, Pennsylvania

Kaddish: Mourner's Prayer . . . . Rabbi Jeffrey A. Wohlberg

Benediction . . . . Sister Gloria Coleman
Cardinal's Committee on Human Relations
Philadelphia, Pennsylvania

Closing Song . . . . Messiah College Choir

THE GENERAL ASSEMBLY OF PENNSYLVANIA
House Resolution

No. 217   Session of 1980
Introduced by Messrs. Greenfield, Pievsky, Rappaport, Berson, Hoeffel,
Geloff, Levin, and Itkin, March 24, 1980
Referred to Committee on Rules, March 25, 1980

In the House of Representatives, March 24, 1980

Whereas, Six million Jews and millions of other people were murdered in concentration camps as part of a program of extermination carried out by the Nazi Party during World War II: and

Whereas, The people of the United States should recognize that all acts of bigotry are rooted in the cruelty of spirit and the callousness that led the Nazis to commit atrocities against millions of people, and should dedicate themselves to the principle of human equality; and

Whereas, The people of the United States should recognize that tyranny creates the political atmosphere in which bigotry flourishes, and should be vigilant to detect, and ready to resist, the tyrannical exercise of power; and

Whereas, On April 28 and 29 of 1945 the Armed Forces of the United States liberated the surviving victims of Nazi internment in the concentration camp in Dachau, Germany, and revealed to the world evidence of a tragic human holocaust that must never be forgotten; and

WHEREAS, The Nazi concentration camp in Dachau, Germany, is not only a shocking symbol of Nazi brutality and destruction, but also a symbol of the danger inherent in tyranny, the pernicious quality of bigotry, and the human capacity to be cruel; therefore be it

RESOLVED, That the House of Representatives of the Commonwealth of Pennsylvania designates April 28, 1980, as "Holocaust Memorial Day," and Governor Dick Thornburgh is authorized and requested to issue a proclamation calling upon the people of the Commonwealth of Pennsylvania to observe the day with appropriate ceremonies and activities; and be it further

RESOLVED, That a copy of this resolution be delivered to Governor Dick Thornburgh.

SENATE OF PENNSYLVANIA
Harrisburg, Pa.

In the Senate, March 25, 1980

WHEREAS, Pennsylvanians for a Civic Commemoration of the Holocaust will be holding a commemorative service April 28, 1980, in the Rotunda of the Capitol in Harrisburg: and

WHEREAS, Six million Jews and many millions of other people were murdered as part of a program of extermination carried out during World War II; and

WHEREAS, On April 28, 1945, the Armed Forces of the United States liberated the surviving victims of the Nazi internment in the concentration camp in Dachau, Germany and revealed to the world evidence of a tragic human holocaust that must never be forgotten; now therefore be it

RESOLVED, That the Senate or the Commonwealth of Pennsylvania recognizes April 28, 1980, as "Days of Remembrance of Victims of the Holocaust"; and be it further

RESOLVED, That a copy of this document, sponsored by Senators W. Louis Coppersmith, George W. Gekas, Robert C. Jubelirer, and Jeanette F. Reibman, be transmitted to Pennsylvanians for a Civic Commemoration of the Holocaust.

Attest: Secretary of the Senate

Ani Maamin

A song of faith and of spiritual resistance sung in the ghettos
and even in the concentration camps.

I believe with complete faith in the coming of the Messiah, and even if he tarries, I will await his coming every day.

Poems written by children in the Theresienstadt concentration camp.
Musical settings by Cantor Charles Davidson.

THE BUTTERFLY

The last, the very last.
So richly, brightly dazzlingly yellow.
Perhaps if the sun's tears
would sing against a white stone...

Such, such a yellow
Is carried lightly 'way up high.
It went away I'm sure
because it wished to
kiss the world goodbye.

For seven weeks I've lived in here,
Penned up inside this ghetto
But I have found my people here.
The dandelions call to me
And the white chestnut candles in the court.
Only I never saw another butterfly.

That butterfly was the last one.
Butterflies don't live in here,
In the ghetto.

—Pavel Friedmann, 1942

BIRDSONG

He doesn't know the worm at all
Who stays in his nest and doesn't go out.
He doesn't know what birds know best
Nor what I want to sing about,
That the world is full of loveliness.

When dewdrops sparkle in the grass
And earth's aflood with morning light,
A blackbird sings upon a bush
To greet the dawning after night.
Then I know how fine it is to live.

Hey, try to open up your heart
To beauty; go to the woods someday
And weave a wreath of memory there.
Then if the tears obscure your way
You'll know how wonderful it is
To be alive.

—Anonymous, 1941

17

An Evening of Commemoration

THE STATE OF NORTH CAROLINA

State of North Carolina Holocaust Memorial Service
Raleigh Civic Center,
Raleigh, North Carolina

A Confession in Memory of the Six Million

Leader: For the sin which we committed before You and before them by closing our ears

People: And for the sin which we committed before You and before them by not using our power;

Leader: For the sin which we committed before You and before them by being overcautious

People: And for the sin which we committed before You and before them by hesitating;

Leader: For the sin which we committed before You and before them by treachery toward brothers and sisters

People: And for the sin which we committed before You and before them by being content with those times;

All: For all these sins, O God of forgiveness,
Forgive us, pardon us, and grant us atonement.

Leader: For the sin which we committed before You and before them by fearing the powerful

People: And for the sin which we committed before You and before them by bowing to their will;

Leader: For the sin which we committed before You and before them by too much patience

People: And for the sin which we committed before You and before them by appeasement,

Leader: For the sin which we committed before You and before them by continued frivolity

People: And for the sin which we committed before You and before them by rationalization;

Leader: For the sin which we committed before You and before them by cowardice

People: And for the sin which we committed before You and before them by apathy;

Leader: For all these sins, O God of forgiveness,
Forgive us, pardon us, and grant us
Strength to say "Never Again!"

HOLOCAUST MEMORIAL SERVICE
Raleigh Civic Center

Presentation of the Colors . . . . Color Guard from Broughton High School
Junior Air Force ROTC, Raleigh

"The Star Spangled Banner" . . . . Raleigh Oratorio Society
Lyrics: Francis Scott Key   82nd Airborne Division Band, Fort Bragg
Music: John Stafford Smith   Bandmaster CW4 Benny R. Easter, Conductor

Opening Comments . . . . Dr. B. Elmo Scoggin
Chairman, N.C. Council on the Holocaust, Raleigh

Invocation . . . . Rabbi Robert J. Eisen
Beth Meyer Synagogue, Raleigh

Governor's Proclamation . . . . Mrs. Ruby T. Hooper, R.D.
Deputy Secretary, N.C. Department
of Human Resources, Raleigh

Mayor's Proclamation . . . . The Honorable Avery Upchurch
Mayor, Raleigh

Responsive Reading: . . . . Rabbi James R. Bleiberg
A Confession in Memory of Six Million   Temple Beth Or, Raleigh

Memorial Prayer . . . . Rev. Richard Brand
First Presbyterian Church, Raleigh

Guest Speaker

Dr. Franklin H. Littell
A Leading Christian Scholar on the Holocaust
Member, United States Holocaust Memorial Council
Professor Emeritus of Religion Temple University
Founder and Honorary Chairman, Anne Frank Institute
Philadelphia, Pennsylvania

El Maleh Rachamim . . . . Rabbi Abe Schoen
Kaddish (Mourners' Prayer)
Beth Meyer Synagogue, Raleigh

Lighting of the Memorial Candles

Silent Meditation

"Ani Ma'amin" ("I Believe") . . . . Raleigh Oratorio Society
Lyrics: Moses Maimonides
Musical Director:
Music: E. D. Fastag
James M. Marshall, Conductor

"Hymn of the Partisans" . . . . Raleigh Oratorio Society
Lyrics: Hirsh Glick
82nd Airborne Division Band
Music: Dmitri Pokras
Bandmaster CW4 Benny R. Easter, Conductor

Benediction . . . . Rabbi Arnold S. Task
Temple Emanuel, Greensboro

"America, the Beautiful" . . . . Raleigh Oratorio Society
Lyrics: Katherine Lee Bates
82nd Airborne Division Band
Music: Samuel A. Ward
Bandmaster CW4 Benny R. Easter, Conductor

Recession of the Colors . . . . Color Guard from Broughton High School
Junior Air Force ROTC

Program Coordinator: Runia Vogelhut

A Memorial Prayer

Exalted, compassionate God, grant perfect peace in your sheltering presence, among the holy and the pure, to souls of our brethren, men, women, and children of the House of Israel who were slaughtered and burned. May their memory endure, inspiring truth and loyalty in our lives. May their souls thus be bound up in the bond of life. May they rest in peace. And let us say: Amen.

Mourners' Kaddish

Magnified and sanctified be the name of God throughout the world which He hath created according to His will. May He establish His kingdom during the days of your life and during the life of all the house of Israel, speedily, yea, soon; and say ye, Amen.

Congregation and Mourners:

May His great name be blessed for ever and ever.

Mourners:

Exalted and honored be the name of the Holy One, blessed be He, whose glory transcends, yea, is beyond all praises, hymns and blessings that man can render unto Him; and say ye, Amen.

May there be abundant peace from heaven, and life for us and for all Israel; and say ye, Amen.

May He who establisheth peace in the heavens, grant peace unto us and unto all Israel; and say ye, Amen.

•

Yis-ga-dal v'yis-ka-dash sh'may ra-bo,
B'ol-mo dee-v'ro hir u-say, v'yam-leeh mal-hu-say,
B'ha-yay-hōon uv-yō-may-hōn, uv-ha-yay d'hol bays yis-ro-ayl,
Ba-a-go-lo u-viz'man ko-reev, v'im-ru o-mayn.

Y'hay sh'may ra-bo m'vo-rah, l'o-lam ul-ol-may ol-ma-yo.

Yis-bo-rah v'yish-ta-bah, v'yis-po-ar v'yis-rō-mam,
V'yis-na-say v'yis-ha-dar, v'yis-a-leh, v'yis-ha-lal
sh'may d'kud-sho b'rih hu;

L'ay-lo (ul-ay-lo) min kol bir-ho-so v'shee-ro-so,
Tush-b'ho-so v'ne-heh-mo-so, da-a-mee-ron b'ol-mo,
V'im-ru o-mayn.

Y'hay sh'lo-mo ra-bo min sh'ma-yo,
V'ha-yeem o-lay-nu v'al kol yis-ro-ayl v'im-ru o-mayn.

Ō-se sho-lōm bim-rō-mov hu ya-a-se sho-lōm
O-lay-nu v'al kol yis-ro-ayl v'im-ru o-mayn.

18

Yom HaShoah: That World That Was

A Remembrance of European Jewry before the Holocaust
Temple Beth-El, San Antonio

Responsive Reading

Reader: I believe that the light will shine, even if I do not live to see the end of the night.

Congregation: *Ani Maamin!*

Reader: I believe in love, even though hatred surrounds me.

Congregation: *Ani Maamin!*

Reader: I believe in the Jewish people united like the fingers of one hand: a hand that can clench in strength, yet reaches out for peace.

Congregation: *Ani Maamin!*

Reader: I believe that I am my brother's keeper, that all Jews are responsible for one another.

Congregation: *Ani Maamin!*

Reader: I believe that, despite the fury and wrath of those who rise up in every generation to destroy us...the people of Israel live.

Congregation: *Ani Maamin!*

Reader: "Now we are a nation like other nations: masters of our destiny for the first time in twenty centuries..."

Reader: "The dream came true, too late to save those who perished in the Holocaust, but *not* too late for the generation to come."

Reader: I believe that the land, the book and the people are one: not only today, but always.

At Temple Beth-El, San Antonio, Texas, coordinated by the Jewish Community Relations Council of the Jewish Federation of San Antonio (Robert Ross, Chairman; Rhonda Abrams, Director).

Congregation: I believe...

Reader: We are one...

Congregation: *Ani Maamin!*

PROGRAM

The Meaning of This Evening . . . . RABBI AMRAM PRERO

Personal Recollection . . . . DR. ISAAC EPSTEIN

"Rojiinkes Mit Mandlen" . . . . BOBBIE FELDSTONE
accompanied by Maxine Cohen

The Light of European Jewry . . . . RABBI ARNOLD SCHEINBERG

Reading . . . . PAUL MARKEY

Personal Recollection . . . . LUDWIG GOTTLIEB

Religious Roots of the Holocaust . . . . RABBI SAMUEL STAHL

Yiddish Poems . . . . SIMON DAVIDSON
translated by Eleanor Siegal

Choosing the Future . . . . REV. T. STEWART COFFMAN

Memorial Service . . . . THE RABBIS AND CANTOR LOUIS GOLDHIRSH

KADDISH

Yis-ga-dal v'yis-ka-dash sh-may ra-bo,
B'ol-mo dee-v'ro hir u-say, v'yam-leeh mal-hu-say,
B'ha-yay-hon uv-yo may-hon, uv-ha-yay d'hol bays yis-ro-ayl,
Ba-a-go-lo u-viz-man ko-reev, v'im-ru o-mayn.
Y'hay sh'may ra-bo m'vo-rah, l'o-lam ul-ol-may ol-ma-yo.

Yis-bo-rah v'yish-ta-bah, v'yis-po-ar v'yis-ro-mam,
V'yis-na-say v'yis -ha-dar, v'yis -a-leh, v'yis-ha-lal sh'may
d'kud-sho b-rih hu,

L'ay-lo min kol bir-ho-so v'shee-ro-so,
Tush-b'ho-so v'ne-heh-mo-so, d-a-mee-ron b'ol-mo,
V'im-ru o-mayn.

Y'hay sh'lo-mo ra-bo min sh'may-yo,
V'ha-yeem o'lay-nu v'al kol yis-ro-ayl v'im-ru o-mayn.

O-se shalom bim-ro-mov hu ya-a-se shalom
O-lay-nu v'al kol yis-ro-ayl v'im-ru o-mayn.

Hatikvah

Kol od balevav pnima
nefesh yehudi homiya
ulefa'atei mizrach kadima
ayin letziyon tzofiya

Od lo avda tikvatenu
hatikvah shnot alpayim
lihoyot am hofshi b'artzenu
eretz tziyon v'yerushalayim

19

Yom HaShoah

*Community-wide Memorial Service
to Commemorate the Holocaust*

CONGREGATION NER TAMID, LAS VEGAS

*"...dedicated to the victims of the Holocaust:
they have no graves, but their memories will live on until the end of time."*

National Anthem . . . . MATTHEW EISENBERG
Cantorial Soloist

Welcome . . . . KENNETH SCHNITZER
President, Congregation Ner Tamid

Proclamations . . . . MAYOR RON LURIE
REV. LARRY GERBER
EDYTHE KATZ, Nevada Liaison to
the U.S. Holocaust Memorial Council
Washington, D.C.

Psalm 23 . . . . CANTOR SIMON BERGMAN
RABBI LOUIS LEDERMAN

The Lord is my shepherd; I shall not want.

He maketh me to lie down in green pastures;
He leadeth me beside the still waters.

He restoreth my soul;
He guideth me in straight paths for His name's sake.

Yea, though I walk through the valley of the shadow of death,
I will fear no evil,
For Thou art with me;
Thy rod and Thy staff, they comfort me.

Service at Congregation Ner Tamid, Las Vegas, Nevada. Sponsored by Congregation Emanu-El, Congregation Ner Tamid, Temple Beth Am, Temple Beth Sholom, and the Jewish Federation.

Thou preparest a table before me in the presence of mine enemies;
Thou hast anointed my head with oil; my cup runneth over.

Surely goodness and mercy shall follow me all the days of my life;
And I shall dwell in the house of the Lord forever.

FROM TOMORROW ON

From tomorrow on, I shall be sad —
From tomorrow on!
Today I will be gay.

What is the use of sadness — tell me that? —
Because these evil winds begin to blow?
Why should I grieve for tomorrow — today?
Tomorrow may be so good, so sunny,
Tomorrow the sun may shine for us again;
We shall no longer need to be sad.

From tomorrow on, I shall be sad —
From tomorrow on!
Not today; no! today I will be glad.
And every day, no matter how bitter it be,
I will say:
From tomorrow on, I shall be sad,
Not Today!

—Motele

THE BUTTERFLY

The last, the very last,
So richly, brightly dazzlingly yellow.
    Perhaps if the sun's tears would sing
    against a white stone...

Such, such a yellow
Is carried lightly 'way up high.
It went away I'm sure because it wished to
    kiss the world goodbye.

For seven weeks I've lived in here,
Penned up inside this ghetto
But I have found my people here.
The dandelions call to me
And the white chestnut candles in the court.
Only I never saw another butterfly.

That butterfly was the last one.
Butterflies don't live in here,
    In the ghetto.

—Pavel Friedmann

"Of Memory and Faith"

Rabbi: All peoples have suffered cruelty, and our hearts go out to them. But this day we think especially of the pain suffered by the House of Israel. Exile and oppression, expulsion and ghettos, pogroms and death camps: the agony of our people numbs the mind and turns the heart to stone. When we consider this, we are tempted to say, with one of our poets: "To me the whole world is one gallows."

Congregation: We can only wonder at the fortitude of our fathers and mothers who said, not once but many times: "Though You slay me, yet will I trust in You." And we can only pray to be blessed with a measure of the faith that enabled them to remain true to God and His Torah, even when He seemed remote from them and life itself might have lost all meaning.

Rabbi: And there was silence! How many stood aside, mute and unconcerned, forgetting the divine command: "You shall not stand idle while your neighbor bleeds."

Rabbi and Congregation:
For the sin of silence,
For the sin of indifference,
For the secret complicity of the neutral.
For the closing of borders,
For the washing of hands,
For the crime of indifference.
For the sin of silence, the world stands accused.

Rabbi: Let there be no forgetfulness before the Throne of Glory, and let memory startle us on sunny afternoons, in sudden silences when we are with friends, when we lie down and when we rise up. O Lord, we shall not forget.

Remember: A Yom HaShoah Responsive Reading . . . . RABBI MEL HECHT

Rabbi: In memory of those who gave their lives for the sanctity of the Jewish people . . . and in living tribute to our fathers and mothers, brothers and sisters destroyed by the Nazi onslaught . . . we are each of us obliged to see ourselves in every generation as survivors of the Holocaust, to the end of time.

Congregation: "We are still haunted by the warning of the Holocaust: that the incredible can become the credible, that the impossible can become possible, if we do not act as we should in time."

Rabbi: "To forget constitutes a crime against memory . . . whoever forgets becomes the executioner's accomplice."

Congregation:	*Remember: do not forget!* (Deut. 9:7) The innocent and pure were murdered — man, woman, and child — with poison gas and in fiery furnaces.
Rabbi:	"All around us were screams, death, smoking chimneys making the air black and heavy with soot and the smell of burning bodies."
Congregation:	"At night, the red sky over Auschwitz could be seen for miles."
Rabbi:	In the face of their oppression, Jews did *not* cringe. "They prayed in secret; their children learned in secret; they held lectures in Jewish history in secret; and they even conducted a symphony in secret."
Congregation:	"They lived as if stretching time itself to prolong existence and to deny to Hitler even for another hour, another minute, another second, the fulfillment of his dream of an earth empty of Jews."
Rabbi:	They did *not* get down on their knees and beg for mercy. They weren't led like sheep to the slaughter. The Jews fought back! "The question is not *why* all the Jews did not fight, but *how* so many of them did. Tormented, beaten, starved — where did they find the strength, spiritual and physical, to resist?"

"THESE THINGS I REMEMBER"

Rabbi:	The earth's crust is soaked with the tears of the innocent. The blood of every people cries out from the ground. Which is the people without its martyrs?
Congregation:	Now, therefore, we remember all: the innocent, the victims, all our companions in death and our partners in grief. Them we honor, them we mourn; may they never be forgotten; may a better world grow out of their suffering.
Rabbi:	And especially do we remember the suffering of the House of Israel, a people of pains and acquainted with grief.
Congregation:	Look and remember. Look upon this land, far, far across the factories and the grass. Surely, there, surely, they will let you pass. Speak then and ask the forest and the loam. What do you hear? What does the land command? The earth is taken: this is not your home.
Rabbi:	Days and years of peace; these too have been our lot. Grandeur, greatness, quiet ages, domestic jobs, times when fear might almost be forgotten. Yet again and again our peace has been shattered, our land usurped, our dwellings razed.

The mind grows numb, and the heart turns to stone,
To see our long travail.
Our foes were not content to give us pain;
Their dream was darker still:
A world without Jews,
A world that would forget our very name!
We cannot forget this or be indifferent to its meaning.
We shall remember!

Rabbi and Congregation:

These things do we remember: through all the years, ignorance like a monster has devoured our martyrs as in one long day of blood. Rulers have arisen through the endless years, oppressive, savage in their witless power, filled with a futile thought: to make an end of that which God has cherished.

Proclamation . . . . Lt. Gov. Robert Miller

Introduction of Guest Speaker . . . . Norman Kaufman
Executive Director,
The Jewish Federation of Las Vegas

Address . . . . Paulette Fink

The Light of Memory . . . . Rabbi Sanford D. Akselrad

Six million died! More than one-third of the Jewish population of the world. The whole world stood by silent. The country that regarded itself as the most civilized nation in the world, Germany, the center of culture, was responsible for the death of six million Jews. Among them were young innocent children, the aged, sick, defenseless, and helpless people. Six million died. We must not forget them. Their death shall not be in vain. This shall never happen again. In our tradition we light a yahrzeit candle for the death of our loved ones. Let us light six candles, one for each million.

All survivors rise.

Processional of Survivors

Sister Klaryta Antoszevska	Lillian Kronberg
Fern Chenin	Sasha Semenoff
Judge Jack Lehman	Gary Sternberg

Yahrzeit candles are lit as Ani Ma'amin is sung.

Ani Ma'amin . . . . CANTOR SIMON BERGMAN

CANTOR GARY GOLBART

(Arrangement by Gary Golbart)

אני מאמין

A-ni ma-a-min be-e-mu-na she-lel-ma

אֲנִי מַאֲמִין בֶּאֱמוּנָה שְׁלֵמָה

be-vi-at ha-ma-shi-ach.

בְּבִיאַת הַמָּשִׁיחַ.

Ve-af al pi she-yit-ma-he-mei-a.

וְאַף עַל פִּי שֶׁיִּתְמַהְמֵהַּ,

Im kol zeh a-ni ma-a-min.

עִם כָּל זֶה אֲנִי מַאֲמִין,

Im kol zeh a-cha-keh lo

עִם כָּל זֶה אֲחַכֶּה לוֹ

be-chol yom she-ya-vo.

בְּכָל יוֹם שֶׁיָּבוֹא.

I believe with perfect faith in the Messiah's coming. And even if he be delayed, I will await him.

Memorial Prayer

God of Abraham, Isaac and Jacob:

We remember this day the nameless millions of martyrs of the children of Israel for whom there exists no monument nor final resting place other than in our own inner recesses. With heavy heart, we bear the tragedy of the death of a full third of your children, our brothers and sisters, offered up by the Nazis on altars of savagery and demonic brutality. There is not the Jewish family over whose home there does not hover a pall of grief at the wanton murder of relatives during the years of the unforgettable Holocaust.

You did bid us to remember from generation to generation the inhumanity of Amalek. Can we ever forget the sadism of the followers of Hitler?

Help us, O Lord, that in remembering the dead, we do not remain in the abyss of hatred, but rise to the mountain of resolve. We must sanctify the names of the Kedoshim whose deaths deepened the holiness of your people. We must dedicate ourselves to the perpetuation of your saving remnant through greater devotion to your teachings and the ideals of Judaism.

May our tears of mourning and sighs of grief be acceptable to you as we accompany them with consecration to the fulfillment of your divine mandate for the exaltation of k'lal Yisrael and the ennoblement of all men. Amen.

All rise.

El Maleh Rachamim . . . . CANTOR JOSEPH KOHN

RABBI SANFORD D. AKSELRAD

We Remember the Six Million... .... Cantor Simon Bergman
Rabbi Sanford D. Akselrad

יִתְגַּדַּל
Kishinev

וְיִתְקַדַּשׁ
Warsaw

שְׁמֵהּ רַבָּא
Auschwitz

בְּעָלְמָא דִּי בְרָא כִרְעוּתֵהּ
Dachau

וְיַמְלִיךְ מַלְכוּתֵהּ
Buchenwald

בְּחַיֵּיכוֹן וּבְיוֹמֵיכוֹן
Babi Yar

וּבְחַיֵּי דְכָל־בֵּית יִשְׂרָאֵל
Baghdad

בַּעֲגָלָא וּבִזְמַן קָרִיב
Hebron

וְאִמְרוּ אָמֵן.

יְהֵא שְׁמֵהּ רַבָּא מְבָרַךְ לְעָלַם וּלְעָלְמֵי עָלְמַיָּא.
Riga, Stutthof

יִתְבָּרַךְ וְיִשְׁתַּבַּח
Kfar Etzion

וְיִתְפָּאַר וְיִתְרוֹמַם
Mayence

וְיִתְנַשֵּׂא וְיִתְהַדָּר
Terezin

וְיִתְעַלֶּה וְיִתְהַלָּל
Treblinka

שְׁמֵהּ דְּקֻדְשָׁא בְּרִיךְ הוּא
Bergen-Belsen

לְעֵלָּא לְעֵלָּא
Vilna

מִכָּל־בִּרְכָתָא וְשִׁירָתָא
Usha

תֻּשְׁבְּחָתָא וְנֶחֱמָתָא
Massada

דַּאֲמִירָן בְּעָלְמָא
Jerusalem

וְאִמְרוּ אָמֵן.

יְהֵא שְׁלָמָא רַבָּא מִן שְׁמַיָּא וְחַיִּים עָלֵינוּ וְעַל כָּל־יִשְׂרָאֵל,
וְאִמְרוּ אָמֵן.

עוֹשֶׂה שָׁלוֹם בִּמְרוֹמָיו הוּא יַעֲשֶׂה שָׁלוֹם עָלֵינוּ וְעַל כָּל־יִשְׂרָאֵל,
וְאִמְרוּ אָמֵן.

All are seated.

All children of survivors rise.

The Light of Life .... Rabbi Sanford D. Akselrad
Children of Holocaust Survivors

Participants:

Helen Edell	Gene Greenberg
Michelle Gelbart	Marsha Miller
Ira Goldberg	Leslie Simon

Rabbi: The Lord has promised us a saving remnant, a thin thread from yesterday to tomorrow. And thus, even though our people was all but consumed with fire and death, yet there emerged into this generation new life. The Children of Survivors are our testimony to and affirmation of life. They carry on the message "Never Forget."

Three candles are lit.

Rabbi: In memory of helpless infants, children and teenagers who were cut down like young trees before their time...before they had a chance to experience life.

Congregation: We shall not forget!

Three candles.

Rabbi: In memory of all mothers who died with their children in their arms.

Congregation: We shall not forget!

Three candles.

Rabbi: In memory of all mothers and fathers who were cruelly separated from their families.

Congregation: We shall not forget!

Three candles.

Rabbi: In memory of the "Heroes of the Resistance" who fought the Nazis so few against so many.

Congregation: We shall not forget!

Three candles.

Rabbi: In memory of the martyrs who gave their lives to help their brothers under the Nazis.

Congregation: We shall not forget!

Rabbi: This one last candle makes eighteen, the symbol of life. The Jewish response to death is the affirmation of life. Our people's death would be altogether in vain if we did not choose life, choose our future, choose tomorrow. The depth of our choice can be fathomed only in the light of our memory. We kindle eighteen candles and dedicate them to life. In doing this simple act of kindling flame, we affirm that the memories of our departed shall not be lost and that each year for now and always, there will be Jews to kindle these lights. To everything there is a season and a time for every purpose under heaven. A time to be born and a time to die. A time to remember the past, and a time to hope for the future.

All rise.

Hatikvah . . . . CANTORIAL SOLOIST MATTHEW EISENBERG
AND CONGREGATION

הַתִּקְוָה

Kol od ba-lei-vav pe-ni-ma.   כָּל עוֹד בַּלֵּבָב פְּנִימָה
ne-fesh Ye-hu-di ho-mi-ya.   נֶפֶשׁ יְהוּדִי הוֹמִיָּה,
U-le-fa-a-tei miz-rach ka-di-ma,   וּלְפַאֲתֵי מִזְרָח קָדִימָה
a-yin le-tsi-yon tso-fi-ya.   עַיִן לְצִיּוֹן צוֹפִיָּה.

Od lo a-ve-da tik-va-tei-nu,   עוֹד לֹא אָבְדָה תִקְוָתֵנוּ,
ha-tik-va she-not al-pa-yim,   הַתִּקְוָה שְׁנוֹת אַלְפַּיִם,
li-he-yot am chof-shi be-ar-tsei-nu,   לִהְיוֹת עַם חָפְשִׁי בְּאַרְצֵנוּ,
be-e-rets tsi-yon vi-ru-sha-la-yim.   בְּאֶרֶץ צִיּוֹן וִירוּשָׁלָיִם.

Benediction . . . . RABBI SANFORD D. AKSELRAD

– 20 –

Service for Yom HaShoah

Madison, Wisconsin

CHARLES FEINBERG

When it comes to the Shoah — the Holocaust — we are all like the fourth child at the Passover Seder, who does not even know how to ask the questions.

The monstrous evil of the Shoah defies the imagination of the novelist, the analysis of the historian, and the eloquence of the preacher.

The Shoah centers about a basic paradox. It imposes silence but demands speech. It defies solutions but requires responses.

Just as the Midrash says: "All Jews were at Sinai," so all Jews were at Auschwitz.

Just as no one really can convey what happened at Sinai, no one can really convey what happened at Auschwitz. Somewhere between the realms of speech and silence swells the secret of Auschwitz.

But one thing may be clearly stated. Just as the Jewish people have never been the same since Sinai, so they can never be the same since Auschwitz. Indeed, the world has not been the same since Auschwitz.

Each of the six million Jews of America must live for two: for himself and for one of the Jews who perished during the Shoah. To live for those who perished means to teach the world the message told by the tale of their deaths. We must show others how to hope where there is no hope. How to live humanely in a brutal world. This is the message of the dead we must bring to the land of the living. May we not be messengers who forget the message. The very existence of the world may depend on it. Lest the Shoah become a prelude to a universal holocaust.

Our generation has come to know people as they really are. They are that being who invented the gas chambers of Auschwitz; however, they are also those who have entered those gas chambers with dignity and with the affirmation of Ani Ma'amin on their lips.

To be a Jew means to perceive light in darkness, to hope when in despair, and to live humanely in an inhuman world.

We have gathered together in observance of a new Holy Day on the Jewish calendar. During the Second World War, six million Jews — men, women, and children — were murdered by the Nazis. We gather today, as a community, to remember them, and to pray for them and for us. This is a very sad Holy Day — but one which is very important, not only for Jews, but for all humankind. For in commemorating that which happened — in remembering — we want to prevent it from ever happening again.

Six Memorial Candles Are Lit

Jewish children were regarded by the Nazis as especially valuable biological material. They were intent on destroying all Jewish children completely and rapidly so as to eradicate the future of the Jewish people. We recall the agony of Jewish children by reading selections of "The Song of the Slaughtered People" by Yitzak Katzenelson. Katzenelson was a noted Yiddish and Hebrew poet who perished with his son in Auschwitz in 1944.

We read responsively:

Reader: They, the children of Israel, were the first in doom and disaster; most of them without father and mother, were consumed by frost, starvation and lice, holy messiahs sanctified in pain. Say then, how have these lambs sinned?

     Why in days of doom are they the first victims of wickedness, the first in the trap of evil are they!...

Congregation: The first ones to be destroyed were the children, little orphans, abandoned upon the face of the earth; they who were the best in the world, the acme of grace on the dark earth;

     Oh, tender orphans!

     From them, the bereaved of the world
     in a house of shelter we drew consolation;
     from the mournful faces, mute and dark,
     we said the light of day will yet break upon us!...

     The first were they detained for death,
     the first into the wagons of slaughter;
     they were thrown into the wagons, the huge wagons,
     like heaps of refuse, like the ashes of the earth —
     and they transported them, killed them,
     exterminated them
     without remnant or remembrance...
     The best of my children were wiped out!
     Oh, woe unto me — Doom and Destruction!

Reader: Do not cry...
     At this station another girl I saw, about five years old;
     She fed her younger brother and he cried,
     the little one, he was sick;
     into a diluted bit of jam she dipped tiny crusts of bread,
     and skillfully she inserted them into his mouth...
     This my eyes were privileged to see!
     To see this mother, a mother of five years feeding her child,
     to hear her soothing words —

My own mother, the best in the world,
had not invented such a ruse.
But this one wiped his tears with a smile,
injected joy into his heart — a little girl in Israel.

—Yitzak Katzenelson, *The Song of the Slaughtered Jewish People*, sec. 6, "The First,"
(Israel: Beit Lohamei Hagettaoth, 1979), 40–42.

Aron Kodesh (Ark) Is Opened

Congregation rises.

As soon as the Germans reached Kubilnick there appeared some hoodlums who began anti-Soviet and anti-Jewish agitation. That very day they burst into the schule and beat the worshipers. They opened the Aron Kodesh (Holy Ark) and commanded the old men, who had not managed to escape, to take the Torah scrolls outside. The hoodlums tore the Torah scrolls, yelling: "Look how strong the parchment is — just like the Jews!"

The next day they called the rabbi of the town, Hirsch Makowsky, and ordered him to burn the scrolls. He answered: "You can burn me, but this I will not do!"

On Succoth 1942, twelve of us were taken about a mile outside of town and ordered to dig two ditches. A troop of Gestapo men stood over us and pushed us on in our work. After we had finished digging we were ordered to stand aside. Suddenly we saw our whole community being driven toward the ditches. The men were told to undress and to kneel at the rim of the ditches. The rabbi told them not to kneel, but to bend over on the tips of their toes and fingers. In the few minutes allowed to them, before they were shot, the rabbi spoke again to them: All will be well, brothers, recite the Sh'ma Yisrael!"

שְׁמַע יִשְׂרָאֵל יְהֹוָה אֱלֹהֵינוּ יְהֹוָה ׀ אֶחָד׃

בָּרוּךְ שֵׁם כְּבוֹד מַלְכוּתוֹ לְעוֹלָם וָעֶד.

וְאָהַבְתָּ אֵת יְהֹוָה אֱלֹהֶיךָ בְּכָל־לְבָבְךָ וּבְכָל־נַפְשְׁךָ וּבְכָל־מְאֹדֶךָ: וְהָיוּ הַדְּבָרִים הָאֵלֶּה אֲשֶׁר אָנֹכִי מְצַוְּךָ הַיּוֹם עַל־לְבָבֶךָ: וְשִׁנַּנְתָּם לְבָנֶיךָ וְדִבַּרְתָּ בָּם בְּשִׁבְתְּךָ בְּבֵיתֶךָ וּבְלֶכְתְּךָ בַדֶּרֶךְ וּבְשָׁכְבְּךָ וּבְקוּמֶךָ: וּקְשַׁרְתָּם לְאוֹת עַל־יָדֶךָ וְהָיוּ לְטֹטָפֹת בֵּין עֵינֶיךָ: וּכְתַבְתָּם עַל־מְזֻזוֹת בֵּיתֶךָ וּבִשְׁעָרֶיךָ:

Warsaw. Jewish girls, stripped of everything by the Gestapo, are commanded to prepare themselves for the pleasure of Nazi soldiers. Rather than submit to this, they follow the path of martyrs who preceded them: they pour out their hearts in a final prayer and they swallow poison.

We have cleansed our bodies and purified our souls.
And now we are at peace.
Death holds no terror; we go to meet it.
We have served our God while alive;
We know how to hallow Him in death.
A deep covenant binds all ninety-three of us;
Together we studied God's Torah; together we shall die.
We have chanted Psalms, and are comforted.
We have confessed our sins, and are strengthened.
We are now prepared to take our leave.
Let the unclean come to afflict us; we fear them not.
We shall drink the poison and die, innocent and pure,
as befits the daughters of Jacob.
To our mother Sarah we pray: "Here we are!
We have met the test of Isaac's Binding!
Pray with us for the people Israel."
Compassionate Father!
Have mercy for Your people, who love You.
For there is no more mercy in man.
Reveal Your lovingkindness.
Save Your afflicted people.
Cleanse and preserve Your world.
The hour of Ne'ilah approaches. Quiet now grow our hearts.
One request we make of our brethren, wherever they may be.
Say Kaddish for us, for all ninety-three, say Kaddish.

— From the *Mahzor for Rosh Hashanah and Yom Kippur,*
ed. Rabbi Jules Harlow (New York: Rabbinical Assembly, p. 561

In 1943, on the first night of Passover, beleaguered Jews of Warsaw got word that the final hour was at hand. The Nazis had decreed their total annihilation. The Jewish Fighters Organization reacted swiftly: "No submission!" was their battle cry. To the people of the world they proclaimed:

Amid the howl of German artillery bombarding our dwellings, our mothers, wives, and children; over the chatter of machine guns that we have captured from gendarmes and SS; through the sheets of flame and in the gushing blood of the Warsaw Ghetto; we — the besieged in the Ghetto — send our heartfelt, brotherly greetings.

Every threshold in the Ghetto has been and will remain a fortress.... At the cost of our lives, we shall not surrender. Along with you, we aim to punish our common foe for all the crimes.... This is a struggle for our common freedom, for common human and social dignity and honor! Long live liberty...

At the same time another Jew, hiding in the sewers in Warsaw, made this observation:

How limited was our understanding about what the Germans were capable of doing! We simply could not imagine that the entire inventory, all the warehouses full of merchandise, all the workshops, factories, and machines worth tens, worth hundreds of millions — that all this would be set on fire on account of us, on account of all those who buried themselves underground and found hiding places between the walls and possess nothing more than their lives and the desire, the strong desire, not to give them up. No, we simply could not imagine it.

—Quoted in David Roskies, *Against the Apocalypse* (Cambridge, 1984), p. 222.

We read together the poem "Es Brent" ("It Burns"), by Mordechai Gebirtig:

Es Brent

S'brent briderlech s'brent!	It's burning, brothers, it's burning!
Oy, undzer orem shtetl nebech brent!	Oh, our poor little town is aflame!
Beyze vintn mit yerugzn	Angry winds full of fury,
Raysn brechn un tseblozn	Tear and break and blow asunder
Shtarker noch di vilde flamen,	Stronger still the wild flames,
Alts arum shoyn brent!	Everything is burning!

Refrain:

Un ir shteyt un kukt azoy zich	And you stand there looking on
Mit farleygte hent,	With folded arms,
Un ir shteyt un kukt azoy zich	And you stand there looking on
Undzer shtetl brent...	While our town goes up in flames...
S'brent! briderlech s'brent!	It's burning, brothers, it's burning!
Oy, es ken cholile kumen der moment,	Oh, the moment can alas, come
Undzer shtot mit undz tsuzamen	When our city with us in it
Zol oyf ash avek in flamen	Can go up in flames,
Blaybn zol — vi noch a shlacht.	Leaving it, like after a battle,
Nor puste, schwartze vent!	With empty, charred walls!
S'brent, briderlech, s'brent!	It's burning, brothers, it's burning!
Di hill iz nor in aych aleyn gevendt.	Help depends only on you.
Oyb dos shtetl iz aych tayer,	If the town is dear to you,
Nemt di keylim lesht dos fayer.	Take the pails and quench the fire.
Lesht mit ayer eygn blut.	Quench it with your own blood.
Bavayzt az ir dos kent.	Show that you can do it.

Refrain:

Shteyt nit brider, ot azoy zich	Do not stand there looking on
Mit farleygte hend.	With folded arms.
Shteyt nit brider, lesht dos fayer	Don't stand there brothers, quench the fire,
Undzer shtetl brent!	Our little town's aflame!

—Ruth Rubin, *Voices of a People* (Philadelphia, 1979), 430–31

We rise for the Memorial Prayer, "El Maleh Rachamim," in memory of the six million:

אֵל מָלֵא רַחֲמִים שׁוֹכֵן בַּמְּרוֹמִים הַמְצֵא מְנוּחָה נְכוֹנָה תַּחַת
כַּנְפֵי הַשְּׁכִינָה בְּמַעֲלוֹת קְדוֹשִׁים וּטְהוֹרִים כְּזֹהַר הָרָקִיעַ מַזְהִירִים,
אֶת־נִשְׁמוֹת כָּל־אַחֵינוּ בְּנֵי יִשְׂרָאֵל, אֲנָשִׁים נָשִׁים וָטַף, שֶׁנֶּהֶרְגוּ
וְשֶׁנִּטְבְּחוּ וְשֶׁנִּשְׂרְפוּ וְשֶׁנֶּחְנְקוּ. בְּגַן עֵדֶן תְּהִי מְנוּחָתָם. אָנָּא בַּעַל
הָרַחֲמִים, הַסְתִּירֵם בְּסֵתֶר כְּנָפֶיךָ לְעוֹלָמִים וּצְרֹר בִּצְרוֹר הַחַיִּים
אֶת־נִשְׁמוֹתֵיהֶם. יְיָ הוּא נַחֲלָתָם, וְיָנוּחוּ בְשָׁלוֹם עַל מִשְׁכְּבוֹתֵיהֶם.
וְנֹאמַר אָמֵן.

Exalted, compassionate God, grant perfect peace in Your sheltering Presence, among the holy and the pure, to the souls of all our brothers and sisters, men, women and children of the House of Israel who were murdered, slaughtered, and burned. May their memory endure, inspiring truth and loyalty in our lives. May their souls thus be bound up in the bond of life. May they rest in peace. And let us say: AMEN.

Song of the Partisans by Hirsh Glick (Yiddish and English)

Zog nit keynmol az du geyst dem letstn veg,
Chotsh himlen blayene farshteln bloye teg;
Kumen vet noch undzer oysgebenkte sho,
S'vet a poyk ton undzer trot'mir zaynen do!

Fun grinem palmenland biz vaysn land fun shney,
Mir kumen on mit undzer payn, mit undzer vey,
Un vu gefaln s'iz a shprits fun undzer blut,
Shprotsn vet dort undzer gvure undzer mut.

S'vet di morgn — zun bagildn undz dem haynt,
Un der nechtn vet farshvindn mitn faynt,
Nor oyb farzamen vet di zun un der kayor —
Vi a parol zol geyn dos lid fun dor tsu dor.

Dos lid geshribn iz mit blut un nit mit blay,
S'iz nit kayn lidl fun a foygl oyf der fray,
Dos hot a folk ts'vishn faindike vent
Dos lid gezungen mit naganes in di hent.

Never say that you have reached the very end,
Though leaden skies a bitter future may portend;
And the hour for which we've yearned will arrive,
And our marching step will thunder: we survive!

From green palm trees to the land of distant snow,
We are here with our sorrow, woe;
And wherever our blood was shed in pain,
our fighting spirits now will resurrect again.

The golden rays of morning sun will dry our tears,
Dispelling bitter agony of yesteryears,
But if the sun and dawn with us will be delayed,
Then let this song ring out to you the call, instead.

Not lead, but blood inscribed this mighty song we sing,
It's not a caroling of birds upon the wing
But a people midst the crashing fires of hell,
Sang this song with guns in hand, until it fell.

(Hirsh Glick wrote this song in the Vilna Ghetto in 1943. It became the anthem of the Jewish partisan fighters. Taken from Ruth Rubin, *Voices of a People* (Philadelphia, 1979), 454–55.)

Aharon Zeitlin was the only survivor of a noted literary and religious family. His poem "Der Sod: Mentsh" captures the extremes of human behavior that the Jews of Europe encountered during the Shoah.

Congregation reads responsively:

THE MYSTERY: MAN

Tell me not man is a beast.
Compared to man beast is angel.
Do beasts build crematoria?
Do they hurl children into the fire?
Do they take pleasure in death?

> Tell me not man is a beast.
> He is more than an angel.
> He is word of an Isaiah.
> He is outcry of a Job.
> He yearns for new worlds.
> Tell me not man is a beast.

Tell me not man is a beast.
Compared to man beast is angel.
Do beasts use napalm on each other?
Do they torture prisoners?
Do they kill their own kind?
Tell me not man is a beast.

> Tell me not man is a beast.
> He is more than an angel.
> He is willingness to help.
> He is ability to fast.
> He is a creature that can cry, confess, and change.
> Tell me not man is a beast.

Tell me not man is a beast.
Compared to man beast is angel.
Man robs, wrecks, and ravages —

> But unlike beast and unlike angel,
> Man can begin again.

So tell me not what man is,
Tell me instead what man can be.
Tell me what you would be,
And then I will know what man is.

—Aharon Zeitlin, from *Lider fun Churbn un Lider fun Gloybn,*
New York: Bergen-Belsen Association, 1967, I, p. 140,
translated by Emanuel Goldsmith

We sing together Ani Ma'amin:

Ani ma-a-min (3)
be-emunah sh'lay-ma
b'vi-at ha-ma-shi-ach (2)
ani ma-a min
v'af al pi she-yit-ma-may-a
im kol zeh ani ma-a-min

I believe with a whole faith in the coming of the Messiah; I believe, although the Messiah tarries — yet, I have faith.

Because of the strength and the beauty and the piety of their lives, because of our hope for the future which they have planted within us — in spite of everything which strangles hope — we say Yes to creation and we say Yes to our Creator and to God's eternity and holiness.

Please rise for the mourner's Kaddish.

Yit-gadal
       Auschwitz ve-yit-kadesh
       Babi Yar
shmei raba
       Bergen-Belsen
b'alma divra khir'uta
       Bialystok
ve-yamlikh mal-khutei
       Buchenwald
be-hayei-khon uve'yomei-khon
       Chelmno
uve-hayei di-khol beit yisrael
       Dachau
ba-agala u-vizman kariv
       Kovno v'imru amen.
Ye-hei shmei raba meva-rakh l'alam ul'almei 'almaya
Yit-barakh ve-yishtabah
       Lodz
ve-yit-pa'ar ve-yitromam
       Maidanek
ve-yitnasei ve-yit-hadar
       Minsk
ve-yit'aleh ve-yit-halal
       Salonika
shmei di-kudsha brikh hu
       Sobibor

l'eila
            Terezin
mikol bir-khata ve-shirata
            Treblinka
tush-be-hata ve-nehe-mata
            Vilna
da-amiran b'alma
            Warsaw
v'imru amen.
Ye-hei shlama raba min shmaya ve-hayim aleinu v'al kol
yisrael v'imru amen.

Oseh shalom bimromav hu ya'aseh shalom aleinu v'al kol
yisrael v'imru amen.

—Adapted from Rabbi Jules Harlow, *Mahzor for Rosh Hashanah
and Yom Kippur* (New York, 1972), 566–69

The service may also conclude with the traditional mourner's kaddish.

Mourner's Kaddish

קדיש יתום

יִתְגַּדַּל וְיִתְקַדַּשׁ שְׁמֵהּ רַבָּא בְּעָלְמָא דִּי־בְרָא כִרְעוּתֵהּ,
Yit·ga·dal ve·yit·ka·dash she·mei ra·ba be·al·ma di·ve·ra chi·re·u·tei,

וְיַמְלִיךְ מַלְכוּתֵהּ בְּחַיֵּיכוֹן וּבְיוֹמֵיכוֹן וּבְחַיֵּי דְכָל־בֵּית
ve·yam·lich mal·chu·tei be·cha·yei·chon u·ve·yo·mei·chon u·ve·cha·yei
de·chol beit

יִשְׂרָאֵל, בַּעֲגָלָא וּבִזְמַן קָרִיב, וְאִמְרוּ: אָמֵן.
Yis·ra·eil, ba·a·ga·la u·vi·ze·man ka·riv, ve·i·me·ru: a·mein.

יְהֵא שְׁמֵהּ רַבָּא מְבָרַךְ לְעָלַם וּלְעָלְמֵי עָלְמַיָּא.
Ye·hei she·mei ra·ba me·va·rach le·a·lam u·le·al·mei al·ma·ya.

יִתְבָּרַךְ וְיִשְׁתַּבַּח, וְיִתְפָּאַר וְיִתְרוֹמַם וְיִתְנַשֵּׂא, וְיִתְהַדָּר
Yit·ba·rach ve·yish·ta·bach, ve·yit·pa·ar ve·yit·ro·mam ve·yit·na·sei, ve·yit·ha·dar

וְיִתְעַלֶּה וְיִתְהַלָּל שְׁמֵהּ דְּקוּדְשָׁא, בְּרִיךְ הוּא, לְעֵלָּא מִן־כָּל־
ve·yit·a·leh ve·yit·ha·lal she·mei de·ku·de·sha, be·rich hu, le·ei·la min kol

בִּרְכָתָא וְשִׁירָתָא, תֻּשְׁבְּחָתָא וְנֶחֱמָתָא דַּאֲמִירָן בְּעָלְמָא,
bi·re·cha·ta ve·shi·ra·ta, tush·be·cha·ta ve·ne·che·ma·ta, da·a·mi·ran be·al·ma,

וְאִמְרוּ: אָמֵן.
ve·i·me·ru: a·mein.

יְהֵא שְׁלָמָא רַבָּא מִן שְׁמַיָּא וְחַיִּים עָלֵינוּ וְעַל־כָּל־יִשְׂרָאֵל,
Ye·hei she·la·ma ra·ba min she·ma·ya ve·cha·yim a·lei·nu ve·al kol Yis·ra·eil,

וְאִמְרוּ: אָמֵן.
ve·i·me·ru: a·mein.

עֹשֶׂה שָׁלוֹם בִּמְרוֹמָיו, הוּא יַעֲשֶׂה שָׁלוֹם עָלֵינוּ וְעַל־כָּל־
O·seh sha·lom bi·me·ro·mav, hu ya·a·seh sha·lom a·lei·nu ve·al kol

יִשְׂרָאֵל, וְאִמְרוּ: אָמֵן.
Yis·ra·eil, ve·i·me·ru: a·mein.

Hallowed and enhanced may God be throughout the world of creation.
May God's sovereignty soon be accepted, during our life and the life of all
Israel. And let us say: Amen

May God be praised throughout all time.

Glorified and celebrated, lauded and praised, acclaimed and honored. extolled and exalted may the Holy One be, far beyond all song and psalm,
beyond all tributes which people can utter. And let us say: Amen.

Let there be abundant peace from Heaven, with life's goodness for us
and for all the people Israel. And let us say: Amen.

May God who brings peace to the universe bring peace to us and to all
the people Israel. And let us say: Amen.

A Yom HaShoah Liturgy for Christians

Franklin H. Littell

In ancient sacred ritual a holocaust was the most costly of animal sacrifices: an offering in which the victim was totally consumed by fire. In the mid-twentieth century the word has acquired a new force: "the Holocaust" means the destruction of European Jewry by the Nazis, 1933–1945.

VOICES OF THE HOLOCAUST

To Reach into the Darkness

A whirlwind cannot be taught; it must be experienced. And we cannot know what happened during the Shoah, that whirlwind of destruction in which Hitler's Germany killed six million Jews — solely by learning historical facts and figures and scholarly explanations. Facts, figures, and explanations are necessary. But we must also touch and feel and taste the dark days and the burning nights. Our hearts must constrict in terror and grief. Our minds must expand to make room for the incredible. And our love for the goodness of life must grow strong enough to reach into the darkness and to discover the heart of that darkness, the experience itself.

Darkness pervaded every street of every town, city, and country occupied by Nazi Germany. The innermost circle of this geography of hell was the concentration camp. Once inside the circle, humanity moved from the light of the day to the valley of the shadow of death. Yet, life did go on. And the testimony of survivors of that life reaches out to us, demanding our concern, our attention, our anguish, and our dedication for tasks left undone, for an expansion of our own existence which must come to encompass those six million lives and bring them back into a world which must not and dares not forget all that took place.

And so we must enter the past. But what passport will gain us entry into hell? Recognizing the fact that the world we are about to enter is utterly alien to the world we know, how can we expand the horizons of our awareness so that hell and the

---

The program was planned by Dr. Elizabeth Wright and conducted in the Chapel at Queens College, Charlotte, N.C., on May 10, 1972. She spoke the transitional parts, read several of the selections, and led the closing prayer. The other selections were ready by students who had been members of a course entitled "The Star and the Swastika: A Study of Jewish Holocaust Literature" during the January term, 1972. The service lasted about thirty-five minutes. It was published in Dr. Littell's book, *The Crucifixion of the Jews* (1975, paperback: 1986.)

experience of it become real? Two paths are open to us: we can add to our knowledge of the past and strive to understand the outer structure and details of the police state achieved by Hitler Germany. And we can add to our knowledge of ourselves, of man's inner nature — of that range of emotions moving from love to hate and fear of death — only as we experience the daily lives of those who lived within the hell that was Nazi Germany. Facts are of little use in this second quest. But in the literature of that period it is not only facts but emotions which are transmitted. And the knowledge of the evil which can reside in us is too heavy a burden for reason or intellect to carry. Somehow, we must enter the Holocaust and its geography in this twofold way: with a clear mind, and with the humility and openness linked in the Bible with the contrite soul. Only then will we see, and seeing, understand.[1]

Why Do I Write?

Some voices of the Holocaust are words written urgently by those who perished soon after in the ghettos or the death camps. Chaim Kaplan kept a secret diary in the Warsaw Ghetto:

The terrible events have engulfed me; the horrible deeds committed in the ghetto have so frightened and stunned me that I have not the power, either physical or spiritual, to review these events and perpetuate them with the pen of a scribe. I have no words to express what has happened to us since the day the expulsion was ordered. Those people who have gotten some notion of historical expulsions from books know nothing. We, the inhabitants of the Warsaw Ghetto, are now experiencing the reality. Our only good fortune is that our days are numbered — that we shall not have long to live under conditions like these, and that after our terrible sufferings and wanderings we shall come to eternal rest, which was denied us in life. Among ourselves we fully admit that this death which lurks behind our walls will be our salvation; but there is one thorn. We shall not be privileged to witness the downfall of the Nazis, which in the end will surely come to pass.

Some of my friends and acquaintances who know the secret of my diary urge me, in their despair, to stop writing. "Why? For what purpose? Will you live to see it published? Will these words of yours reach the ears of future generations? How? If you are deported you won't be able to take it with you because the Nazis will watch your every move, and even if you succeed in hiding it when you leave Warsaw, you will undoubtedly die on the way, for your strength is ebbing. And if you don't die from lack of strength, you will die by the Nazi sword. For not a single deportee will be able to hold out to the end of the war."

And yet in spite of it all I refuse to listen to them. I feel that continuing this diary to the very end of my physical and spiritual strength is a historical mission which must not be abandoned. My mind is still clear, my need to record unstilled, though it is now five days since any real food has passed my lips. Therefore I will not silence my diary!" (July 26, 1942).[2]

---

1. Albert H. Friedlander, ed., *Out of the Whirlwind: A Reader of Holocaust Literature* (New York: Union of American Hebrew Congregations and Doubleday & Co., 1968), 11–12.

2. Chaim A. Kaplan, *Scroll of Agony*, in Friedlander, ed., *Out of the Whirlwind*, 189. *From Scroll of Agony*, ed. and trans. Abraham I. Katsh (New York: Macmillan, 1965).

The Voice of a Child in the Terezin Camp

"The Butterfly," a poem written in camp by Pavel Friedmann, age eleven:

The last, the very last
So richly, brightly, dazzling yellow.
Perhaps if the sun's tears would sing
against a white stone...

Such, such a yellow
Is carried lightly 'way up high
It went away I'm sure because it wished to kiss the world goodbye.

For seven weeks I've lived in here,
Penned up inside this ghetto
But I have found my people here,
The dandelions call to me
And the white chestnut candles in the court,
Only I never saw another butterfly.

That butterfly was the last one.
Butterflies don't live in here,
In the ghetto.[3]

Our Bodies Beginning to Devour Themselves; One Literally Became a Number

Others who survived the Nazi years speak to us of their experience as prisoners. Viktor Frankl, a doctor:

When the last layers of subcutaneous fat have vanished, and we looked like skeletons disguised with skin and rags, we could watch our bodies beginning to devour themselves. The organism digested its own protein, and the muscles disappeared. Then the body had no powers of resistance left. One after another the members of the little community in our hut died. Each of us could calculate with fair accuracy whose turn would be next, and when his own would come. After many observations we knew the symptoms well, which made the correctness of our prognoses quite certain. "He won't last long," or "This is the next one," we whispered to each other, and when, during our daily search for lice, we saw our own naked bodies in the evening, we thought alike: This body here, my body, is really a corpse already. What has become of me? I am but a small portion of a great mass of human flesh... of a mass behind barbed wire, crowded into a few earthen huts; a mass of which daily a certain portion begins to rot because it has become lifeless.

It is very difficult for an outsider to grasp how very little value was placed on human life in camp. The camp inmate was hardened, but possibly became more conscious of this complete disregard of human existence when a convoy of sick men was arranged.

---

3. Hana Volavkova, ed., *I Never Saw Another Butterfly* (New York: McGraw-Hill Book Co., 1964). Used with permission of the publisher.

The emaciated bodies of the sick were thrown on two-wheeled carts which were drawn by prisoners for many miles, often through snowstorms, to the next camp. If one of the sick men had died before the cart left, he was thrown on anyway — the list had to be correct! The list was the only thing that mattered. A man counted only because he had a prison number. One literally became a number: dead or alive — that was unimportant; the life of a "number" was completely irrelevant. What stood behind that number and that life mattered even less: the fate, the history, the name of the man.[4]

These voices are vitally important to us, the survivors. For in a sense we are all survivors. What our generation has to live with — not just Jews, but all of us — is the fact that the Nazi Holocaust brought an end to a certain kind of innocence. In the light of what happened, we now know that there is practically no limit to the horror which men are capable of perpetrating and that only we ourselves can stand in the way to prevent its happening again.

Terrifying Torment of the Spirit

The physical agony suffered during the Holocaust was appalling. But these voices tell us also of a truly terrifying torment of the spirit, dominated by the victims' feeling of complete isolation from the rest of the world. And beyond this human silence lay the even more terrifying silence of God.

> In any case, by one road or another, they almost all reached the "Heart of Darkness," fell victims to the "Final Solution." The physical agony suffered requires no further comment. But what comes through in all the books written on the subject is the truly terrifying torment of the spirit — the feeling of complete isolation from the rest of the world, the feeling (amply justified) that in their hour of agony they were abandoned by nearly all of mankind. We are concerned here not with the moral implications of this failure of mankind (though there were notable exceptions, such as the case of the Danes who saw to it that almost no Jews fell into Nazi hands); we are concerned, rather with the impact this failure had on the spirit of the camp inmates. The eyes and ears of humanity seemed shut, and not a move, not even a token gesture was forthcoming to bring, if not help, at least a message of hope.[5]

Never Shall I Forget that Night

Elie Wiesel was fourteen years old, a village boy, sheltered and deeply religious, when he was taken in a convoy to Auschwitz. He writes of that midnight when they reached the camp:

> Never shall I forget that night, the first night in camp, which has turned my life into one long night, seven times cursed and seven times sealed. Never shall I forget that smoke. Never shall I forget the little faces of children, whose bodies I saw turned to wreaths of smoke beneath a silent blue sky.

---

4. Viktor Frankl, *Man's Search for Meaning* (Boston: Beacon Press, 1963), 47–48, 83.
5. Ernst Pawel, film lecture, "Writings of the Nazi Holocaust," available from the Audio-Visual Department, Anti-Defamation League; pamphlet 10–11.

Never shall I forget those flames which consumed my faith forever.

Never shall I forget that nocturnal silence which deprived me, for all eternity, of the desire to live. Never shall I forget those moments which murdered my God and my soul and turned my dreams to dust. Never shall I forget these things, even if I am condemned to live as long as God Himself. Never.[6]

One Day, When We Came Back from Work, We Saw Three Gallows

Again Elie Wiesel, describing an execution ceremony in the concentration camp:

One day, when we came back from work, we saw three gallows rearing up in the assembly place, three black crows. Roll call. SS all around us, machine guns trained: the traditional ceremony. Three victims in chains — and one of them, the little servant, the sad-eyed angel.

The SS seemed more preoccupied, more disturbed than usual. To hang a young boy in front of thousands of spectators was no light matter. The head of the camp read the verdict. All eyes were on the child. He was lividly pale, almost calm, biting his lips. The gallows threw its shadow over him.

This time the Lagerkapo refused to act as executioner. Three SS replaced him.

Three victims mounted together onto the chairs.

The three necks were placed at the same moment within the nooses.

"Long live liberty!" cried the two adults.

But the child was silent.

"Where is God? Where is He?" someone behind me asked.

At a sign from the head of the camp, the three chairs tipped over.

Total silence throughout the camp. On the horizon, the sun was setting.

"Bare your heads!" yelled the head of the camp. His voice was raucous. We were weeping.

"Cover your heads!"

Then the march past began. The two adults were no longer alive. Their tongues hung swollen, blue-tinged. But the third rope was still moving; being so light, the child was still alive....

For more than half an hour he stayed there, struggling between life and death, dying in slow agony under our eyes. And we had to look him full in the face. He was still alive when I passed in front of him. His tongue was still red, his eyes were not glazed.

Behind me, I heard the same man asking: "Where is God now?"

And I heard a voice within me answer him: "Where is He? Here He is — He is hanging here on this gallows...."

That night the soup tasted of corpses.[7]

---

6. Elie Wiesel, *Night* (New York: Hill & Wang, 1969), 44.
7. Ibid., 75–76.

O the Chimneys

The spiritual night of the concentration camps destroyed not only the intended victims but the executioners themselves, those clever technicians of death. The poet Nelly Sachs invokes the smoking chimneys of the crematories:

> O the chimneys
> On the ingeniously devised habitations of death
> When Israel's body drifted as smoke
> Through the air —
> Was welcomed by a star, a chimney sweep,
> A star that turned black
> Or was it a ray of sun?
>
> O the chimneys!
> Freedomway for Jeremiah and Job's dust —
> Who devised you and laid stone upon stone
> The road for refugees of smoke?
>
> O the habitations of death,
> Invitingly appointed
> For the host who used to be a guest
> O you fingers
> Laying the threshold
> Like a knife between life and death
>
> O you chimneys,
> O you fingers
> And Israel's body as smoke through the air!⁸

On Jewish Resistance

At the time of Hitler and ever since, Jews have energetically debated the question of their resistance against the Nazis: whether to resist, why, how, to what avail. One view in this continuing debate is that of Alexander Donat, in his memoirs of the Warsaw Ghetto:

There was a stubborn, unending, continuous battle to survive. In view of the unequal forces, it was a labor of Sisyphus. Jewish resistance was the resistance of a fish caught in a net, a mouse in a trap, an animal at bay. It is pure myth that the Jews were merely "passive," that they did not resist the Nazis who had decided on their destruction. The Jews fought back against their enemies to a degree no other community anywhere in the world would have been capable of doing were it to find itself similarly beleaguered. They fought against hunger and starvation, against epidemic disease, against the deadly Nazi economic blockade. They fought against the German murderers and against the traitors within their own ranks, and they were utterly alone in their fight.

---

8. Nelly Sachs, *O the Chimneys*, trans. Michael Hamburger (New York: Farrar, Straus & Giroux, 1967), 3. Copyright 1967 by Farrar, Straus and Giroux, Inc. Reprinted with the permission of Farrar, Straus and Giroux, Inc.

They were forsaken by God and man, surrounded by the hatred or indifference of the Gentile population.

Ours was not a romantic war. Although there was much heroism, there was little beauty; much toil and suffering, but no glamor. We fought back on every front where the enemy attacked — the biological front, the economic front, the propaganda front, the cultural front — with every weapon we possessed.

In the end it was ruse, deception, and cunning beyond anything the world has ever seen, which accomplished what hunger and disease could not achieve. What defeated us, ultimately, was Jewry's indestructible optimism, our eternal faith in the goodness of man — or rather, in the limits of his degradation. For generations, the Jews of Eastern Europe had looked to Berlin as to the very symbol of lawfulness, enlightenment, and culture. We just could not believe that a German, even disguised as a Nazi, would so far renounce his own humanity as to murder women and children — coldly and systematically. We paid a terrible price for our hope, which turned out to be a delusion: the delusion that the nation of Kant, Goethe, Mozart, and Beethoven cannot be a nation of murderers. And when, finally, we saw how we had been deceived, and we resorted to the weapons for which we were least well prepared historically, philosophically, psychologically — when we finally took up arms, we inscribed in the annals of history the unforgettable epic of the Warsaw Ghetto uprising.[9]

Why Do the Christians Hate Us?

Among the many and complex factors which made possible the rise of Nazism, there is no doubt that one essential factor was the centuries-long history of Christian hostility, oppression, and sporadic violence against Jews. Without this potent anti-Jewish poison in the bloodstream of Christian Europe, without the superstitions and religious dogmas which had long been used to justify it, the Nazi program would never have been so hideously successful.

This ancient evil of Christian hostility toward the Jew is the theme of a conversation in André Schwarz-Bart's novel *The Last of the Just*. Ernie and Golda are two young Jews who meet in Paris during the Nazi occupation.

"Oh Ernie," Golda said, "you know them. Tell me why, why do the Christians hate us the way they do? They seem so nice when I can look at them without my star."

Ernie put his arm around her shoulders solemnly. "It's very mysterious," he murmured in Yiddish. "They don't know exactly why themselves. I've been in their churches and I've read their gospel. Do you know who the Christ was? A simple Jew like your father. A kind of Hasid." Golda smiled gently. "You're kidding me."

"No, no, believe me, and I'll bet they'd have got along fine the two of them, because he was really a good Jew you know, sort of like the Baal Shem Tov — a merciful man, and gentle. The Christians say they love him, but I think they hate him without knowing it. So they take the cross by the other end and make a sword out of it and

---

9. Alexander Donat, "The Holocaust Kingdom" in Friedlander, ed., *Out of the Whirlwind*, 57–58. From *Jewish Resistance* (Flint, Mich.: Walden Press, 1964).

strike us with it! You understand, Golda, he cried suddenly, strangely excited, *"they take the cross and they turn it around, they turn it around, my God...."*

'Sh, quiet," Golda said. "They'll hear you." And stroking the scars on Ernie's forehead, as she often liked to do, she smiled. "And you promised you wouldn't think all afternoon...."

Ernie kissed the hand that had caressed his forehead and went on stubbornly, "Poor Jesus, if he came back to earth and saw that the pagans had made a sword out of him and used it against his sisters and brothers, he'd be sad, he'd grieve forever. And maybe he does see it. They say that some of the Just Men remain outside the gates of Paradise, that they don't want to forget humanity, that they too await the Messiah. Yes, maybe he sees it. Who knows? You understand, Goldeleh, he was a little old-fashioned Jew, a real Just Man, you know, no more nor less than... all our Just Men. And it's true, he and your father would have got along together. I can see them so well together, you know. "Now," your father would say, "now my good rabbi, doesn't it break your heart to see all that?" And the other would tug at his beard and say, "But you know very well, my good Samuel, that the Jewish heart must break a thousand times for the greater good of all peoples. That is why we were chosen, didn't you know?" And your father would say, "Oi, oi, didn't I know? Oh, excellent rabbi, that's all I do know, alas...."

They laughed. Golda took her harmonica from the bottom of the basket, flashed sunlight off it into Ernie's eyes, and still smiling brought it to her lips and played a forbidden melody. It was Hatikvah, the ancient chant of hope, and as she inspected the Square Mouton-Duvernet with uneasy eyes, she tasted the sweetness of forbidden fruit. Ernie leaned down and plucked a tuft of slightly mildewed grass and planted the blades in Golda's still moist hair. As they got up to leave he tried to strip her of that poor garland, but she stopped his hand. "Too bad about the people who see. And too bad about the Germans too. Today I say too bad about everybody. Everybody..." she repeated, unexpectedly solemn.[10]

Chorus of the Rescued

Within a few months, both Ernie and Golda were dead in a gas chamber. For those Jews who did not die, but somehow outlasted the wreckage of the Third Reich, there was the pain of learning to re-enter the world. The poet Nelly Sachs gives them voices in her "Chorus of the Rescued":

> We, the rescued
> From whose hollow bones death had begun to whittle his flutes,
> And on whose sinews he had already stroked his bow —
> Our bodies continue to lament
> With their mutilated music.
> We, the rescued,

---

10. André Schwarz-Bart, *The Last of the Just,* trans. Stephen Becker (New York: Atheneum, 1960), 365–67. Copyright 1960 by Atheneum House, Inc. Copyright 1959 by Editions du Seuil, Paris. Reprinted by permission of Atheneum Publishers U.S.A. and Martin Secker & Warburg Lt.

The nooses would for our necks still dangle
before us in the blue air —
Hourglasses still fill with our dripping blood.
We, the rescued,
The worms of fear still feed on us.
Our constellation is buried in dust.
We, the rescued,
Beg you:
Show us your sun, but gradually,
Lead us from star to star, step by step.
Be gentle when you teach us to live again.
Lest the song of a bird,
Or a pail being filled at the well,
Let our badly sealed pain burst forth again
and carry us away —
We beg you:
Do not show us an angry dog, not yet —
It could be, it could be
That we will dissolve into dust —
Dissolve into dust before your eyes.
For what binds our fabric together?
We whose breath vacated us,
Whose soul fled to Him out of that midnight
Long before our bodies were rescued
Into the ark of the moment.
We, the rescued,
We press your hand
We look into your eye —
But all that binds us together now is leave-taking,
The leave-taking in the dust
Binds us together with you.[11]

The Resurrection — An Elegy for the Six Million

The voices of the dead, the rescued, and the living have become a growing chorus in our time as Jews take up the task of remembering, of teaching their children, of bearing witness before the world. Some congregations now use this poem by David Polish in their liturgy for the Days of Awe (the solemn period of the Day of Atonement and the New Year). It is entitled "The Resurrection — An Elegy for the Six Million":

One day they will assemble in the valley of bones —
Ashes sifted out of furnaces, vapors from Lunenberg,

---

11. "Chorus of the Rescued," a choral reading by three, Nelly Sachs, *O the Chimneys,* trans. Michael Hamburger (New York: Farrar, Straus & Giroux, 1967), 25–27. Copyright 1967 by Farrar, Straus and Giroux, Inc. Reprinted with the permission of Farrar, Straus and Giroux, Inc.

Parchments from some friend's books, cakes of soap,
Half-formed embryos, screams still heard in nightmares.
God will breathe upon them. He will say: Be men.

But they will defy Him: We do not hear you. Did you hear us?
There is no resurrection for us. In life it was a wondrous thing
For each of us to be himself, to guide his limbs to do his will.
But the many are now one. Our blood has flowed together,
Our ashes are inseparable, our marrow commingled,
Our voices poured together like water of the sea.
We shall not surrender this greater self.
We the Abrahams, Isaacs, Jacobs, Sarahs, Leahs, Rachels
Are now forever Israel.

Almighty God, raise up a man who will go peddling through the world.
Let him gather us up and go through the world selling us as trinkets.
Let the peddler sell us cheaply. Let him hawk his wares and say:
Who will buy my souvenirs? Little children done in soap,
A rare Germanic parchment of the greatest Jew in Lodz.
Men will buy us and display us and point to us with pride:
A thousand Jews went into this and here is a rare piece
That came all the way from Crakow in a box car.
A great statesman will place a candle at his bedside.
It will burn out but never be consumed.
The tallow will drip with the tears we shed.
And it will glow with the souls of our children.
They will put us in the bathrooms of the United Nations
Where diplomats will wash and wash their hands
With Polish Jews and German Jews and Russian Jews.
Let the peddler sell the box of soap that was once buried
With Kaddish and Psalms by our brothers.

Some night the statesman will blow upon the candle
And it will not go out.
The souls of little children will flicker and flicker
But not expire.
Some day the diplomats will wash their hands and find them stained with blood.
Some day the citizens of the German town
Will awake to find their houses reeking
With all the vapors from all the concentration camps,
From Hell itself, and the stench will come from the soap box.

Then they will all rise up, statesmen, diplomats, citizens
And go hunting for the peddler: You who disturb our rest

And our ablutions, you who haunt us with your souvenirs,
You who prick our conscience, death upon you!

But the peddlers shall never cease from the earth
Until the candles die out and the soap melts away.[12]

Let us Pray

Let the mind never cease to forget what was done to us

God of Israel, our God, God of all humanity, help us to learn how to listen to such messengers. We have so little bravery of mind, so little of the humble and contrite heart, which would enable us to heed their words. In many and various ways you spoke of old to our fathers by the prophets and through Jesus the Jew, our fellow man whom we allege to be your Son. Help us to hear the voices which you send today. Strengthen now our trust in the goodness of life, strengthen us for tasks yet to be done, so that no earthly darkness may be able to overwhelm us.

Amen
Shalom Aleichem!

---

12. David Polish, in Mordecai M. Kaplan, Eugene Kohn, and Ira Eisenstein, eds., *High Holy Day Prayerbook* (New York: Jewish Reconstructionist Foundation, 1948), 2:404–5.

22

A Christian Witness in Memory of the Holocaust of Six Million Jews

A Good Friday Statement

The Ministers of Claremont, California

We are a group of Christians, of several denominations, who are moved on this Good Friday to make a public witness, in sorrow and soul-searching, in memory of the six million Jews whose lives were extinguished during the Holocaust. While this terrible act was carried out by a neo-pagan regime, we believe it was not unrelated to historic Christian attitudes toward Judaism and Jews. We believe these attitudes have not reflected, but rather have distorted, the spirit and intent of Christ. We believe it fitting to make this witness on the day in which we remember the death on a cross of Jesus Christ.

We seek to understand better and help in some part to heal the tragic rupture, nearly two millennia ago, between the parent experience of Judaism and the separated career of its giant child, Christianity.

We believe that, as Christians, we should remember that, not long after its beginning, the Christian church assumed that it was the successor to and displacer of the Jewish faith, and hence could see little reason for the continued existence of Jews except as candidates for conversion to Christianity; that, in alliance with military states, it often sought to coerce such conversions; that, in the same alliance, it segregated Jews, limited their civil rights, and from time to time condoned their persecution; in short, made them a pariah people in Western civilization. Were they not thus ready-made as scapegoats in the design of a desperate dictator?

We believe that, in allowing and often even sanctioning an idolatrous nationalism in their respective countries and many blood wars, Christians had a part in bringing about Naziism itself. We observe that, while there was still opportunity, this same selfish nationalism, in many countries, refused to open the door to the possible rescue of Jews from their fate under their Nazi oppressors.

Made in conjunction with the annual Good Friday Community Service of the Claremont Committee of the Pomona Valley Council of Churches, held at the Claremont United Methodist Church, Claremont, Calif., March 24, 1978. The observance was in the nature of a silent prayer vigil. One person held a sign saying: "A Christian Witness in Memory of the Holocaust of Six Million Jews." Signatories of the statement included many of the religious and academic leaders of the community of Claremont. Among denominations represented were United Church, Methodist, Quaker, Roman Catholic, Presbyterian, Lutheran, Baptist, Disciples, and Episcopalian. Rev. Ferner Nuhn, Coordinator.

Happily, especially since the conciliar statement of Vatican II, Christian views of Judaism are being revised. A new dialogue is opening up between Christians and Jews. But we ask Christians to ponder this whole matter in the spirit of Christ whose death we commemorate. We seek forgiveness for the transgressions which led, with other evils, to the Holocaust. We strive for justice, reconciliation, and peace among all peoples.

•

The clergy of Claremont continue to finds ways to achieve reconciliation. This press release describes the activities of the Claremont United Methodist Church.

CHURCH HYMNAL "TELLS IT LIKE IT IS"

CLAREMONT, CA — If other churches would follow the lead of the Claremont United Methodist Church, antisemitism would have its greatest enemy.

The following message appears on the inside cover of each of the hymnals used in the church:

> The Claremont United Methodist Church publicly states its affirmation that Judaism is a continuing bulwark of faith, that it has not been superseded by Christianity, that God has not rejected the Jewish people, that the Jewish people have never lost their covenant with God, that salvation is available to Jews as a covenant people, that the Jews as an historic nation are not responsible for, and therefore not to be blamed for, the death of Jesus, and that Jews should not be pressured to convert to Christianity.

The message adds,

> Furthermore, we state that anti-Judaism in all forms should be universally condemned. We ask forgiveness for past sins and persecutions against the Jewish people. We pray that old barriers to communication and understanding will be removed and that the relationships of this church with the congregations of the local Jewish community will be enhanced.

The statement was published in the bulletin of Congregation Emanu El of San Bernardino, whose rabbi, Hillel Cohn, is an old friend of Dr. Robert Davis, Claremont's pastor, who previously served in San Bernardino.

Rabbi Cohn noted that he was moved by the statement and the "fact that it is read by the members of that church each week as they open their hymnals is most meaningful. May the season during which there is so much talk of 'peace on earth and good will' be accompanied by acts of good will. The affirmation of the Claremont United Methodist Church is surely such an act."

23

"Where Can We Find God?"

The Mormon Tabernacle Choir

March 5, 1995
Salt Lake City, Utah
The Church of Jesus Christ of Latter-Day Saints

The Salt Lake Mormon Tabernacle Choir
Conducted by Jerold Ottley
At the Organ — Clay Christiansen

"Gently Raise the Sacred Strain"
by Thomas C. Griggs
words by William W. Phelps

"Sing unto God"
from Judas Maccabaeus
by George Frederick Handel
edited by Richard P. Condie

"Even When God Is Silent"
by Michael Horvit

"Praise to the Living God"
music attributed to Meyer Lyon
words adapted from Maimonides'
"13 Articles of Faith"

Organ Solo
"Adagio"
from *Sonata on Psalm 94*
by Julius Reubke

"Sunrise, Sunset"
from *Fiddler on the Roof*
by Jerry Bock
arranged by Arthur Harris
words by Sheldon Harnick

"God Moves in a Mysterious Way"
by William B. Bradbury
words by William Cowper

"O Father, Whose Almighty Power"
from Judas Maccabaeus
by George Frideric Handel

The Spoken Word: "Where Can We Find God?" . . . . Lloyd Newell

Where can we find God? Where is He to be found? Amid the rubble and fire of an earthquake, in the whipping wind of a hurricane, through the noisy destruction of war, dazed survivors look heavenward and in anguished cries ask the great questions: Where? Where can we find God? Where is He to be found?

Some turn their gaze downward in hopelessness; it is a question without an answer. But others, searching skyward, can testify that God can be found. He is with us in the most unexpected places, under the most trying of circumstances.

The courage and hope of Anne Frank's diary reminds us that He can be found in a small attic, hidden carefully above an office; the bravery and faith of Zlata Filipovic's journal testifies that He walks through the shell-pitted streets of Sarajevo. Albert Einstein found Him in the nucleus of the atom, while Stephen Hawking searches for Him in the furthest reaches of the stars. He spoke to Alexander Solzhenitsyn in the cold, dark loneliness of a Siberian labor camp. And God ministered to the ill and starving poor of Calcutta through an elderly nun named Teresa.

God can be found in a friend's loving counsel, a word of encouragement, in a handclasp and a smile. God can be found in a classroom, a boardroom, or a prison. God can be found on a highway — in a stranger changing our flat tire. Or God can be found at home.

To many of us, God speaks through scribbled papers, lovingly displayed on a refrigerator door. God dwells in families and communities — wherever two or three are gathered in His name. And, as Elie Wiesel reminds us, "A child always suggests the presence of God."[1] Perhaps nowhere is He closer than in the trusting eyes and loving embraces of small children.

Where can we find God? Where is He to be found? In the heart that is pure, in the soul that longs for His comfort. In earthquakes and hurricanes and war itself — in quiet repose and noisy tumult — God is where we seek Him.

Editors note: This program was created in honor of the 25th Anniversary Scholars' Conference on the Holocaust and the Churches, which was held March 5–8, 1995, at Brigham Young University, in Provo, Utah. The Annual Scholars' Conference has been held since 1970, the year it was founded by Franklin H. Littell and Hubert G. Locke. From the beginning the conference has been committed to examining issues raised by the Holocaust in tandem with the study of the churches' struggle and failure to confront antisemitism and the final solution. It is international, interfaith, and interdisciplinary in scope.

---

1. Harry James Cargas, *Conversations with Elie Wiesel* (South Bend, Ind.: Justice Books, 1992), 103.

24

The Meaning of "Good Friday"

Richard L. Ullman

Rabbi Yaakov Rosenberg of Congregation Adath Jeshurun in Elkins Park, Pennsylvania, was speaking to a group of Episcopal clergy. In all the Torah, he was saying, there are three laws a pious Jew would never break — even under threat of death. The pious Jew will die rather than worship any but the One God who has commanded "I am the Lord your God who brought you out of bondage. You shall have no other gods but me." Equally, in obedience to the One God and as a sign of faithfulness to the Redeemer of Israel, the pious Jew would rather die than commit adultery. Finally, among all the laws of the Torah, the third of those three which a pious Jew must never transgress is the law against murder. For every human being is created in the image and likeness of God. Therefore, to murder another human being is not simply to kill a brother or sister, it is to diminish the image of God in the world.

Good Friday is, first of all, about the diminishment of the image of God in the world. On the sheerly human level, without an ounce of interpretation about the meaning of the ministry of Jesus, to crucify him was to diminish the image of God in the world. When Jesus was, all innocently, put to death, the same thing took place that always takes place in the presence of deliberate killing of human beings: God's living image in the world was wantonly diminished.

There is, of course, another level of interpretation of the death of Jesus upon the cross. When the eyes of faith behold in Jesus God's own Anointed One, the Messiah, then the crucifixion is seen even more intensely as deliberately to diminish God's image in the world. If Jesus is God's incarnation, then the crucifixion is a terrible blasphemy, an attempt to blot out God's earthly presence.

There have been times when this theme was greatly stressed on Good Friday. In killing Jesus, said the preachers, a terrible thing had been done — not simply terrible on a human level, but on a divine level as well. And, the preachers argued, the offense against the divine must be avenged. For vengeance to be done, blame must be fixed, and the Good Friday preachers found someone to blame: "The Jews," they said, "killed Christ; and so the Jews must suffer." So it came about that Good Friday, the day on which all of his disciples abandoned the Jew Jesus, the day on which the Roman governor imposed with his troops of occupation the pagan Roman sentence of crucifixion, Good Friday became a day on which Christian preachers incited Christian congregations to violence and hatred against their Jewish neighbors. Good Friday became a day of terror for Jews in so-called Christian lands.

Rev. Richard L. Ullman, Church of the Redeemer, Springfield, Pa.

What irony! Pious priests of Christ preached blind hatred, in direct conflict with the "Father, forgive" Jesus proclaimed from the cross. Pious Christian priests, assuming the role of spokesmen for divine vengeance, fomented blood-letting that no pious Jew before or after Jesus' day could take part in other than as victim.

Even when our preachers were without a trace of antisemitic vengeance, the Church for centuries on Good Friday perpetuated an attitude toward Jews which is unhealthy, uncharitable, and in conflict with Jesus' own conduct during his Passion and death. In the noble Book of Common Prayer, in the 1662 book still used in England and up until the 1892 revision in this country, a Good Friday prayer looked upon Jews, along with "Turks, Infidels and Heretics," as people of "ignorance, hardness of heart, and contempt of [God's] Word." They were beyond the pale of salvation, not to be counted as "among the remnant of the true Israelites" (*Book of Common Prayer,* 3rd Collect of Good Friday).

Anglican liturgy and tradition have but mild traces of Christian antisemitism, and we have eliminated most of that in the 1976 Book of Common Prayer. But we do well to keep aware of this evil seed in the common Christian heritage, the bitter seed of misplaced, unwarranted vengeance which has more than once in history borne poisonous fruit of murderous persecution of Jews, the people of the Scriptures, heritage, and blood of Jesus, the Chosen People of the Holy One whom Jesus and his followers call "Abba, Father."

There is a direct line from such prayers, and the yet more scandalous sermons of which I spoke, to this scene, recounted by a reliable witness at the trial of Adolf Eichmann:

"One day all children were told to step aside," recalled (the witness who was) testifying on the horrors of (a Nazi) "labor" camp. "There was a great commotion in the camp. Mothers rushed forward, crying and shouting. They felt that their children were being sent away. Then two things happened at once. Machine guns were mounted and loaded for action. The other thing was the sounding of lullabies over the loudspeakers.... Thus the children were carried away to the tunes of lullabies and their mothers, half-paralyzed with fear and half-fooled, stopped in their tracks."

And from another witness, this scene from the Jewish ghetto in a city in Lithuania:

The climax of the horrors was "the children's operation...." (They) entered all the courtyards in the ghetto and tore away every child they encountered.... I saw one mother beseech the guards near the hospital. "How many do you have there?" the German asked. "Three," said the mother. "You may have one back," said the German and climbed into the car with the mother. All three children looked at her and stretched out their little hands. All of them wanted to go with the mother: she did not know which child to select, looked from one to the other, and finally went away alone." (Gideon Hausner, *Justice in Jerusalem,* 330)

It is crucial that, when we look at the cross on Good Friday, we see there the diminishment of the living image of God in the world. It is entirely right that the sight of Jesus hanging there, dying, should arouse within us the deepest of emotions: grief, terror, anger, fear. But it is a shallow and finally evil piety that turns those deep emotions outward on others. Shallow and evil — and finally death-dealing. So much so that now, these nineteen and a half centuries from the crucifixion, when Christians look at the cross on Good Friday, we must see not only Jesus there, but the children of that labor camp, and of that Lithuanian ghetto, and all the other six million Jews of the Holocaust, and the hundreds of thousands more Jews murdered by those who called themselves Christians from the time of the Emperor Constantine through the Crusades and the Spanish Inquisition down to antisemites of this very hour.

When we look at the cross in this manner, we see there an even greater diminishment of the living image of God in the world. And so we might rightly respond with even deeper grief, terror, anger, and fear. And in time in our response we will be led to deeper, fuller, more honest piety if we turn the energy of these emotions toward self-examination.

Upon self-examination, we come to understand that:

> if we had been among the disciples, we would have
>   slept as Jesus prayed in the Garden;
> if we had been in Peter's shoes, we would have
>   denied knowing the prisoner;
> if we had been among Pilate's Praetorian Guards, we would have
>   helped weave the crown of thorns;
> if we had been in Pilate's judgment seat, we would have
>   seen the political wisdom of letting one man die to prevent a riot;
> if we had been among the chief priests, we would have
>   wished this trouble-maker silenced;
> if we had been among the crowds, we would have
>   shouted "Crucify him";
> if we had been among the soldiers at the foot of the cross, we would have
>   joined in throwing dice for his garments.

In this Good Friday piety, we know better than to seek vengeance upon the Christ-killers, for we know that we ourselves are quite capable of that; we ourselves are capable of "ignorance, hardness of heart, and contempt of God's Word"; we ourselves have helped if only by silence to diminish the living image of God in the world.

Our Good Friday devotions now become not incitement to vengeance but a call to repentance.

> We sing then, full-heartedly:
>   "Were you there when they crucified my Lord?"
>   —*Hymnal 1940,* No. 80
>
> And we answer, full-grievingly,
>   "Yes, I was there none other but me."
> Again we sing:
>   "Who was the guilty? Who brought this upon thee?"
> And in the next breath we answer:
>   "Alas, my treason, Jesus,
>   hath undone thee.
>   'Twas I, Lord Jesus,
>   I crucified thee."
>   —*Hymnal 1940,* No. 71, verse 2

– 25 –

Your People, My People

THEODORE W. LODER

Luke 13:1–5

The word "Holocaust" literally means burnt offering. Thirty years have passed, a whole generation, since six million Jews were systematically tortured, starved, murdered, and burned in the Nazi death camps, a historical event which has come to be called the Holocaust. Yet time has only added urgency to the question: a burnt offering of whom, by whom, to whom? After thirty years, we are just beginning to face the Holocaust as a decisive event in human history. Six million Jews deliberately, efficiently murdered, simply, and for no other reason than because they were Jews.

Of the Holocaust, Elie Wiesel says: "How does one remember? It defies memory, it defies categories. Yet one *can* remember and one must. Something happened then. Something of an ontological nature." To look into Elie Wiesel's eyes is to know something happened then, something beyond words, something unbearable that somehow must be borne...and is borne by men like him. How then do we remember? What meaning is there in the Holocaust? It is almost obscene to ask that question. Yet ask we must: look we must. For to fail to see this evil, to fail to grasp what happened there to the soul of man would be to finally fail our already fragile humanity. We can and we must look at the Holocaust as human beings and as Christians. We dare not draw any easy, simple conclusions that will violate the witness of the six million Jews or those who survived. So it is a painful, humble, and tentative exploration I invite us to make together now.

How did it happen? That is the first question that comes to mind when you read about the Holocaust, when you see pictures of the death camps, the gas chambers, the ovens, the mountains of gaunt bodies, the mounds of ashes and bones. Six million Jews — babies, children, old people, men, women — tortured, subjected to painful medical experiments, victims of unspeakable atrocities, murdered in cruel ways — how did it happen?

I suppose it would be disturbing but yet convenient to say it was a singular unique eruption of something irrational and demonic in human affairs. But that is simply not true. John Pawlikowski, professor of theology at Catholic Theological Union, is closer to the truth when he says, "The real issue that we must confront in the Holocaust is its rationality. It was a planned event whose origins lie in philosophies developed by thinkers some consider to be giants of liberal Western thought, and in theological attitudes central to Christianity

Sermon preached by Rev. Theodore W. Loder, First United Methodist Church of Germantown, Philadelphia, Pennsylvania, June 15, 1975.

almost since its inception." Jacob Bronowski, the Jewish scientist, in that TV series *The Ascent of Man,* stood up to his ankles in the pond of Auschwitz into which the ashes of four million people were flushed. Those who saw him will never forget as Bronowski reached into the water and took a handful of those ashes and spoke this urgent truth:

> This is where people were turned into numbers.... And that was *not* done by gas. It was done by arrogance. It was done by dogma.... When people believe that they have absolute knowledge... this is how they behave. This is what men do when they aspire to the knowledge of gods.

How did the Holocaust happen? Don't you suppose it has something to do with giving religious status to our perverse need to be right and so to have others be wrong? Don't you suppose the Holocaust grows out of giving divine sanction to our insidious assumptions that we *are* right and that others are wrong so that we can define our rightness by their wrongness? Do you remember that argument in the early church between Peter and Paul recorded in the book of Acts? Peter, you remember, understood the Christian church to be essentially Jewish in its roots, in its nature. Peter believed that to become a Christian you must first become a Jew, acknowledge and observe Jewish teaching and Jewish law and not ignore it, go beyond it perhaps but not be separate from it. But Paul said no. He insisted that Christians do not have to become Jews first or obey the Jewish law and teaching. Paul won the debate, unfortunately. So Christianity began to be ripped away from its Jewish roots. All through the New Testament and all through early Christian thought there is the determined compulsive effort by the young church to define itself over against, distinct from, and superior to the Jews. It was the early church which remembered the events and sayings of Jesus' life, and which selected, edited, and compiled the story according to its own needs, one such need being the need to be right, and for the Jews to be wrong, so that the church could gain new members. There is a strong and tragic note of antisemitism in the Scripture and in the church and its history from the beginning, a note resonating in our need to be superior, religiously, to other people. Jews are presented as breaking the covenant with God, and killing the messiah, and somehow deserving the ostracism, if not outright persecution, of the Christian world. I am not saying that such attitudes are indigenous and essential traits of the Christian gospel or the Christian faith. I believe Jesus and Peter and Paul would have died in the death camps. But antisemitism clearly came to be part of the New Testament and of church history.

How did the Holocaust happen? "It was done by arrogance. It was done by dogma!" It was made possible by people who had to be right and claimed to know the mind of God. It is not far, is it, from the claims of religious superiority to the claims of racial superiority at the heart of the Nazi policies of the death camps. It is not far, is it, from accusing Jews of being Christ killers to accusing them of being responsible for Germany losing World War I, or for causing depressions, or for originating and perpetuating communism, or for whatever else anyone might say is wrong in world history, even the enmity of Arab oil-producing nations toward supporters of Israel.

How did the Holocaust happen? In the little book called simply *The Holocaust,* there is this line: "Most of those who planned this genocide were seemingly ordinary members of society and, in the main, educated men. They were, however, inculcated with the belief that every Jew was a powerful enemy of the German people and had to be destroyed."

Now as we go along, I want to relate a story, to lay it alongside this sermon, so to speak. I want to do this partly because I love stories, and partly because of something Martin Buber, a great Jewish thinker, has written about stories, which is this:

A story must be told in such a way that it constitutes help in itself. My grandfather was lame. Once they asked him to tell a story about his teacher. And he related how [his teacher] used to hop and dance while he prayed. My grandfather rose as he spoke, and he was so swept away by his story that he himself began to hop and dance to show how the master had done. From that hour he was cured of his lameness. That's the way to tell a story.

[handwritten margin note: help for the teller?]

That is my hope for us, and the story I would relate to you is of Ruth, a story written at least twenty-four hundred years ago, and buried there in our Old Testament. I want to tell you the story in three parts and each part relevant to a section of the sermon. I know it is hard for a story to be told this way and yet I'm going to ask you to hold each part in your mind until the whole is told. The first part of the story is the beginning, which is:

In the day when the judges ruled there was a famine in the land, and a certain man of Bethlehem in Judah went to sojourn in the country of Moab, he and his wife and his two sons. The name of the man was Elimelech and the name of his wife, Naomi, and the names of his two sons were Mahlon and Chilian.... They went into the country of Moab and remained there. But Elimelech, the husband of Naomi, died and she was left with her two sons. These took Moabite wives. The name of the one was Orpah and the name of the other was Ruth. They lived there about ten years; and both Mahlon and Chilian died, so that the woman was bereft of her two sons and her husband.

So death and sorrow and loneliness are at the beginning of the story, and in it is the seed of a secret, somehow. Hold it and wait for it to whisper to you and begin to relate it to this: Six million Jews murdered and as the book *The Holocaust* put it, "The very few who survived...and returned to their native cities and villages...were received with anger and hostility."

So the second question surfaces in the struggle to face the Holocaust. That question is: To whom did it happen? Before he begins his novel *The Oath*, Elie Wiesel quotes a line from the Talmud, "Had the peoples and nations known how much harm they brought upon themselves by destroying the Temple at Jerusalem, they would have wept more than the children of Israel." Alain de Rothschild, a leader of the Jewish community in Paris, puts it this way: "When they carried out their genocide the Nazis made the impossible possible. From the moment the Germans set up crematoria, a breach opened up in the human conscience."

[handwritten margin note: Christian creed to mourn?]

The first death camp was established in Dachau in March of 1933, three months before the Nazi Party became the only recognized legal political party in Germany. Random and constant pogroms were perpetuated against Jews through the centuries: murder, confiscation of property, denial of civil rights. But never anything quite like what began at Dachau in 1933. "From the moment the Germans set up crematoria, a breach opened up in the human conscience." I wonder what obscene atrocities have poured through that breach since 1933, Dachau. Who dares contemplate that?

Elevation of "truth" over love

To whom did the Holocaust happen? Until the outbreak of World War II, the press of Western nations consistently reported the Nazi policy of brutal victimization of the Jews. No effective protest was raised. In 1938, the Evian Conference of several nations was convened by President Roosevelt to help emigration of refugees from Germany. No country, including our own, committed itself to any practical measures, and the United States did not relax its stringent immigration quotas. That was taken by the Nazis as an expression of support for their antisemitic policies and eased their taking their step toward their "Final Solution." With rare exceptions, the church and its leaders inside Germany made common cause with the Nazis, and the church and its leaders outside Germany remained silent. In the years 1942–43 the *New York Times* reported every massacre of Jews in full detail. But pleas from the Jewish community to exchange German war prisoners for Jews were ignored by the government and by the public. No food or aid to Jews in Germany was allowed by our country because it was regarded as aiding the enemy. But enough . . . enough recounting the ugly history.

To whom did the Holocaust happen? We know. In our hearts we know. After Elie Wiesel's talk here a few weeks ago, the family of Rabbi Charry and our family met with him for supper. When we were together, Rabbi Charry's daughter-in-law asked me how Christians could ever feel anything but enormous guilt about the Holocaust. I said that I did feel enormous guilt, and that many Christians did. Elie Wiesel said very softly, "The more guilt a man feels, the closer to him I feel." In that somewhere is the beginning of something beautiful which I hesitate to call forgiveness for fear of cheapening it. But please, let the closeness begin.

Even so, of what are we guilty? Father Pawlikowski makes this observation:

> The Holocaust . . . lays bare another strain in Christian teaching. It is the attitude that truth is more important than love, an attitude which in concrete practice meant the persecution and slaughter of those who might disagree with Christians on the meaning of ultimate truth."

I find Father Pawlikowski persuasive. For, you see, the claim to know truth presumes the power to destroy error, doesn't it, especially if it's God's truth. Isn't that why we are forever defensive and scurrying about to justify our behavior? But love? Love suffers with and struggles on behalf of the wronged, the oppressed, the victims of injustice and hate . . . even the enemy. "From the moment the Germans set up their crematoria, a breach opened up in the human conscience."

The elevation of truth over love does several things. It gives me an escape, a rationalization for saving my own skin. I can always find something wrong in the views or lifestyles of those who make me uncomfortable or need my love beyond my inclination to give it. Moreover, the elevation of truth over love is a key factor which leads to the privatization of religion in which the salvation of my soul or my personal growth as an individual, or my God-given right to be me all take priority over the welfare of the community. The Christian emphasis on the worth of the individual is a half truth which has perverted the other half of the truth which is our responsibility for the community and for the earth, an insight so essentially, wonderfully Jewish and part of their healthy this-world emphasis. Our churchly privatization of religion has also led to a kind of stifling uniformity and conformity which has often made the church into a club of like-minded people who cannot sustain difference of opinion and style, and who cannot endure the ambiguities and insecurities of not being able to claim absolute certain truth for their religious views. One result of this blind arrogance is the attitude that religion has to do with spiritual matters, only matters which are relatively safe and harmless. So religion does *not,* must not touch on the more dirty, complicated, but important, matters of politics, economics, racism, sexism, and war. But this assumption also fosters the attitude that what doesn't directly affect my well-being isn't really important, even to God...even to God! "The more guilt a man feels, the closer to him I feel." Beloved friends, not all guilt is neurotic. Some guilt is real and it is sick not to feel it and acknowledge it.

Six million Jews murdered. "The very few who survived...and returned to their native cities and villages...were received with anger and hostility." To whom did the Holocaust happen? "Had the peoples and nations known how much harm they brought upon themselves by destroying the Temple of Jerusalem, they would have wept more than the children of Israel."

But again, our story of the three widows: Naomi who lived in the land of Moab with her husband and her sons, all who died, leaving her and her two Moabite daughters-in-law alone. Here's the second part of the story:

> Then Naomi started with her daughters-in-law to return from the country of Moab. ...So she set out...with her two daughters-in-law, and they went on the way to re- turn to the land of Judah. But Naomi said to her two daughters-in-law, "Go, return each of you to her mother's house. May the Lord deal kindly with you....The Lord grant that you may find a home, each of you in the house of her husband." Then she kissed them, and they lifted up their voices and wept. And they said to her, "No, we will return with you to your people." But Naomi said, "Turn back, my daughters, why will you go with me?...Even if I should have a husband this night and should bear sons, would you therefore wait till they were grown? Would you therefore refrain from marrying? No, my daughters, for it is exceedingly bitter to me for your sake that the hand of the Lord has gone forth against me!" Then they lifted up their voices and wept again; and Orpah kissed her mother-in-law, but Ruth clung to her. And she said, "See, your sister-in-law has gone back to her people and her gods; return after your sister-in-law."

So the story unfolds and the secret grows. Hold it and wait for it to whisper to you. Now this final question that stares at us out of the face of the Holocaust: What does it mean that it happened? It means many things, I suppose, some not yet apparent at all, some quite unclear as yet. But if nothing else, it means for me, and I suspect perhaps for the church, a crisis of faith, a profound, disturbing disruption of much, if not all, we have come to assume we are or have. Let me refer to two sources to help define the crisis I perceive and experience.

One is in Franklin Littell's book, *The Crucifixion of the Jews,* a book I commend to you. More than almost any Christian, Franklin Littell has pressed upon the Christian community the fact and the consequences of the Holocaust, and I am grateful he is in this church family. In his book, he quotes Jewish theologian Rabbi Richard Rubenstein, who wrote of his experience with Heinrich Gruber after the war. Heinrich Gruber was one of the great men of Christian resistance to Hitler. Hear that! Gruber said to Richard Rubenstein that if one takes the biblical theology of history seriously, Adolf Hitler is no more nor less an instrument of God's wrath than Nebuchadnezzar. It struck Rubenstein, the Jew, that he agreed with Gruber, the Christian, on that. Now hear what Rubenstein writes:

> I had what was perhaps the most important single crisis of faith I have ever had...I have had to decide whether to affirm the existence of a God who inflicts Auschwitz on his guilty people or to insist that nothing the Jews did made them more deserving of Auschwitz than any other people...I have elected to accept...the courage to live in a meaningless, purposeless Cosmos rather than believe in a God who inflicts Auschwitz on his people.

What does it mean that the Holocaust happened? It means a profound crisis of faith like that of Rubenstein, a crisis very painful and disturbing, which is surely one reason we have avoided facing the Holocaust. But it is a crisis of faith my friends, about which we cannot lie and which we dare not resolve with pious, easy clichés.

The other source I refer to in order to point up the crisis of faith is Elie Wiesel; first a line from his book *The Oath,* and second in a story he tells. The line is, "And what if I told you that the Creator of past and future worlds is to be found in fear and not in mercy? In anguish and not in grace?" Well, I've been told that and I say I've heard a prophet speak to where I am.

The story Wiesel tells is about a shammes. A shammes is someone who performs certain tasks in the synagogue, usually a poor man, often hunchbacked, usually taciturn.

> Somewhere in Russia, in a ghetto, a shammes called Moishe went mad. Day after day he would come to the synagogue...bang his fist on the pulpit and say to God, "Ribbono shel Olam, Master of the Universe, I want you to know we are still here...." Then began the transports. The ghetto was decimated. Still the shammes came, mad as he was, and with anger or was it laughter, he would pound his fist on the table saying, "Master of the Universe, I want you to know, we are still here." Finally came the last transport, and he was the only Jew who remained in the ghetto. For some reason, the madmen were left behind....He was alone in the ghetto. He came to the synagogue...and banged his fist against the sanctuary, "Master of the Universe, I want you to know I am still here." And then he stopped, only to murmur, "But you—where are you?"

What does it mean that the Holocaust happened? A painful, frightening crisis of faith. I do not believe that we live in a meaningless Cosmos. I have, as yet, less reason than Richard Rubenstein to believe that and/or perhaps less courage. But I do think we have a crisis of faith which is summed up, for me, in the affirmation "Master of the Universe"; in the assertion, "I want you to know, I am — we are — still here"; and in the question, "But you — where are you?" I believe, I feel deeply, that faith is precisely the honest, demanding, living of the tension of that, and especially living that question, trusting that it will be answered somehow. But if so, it will be answered in a different way, in different categories, perhaps, than those we have become so familiar and comfortable with. It will be answered, partly at least, "...in fear and not in mercy, in anguish and not in grace." Elie Wiesel, in a dialogue with Richard Rubenstein, said this, and I find it persuasive: "Dick...you say that it is more difficult to live today in a world without God. No! If you want difficulties choose to live with God. . . . The real tragedy, the real drama, is the drama of the believer." "Master of the Universe we want you to know we are still here. But you — where are you?" Perhaps an honest, and I hope loving, faith can do no more right now than live that question.

And what does living it mean? It means at least pledging our lives to the words inscribed on the international memorial sculpture at the death camp of Dachau. The words are, "Never Again."

Never again, because we shall recover the Jewish spirit of aggressive worldliness and take responsibility for the world, its peoples and creatures!

Never again, because we will be vigilant and act against the world's inhumanities, and ours, wherever and however we encounter them, whether in corrupt politicians, in perverted technologies, in misguided, secret arrogant spying operations of CIA's, in bloated defense budgets and reduced funds for human services.

Never again, because we will support Israel, pressure for release of Soviet Jews, and oppose the cowardly silence of the church.

Never again, because we shall join ourselves in a relationship with a Jewish congregation and learn our common history, be part of the Jewish-Christian task force of NIH*; begin an observation of the Holocaust in our litanies; examine our faith and Scripture for its essential character and affirm its pro-Jewish roots; continue teaching our children that we are Jews as well as Christians!

Never again, for we shall live out the pain and the promise of what it means that the Holocaust happened. "Master of the Universe, we want you to know, we are still here. But you, where are you?"

And so the last part of our story of Ruth to add to those in your mind now. It is this:

And Naomi said, "See, your sister-in-law has gone back to her people and her gods; return after your sister-in-law." But Ruth said, "Entreat me not to leave you or to return from following you; for where you go I will go, and where you lodge I will lodge; your people shall be my people and your God my God; where you die I will die, and there will I be buried. May the Lord do so to me and more also if even death parts me from you."

Maybe someday we shall learn to tell a story, live a story like that. Maybe then our question may be answered beyond words. Maybe then the fire that burns our house will be taken away. Shalom.

A kaddish is said every day in the synagogue. It will be said now! It is a prayer of mourning. Here are the words:

> May Thy glory, O King of Kings, be exalted.
> O Thou who shallst renew the world
> and let the defunct rise again.
> Thy rule, Adonai, shall be proclaimed by us,
> the children of Israel, today, tomorrow, always.
> Let us say: Amen.
> May it be loved, may it be cherished,

---

*National Institute on the Holocaust (now the Philadelphia Center on the Holocaust, Genocide and Human Rights)

may it be praised and glorified,
Thy radiant name.
May it be blessed, sanctified, may it be worshiped,
Thy name that soars in the skies,
in our praises, in our hymns,
in all our benedictions.
May merciful Heavens grant us a quiet life,
peace, and happiness.
Let us all say: Amen."

26

A Midrash on Job for Yom HaShoah

Michael D. Ryan

Rabban Shimon ben Gamliel said: Upon three things the world stands, on Truth, on Judgment and on Peace. As it is said: Truth and judgment of peace judge ye in your gates (Zech. VIII. 16). Pirke Aboth I. 18.

How does truth come to us? Naturally, like water rushing toward the lowlands? Like sunlight calling forth the blossoms of earth? In pain, like the birth of a lamb, of a calf, of a human child? Perhaps in all of these ways and many more, but not without one ingredient in *none* of these. Before truth can come to human beings, there first must be present a will to truth. A will to truth as mysterious, as imponderable as the very givenness of life itself, as amazing in its concrete "is-ness" as sunlight and air and water and earth and the interaction between these that is the occasion for our kind of life.

The will to truth is more profound and more radical than the will to meaning, and so they are not the same and must therefore be distinguished. The will to truth is more radical than the will to meaning because it is open to the possibility of meaninglessness as truth, as that with which humans may have to reckon in their sojourn through life. It is more profound because it does not cover over the mystery of the unknown with a construct of human thought, with a dogma, with a doctrine, with an ideology to protect oneself from radical questioning about that which slips away from all such artifices of the human mind.

On this evening on the day before Yom HaShoah, the day to remember the destruction of European Jewry by the National Socialism of Germany under Adolf Hitler, we are gathered in an act of remembrance. In this act it must not simply be a matter of our corporate fascination with the macabre, with the remembrance of realities too horrible, too ugly, too despicable to be the product of fiction, but rather the will to truth must guide us lest we lose our equilibrium and fall victim in retrospect to the Holocaust mind, to the human mentality, the corporate social-pathology that created the death camps in the first place.

In a sensitive and remarkable lecture on the Holocaust given at Montclair State College last fall, Terence Des Pres, author of the book *The Survivor: An Anatomy of Life in the Death Camps* (New York: Oxford University Press, 1976), declared that to allow one's consciousness to feel and to absorb the complete implications of the Holocaust for Western culture is to find oneself torn loose from cultural moorings, without ideology, without traditional values and faith, without even an appropriate vocabulary for expressing one's

Prepared by Dr. Michael D. Ryan. An address given at *Yom HaShoah* observance at Drew University, April 14, 1977.

meanings in the post-Holocaust world. Two sentences of his stabbed *me* as a theologian, which I am quoting from his unpublished manuscript with his permission:

> To the extent that we must ignore the Holocaust in order to affirm inherited *beliefs,* our heritage becomes dishonest. To the extent that we use these same beliefs to interpret and make sense of the Holocaust, we make no sense at all![1]

I fully agree with both of these statements. Indeed, to ignore the Holocaust while writing books of theology and biblical interpretation, especially those that involve making Christian judgments about the meaning of Judaism and of Jewish history, does render our acts of interpretation dishonest in face of the current situation of Christianity after the Holocaust. And surely, to use traditional belief to interpret the Holocaust makes no sense at all. First, because it attempts to give a meaning for that which is incomprehensible; this is to superimpose a Christian structure of meaning on the reality of the Holocaust. Secondly, like the friends of Job, theologians who give theological interpretations of the Holocaust necessarily end up defending the ways of God to suffering persons, who from the standpoint of their suffering are closer to reality, closer to truth, than the propounders of theodicy. So what must be said is that there can be no theology of the Holocaust without committing blasphemy, both against God and the memory of those who suffered there and died there, and not without insulting the personal presence of those who suffered there and survived and are in our midst.

But is this to say that theology as such is impossible after the Holocaust? Is this to say that one may not take up sacred writings and read them with new eyes, as it were, with a new understanding after facing the horrors of Auschwitz, Maidanek, and Treblinka? If one may not capture the Holocaust with traditional teachings, with the mediated meaning of a community of faith, is it still not possible to illuminate and perhaps even transform that mediated meaning by searching the Scriptures, by performing a midrash, in the light of the Holocaust flames? With all the great risk of distortion and of reading our own stories back into the stories of Scripture, I propose to venture such a midrash here. I do so in hope of lending to the Book of Job and to the Holocaust, to each, its own uniqueness; but also in hope of finding in the tension between them a genuine insight for which to be grateful.

The Book of Job represents in eloquent, dramatic fashion, like a magnificent play spun out of the internal dialogue of a great sad spirit, the very essence of human suffering.

For literally millions who have been exposed to biblical religion, whether Jewish or Christian, the Book of Job has provided a language to express their sorrow, their despair, their anguish in suffering. Elie Wiesel is correct to refer to Job in his own midrash as "our contemporary," for Job represents every person who has been pulled by an unforeseeable chain of events into an abyss of despair and who has to return again from the brink of disaster to equanimity and to the normal acquiescences of life.

Job, the wealthy and just Gentile of the Land of Uz, was the subject of a legend passed down through generations of multiple cultures until the legend found a definitive telling in the fluent Hebrew of probably an Exilic or perhaps Post-Exilic Jew. In this telling of the

---

1. Terence Des Pres, Julian Jaffe Memorial Lecture, Montclair State College, Upper Montclair, N.J., October 25, 1976.

legend of the Gentile Job, the story of Israel in Exile and bondage and return find symbolic expression. And in it a very Jewish questioning of God occurs, but in a definitive form rendered by creative genius.

Job, the good and pious and just man of the Land of Uz, in his strength and prosperity represents every person living well and happily before disaster strikes. Job's lifestyle and his religious attitude and beliefs were commensurate with every person living in earthly *shalom,* in the relative peace and quiet of an orderly and quite predictable world in which tomorrow will be pretty much like today, next week pretty much like this week, and next year at harvest time, pretty much like this year's reaping and threshing and rejoicing in work and celebration.

Then, quite suddenly, things began to happen that shook the foundations of this world. Sabean raiders made off with his oxen and slew his servants who cared for them. Fire fell from heaven and destroyed his sheep and their shepherds. Chaldeans attacked his camel herders and killed them and stole the camels; a great wind destroyed the house where his children and servants were feasting. One calamity followed another in swift succession. Job was shriveled by his grief. He rent his robe, shaved his head in mourning, and fell upon the ground and worshiped, saying:

> Naked I came from my mother's womb, and naked I shall return; the Lord gave, the Lord has taken away; blessed be the name of the Lord. (1:21)

Job was shaken, but yet faithful in his suffering.

Then the day came when he himself was afflicted, breaking out with loathsome sores from head to foot. He took a potsherd with which to scrape himself, and went and sat among the ashes. His wife, portrayed as unsympathetic in the book, more generously by the Midrashists, so Wiesel says, invites him to complete his misery by cursing God and dying. Job is here every person whose neat, orderly, tomorrow-is-going-to-be-like-today world has suddenly become unpredictable and horrible — a world rapidly torn into a *before* and an *after* by the excruciating experience of sudden suffering.

In this break-up of the familiar world, all of the old relationships are strained, if not shattered. Spouse and friends are there, but their words do not reach to his center. Job felt all alone, a discarded piece of rotten flesh there in the ash pile. Three of his friends come and out of respect for his grief they remain silent. Job makes them wait a good long time before he breaks silence with a curse. But he doesn't curse God, or the world at large — he curses the day he was born. What person in great pain and hurt has not wished in passing that he or she had never been born? Job rails at his life. His *shalom,* his peace is completely gone.

Having lost his world in an agony of pain and humiliation before wife and friends, Job experiences as a correlate with that the losing of himself, but not quite. What made it all so hellish is that he had not completely lost himself. He still knew what was happening to him, and he wished that he wouldn't have to know it.

> Why is light given to him that is in misery? And life to the bitter in soul, who long for death, but it comes not.... Why is light given to a man whose way is hid, whom God has hedged in? (3:20–23)

Put the word "consciousness" where you find "light" in the foregoing passage and you catch a glimpse of Job's predicament. Job is here asking for death like one seeking an anesthesia, a relief from having to know what is happening to him.

Having lost his everyday home world, losing himself but not quite, Job then plunges in the depth of yet another loss. The loss of the sense of the presence of God. At first, he is angry. And his anger draws the fire of his friends. But one of them goes too far when he says:

> Does God pervert justice? Or does the Almighty pervert the right? If your children have sinned against Him, He had delivered them into the power of their transgression. ...Behold God will not reject a blameless man. (8:3–4)

But Job from his broken world saw things quite differently.

> I *am* blameless: I regard not myself. I loathe my life. (9:21)

Or in modern times, "Look, I really don't like me! If I had anything to confess that would account for all my disasters to my servants and to my children and myself, I would do so, but in all honesty, I can see no relationship between these events and my own conduct." So

> It is all one: therefore I say, God destroys both the blameless and the wicked. When disaster brings sudden death, he mocks at the calamity of the innocent. The earth is given into the hand of the wicked, he covers the faces of its judges. (9:22–24)

As far as Job is concerned, there is no justice in the earth. God destroys both the innocent and the wicked; both of them die just as easily from sickness, from the weapons of war, so what difference does it make to be good, if goodness is not protection from suffering? Job knew that it was giving false hope to teach that goodness protects from harm and tragedy, because the harm happens anyway. And Job demands an accounting of God.

> Thy hands fashioned and made me and now dost Thou turn about and destroy me? Remember that Thou has made me of clay; and will Thou turn me to dust again? Didst Thou not pour me out like milk, and curdle me like cheese? (10:8–10)

In the last sentence we have expressed the essence of human suffering and Job wishes to find God, to come before his seat and demand an accounting for this experience of an absurd world. The twenty-third chapter expresses the pathetic frantic searching for God, and his not finding. Everywhere Job looks — forward, backward, this way and that, but God is nowhere to be found. The chapter ends with a poignant expression of what Martin Buber called the eclipse of God:

> ...for I am hemmed in by darkness, and thick darkness covers my face. (23:17)

What? Where? When was the darkness that blacked out the light of God in such a way that the Book of Job was written to give expression to it? We do not know. We can only speculate. Was it perhaps the Exile, when Jews were uprooted from their homeland and carried off once more into slavery? Perhaps. It must have been a darkness occurring at a juncture of nature and history, at the interaction of human violence with natural disaster in such a way as to blot out the presence of God. What that creative genius did with the Book was to describe the anguish of Job with such power and poignancy that all who ever since have experienced loss of world, loss of self, loss of God, find that the Job story is their story because it expresses these dimensions of human suffering.

Does the Job story perform the same sense of human bonding, of unity in suffering for the victims of the Holocaust? The answer to this question depends upon how one understands the Book of Job. If it is taken as a kind of answer to the problem of human suffering, such as: one must suffer to be human, or even if it furnishes the conclusion that there is no answer to the problem of human suffering — even that is an answer — for "there is no answer" is an answer, then the Book of Job becomes a structure of meaning projected over the black abyss of meaninglessness. It then hides and distorts the uniqueness of the Holocaust experience.

But if one understands the Book of Job as radical questioning of all of life from the midst of suffering, then the Holocaust experience loses none of its uniqueness as a new occasion for such radical questioning, for a new spontaneous outburst of the will to truth as a response to the attempt to repress all will to truth in human being. The Holocaust in this perspective does not abrogate or invalidate the radical character of human being disclosed in the Book of Job — namely, the human person as born of radical questioning of the very foundations of life. Rather the uniqueness of the Holocaust is such that it profoundly transforms and deepens the essence of human being as radical questioning.

The uniqueness of the Holocaust, therefore, can be discerned in this, that it was a new and powerful disclosure of the quintessential character of being human, of the ambivalence, the twofold propensities of human beings. On the one hand it revealed the horrible degrading depths of monstrosity and perversity to which human beings may sink. On the other hand, it revealed the will to love, to truth, to cooperation to which humans may rise even in the midst of degradation calculated to destroy and root out every trace of human fellow feeling and concern.

The Holocaust revealed new depths and new dimensions to radical evil as human being. The evils in the world of Job were largely the result of the happenstance concurrence of human aggression and natural threats to human well-being. Evil gave life an altogether capricious character, like the tossing of dice in a game of chance. Satan was the mythical expression for evil as whimsy and caprice. In the Holocaust world, evil appeared neither in mythical nor in natural guises, but rather took specifically human form. The Nazis feared neither devil nor demons because regarding them as mere myths demonstrated the power of evil in a purely human form. Evil here was not capricious, but occurred with remorseless intentionality as the calculated human attempt to strip other human beings of their dignity, their personal identities, their faith, their home, their love by a process that reduced them to things, to waste material to be disposed of by fire. Hell literally came on earth as the *human world* of Germans and Jews and Poles and French and Italians and all of the peoples of Europe was radically inverted, turned upside down in the Nazi social organization, and became the kingdom of death. It was not death as the inevitable outcome of all organic life, not natural death, but rather unnatural willed death as both the symbol and the reality of power. The artist Naftali Bezem very appropriately portrayed this inverted Nazi world in the Yad Vashem Memorial in Israel with the figure of a woman holding two flaming candlesticks upside down with the flames burning her breast.

From the moment that the Nazis placed the Jews of Poland on a starvation diet and

The Holoc. mentality

applied a social policy of containment and random terror perfected in the concentration camps of Dachau and Buchenwald, in that moment all of Poland became the hub of the kingdom of death. Never have human beings willed the death of others in precisely this way — slowly to starve them so that their last months of life can be spent in slave labor and they can be rendered into walking corpses with the light of self-consciousness literally burnt out before the body itself is disposed of.

Motivating the formation of the Nazi kingdom of death was the all too human desire to control human destiny totally. From this there followed the utterly naive assumption that one could create the good world by identifying the evil presence and then radically eliminating it. Lionel Rubinoff, commenting on this feature of the Nazi mind, wrote:

> there is something magical and paranoiac about believing one need only to eliminate evil to bring about good — which completely ignores the fact that the good society is the product of labor, the labor of the mind as well as of body, to be achieved through the sweat of his brow.[2]

Without the presence of some such belief shared in a social pathological sense by most of the persons who participated in the factory-like process of harvesting Jews in death mills, their acquiescence to play a role in it can scarcely be imagined. That might be a rule of thumb for identifying the all too human pathological spirit that produced the death camps. Whenever it is claimed that the good life can result from the radical elimination of evil through "search and destroy" — there is the Holocaust mentality! Whenever persons are viewed as things, there the perversion has already occurred.

I say this fully aware that such a mentality characterized the American pursuit of the Vietnam War, and it is present today in many different places throughout the world; terror and torture are even now used to maintain control in Russia, Chile, Argentina, and Brazil, in South Korea, the Philippines, and Indonesia. And once again antisemitism is on the rise with 14 million Jews out of the world's 3.8 billion people being blamed for the world's morbid condition. *The Protocols of the Elders of Zion* are being widely distributed in South America, especially in Argentina, and in the United States they are being distributed by a West Virginia press along with Henry Ford's Dearborn Papers and Martin Luther's *Against the Jews and Their Lies.*

Do I say this to suggest an anti-terrorist terrorist campaign? — a crusade once more — a new search and destroy operation? That would simply mean reenacting the cosmic myth in a new key with the promise of the same results for the bearers of such a myth — namely, self-destruction in the crusade as the good fight. It has come home to me with special force in this semester of Holocaust studies. The Jews were not the only victims of the Nazi social myth, nor were the next largest number, that is, the Gypsies and Jehovah's Witnesses. The Germans, too, were victims, and especially those who became Nazis and obediently goose-stepped their way off to war to die in suicidal military operations such as at Stalingrad.

So, on this day of destruction I remind you of all the victims, especially the Nazi victims, and I do so because the Holocaust mentality, the temptation to quick and easy solutions to human problems, is still abroad in the world. This mentality did not die with Nazism;

---

2. Lionel Rubinoff, "Auschwitz and the Pathology of Jew Hatred," in Eva Fleischner, ed. *Auschwitz: Beginning of a New Era?* (New York: KTAV Press, 1976), 369.

indeed Nazism itself is not dead. There are those who rise out of their wretched existence to proclaim their loyalty to Hitler, and even in our midst don brown shirts and swastika arm bands. More subtle, and hence far more dangerous, are the technicians who refuse to make distinction between human problems and technical problems, and they are a pervasive presence in a technically oriented social system.

Wherein then lies hope? Our hope must come from the other, opposite propensity of human being disclosed in the Holocaust, namely, from the will to care for others, from the will to resist the total oppression, the will to maintain one's humanity by finding spheres of freedom in one's ambience and from these having a basis to reach out in loving kindness and creating a sphere of peace. The Job story symbolizes this hope through the radical questioning of Job — who keeps seeking, not settling for cheap and easy answers until quite suddenly and expectedly his Shalom returns and he finds himself in the presence of God. Job the radical questioner, the one who exercised his freedom, is justified, not the defenders of God. As Wiesel once said to me, "Job suffered. His friends developed a theory of suffering."

Our hope becomes even more concrete in discerning the miracle of rebirth in the lives of survivors who emerged from the camps and have become a leavening, humanizing force in our midst. These survivors bear in their lives even more than in their words the message of hope. Where humans perversely will to turn other humans into things, there arises a will to fight and struggle for one's humanity. One discovers one's freedom in the power to choose responses to suffering and learns to exercise that freedom in radical questioning. One then finds the appropriate expression of that freedom in caring for one's fellow human beings and at this stage finds that a new world has emerged.

The message of the Holocaust that deepens the Job story of suffering is simply this: human beings playing "God" constitute the greatest threat to human being. Human beings radically questioning the self-made gods constitute the hope for genuine peace.

Elie Wiesel put it this way at the end of his midrash on Adam in *Messengers of God*:

according to Jewish tradition, creation did not end with man, it began with him. When He created man, God gave him a secret — and that secret was not how to begin but how to begin again.

In other words, it is not given to man to begin; that privilege is God's alone. But it is given to man to begin again and he does so every time he chooses to defy death and side with the living. Thus he justifies the ancient plan of the most ancient of men, Adam, to whom we are bound both for the anguish that oppressed him and the defiance that elevated him above the paradise we shall never enter.[3]

---

3. Elie Wiesel, *Messengers of God* (New York: Random House, 1976), 39.

27

A Yom HaShoah Message

Franklin H. Littell

To speak at Yom HaShoah is a very hard assignment. It's also a privilege, and I'm grateful to you. But whenever I come forward as a Christian — and perhaps especially as a clergyman — to address my thoughts and the thoughts of the listeners to remembering the Holocaust, I have to struggle hard to contain my emotions and to say something that will be helpful to all present.

Of course it is strengthening to all of us to know that since 1980, by Act of Congress, the Days of Remembrance are a national observance — an observance for all Americans. And in the last four or five years the president, the Congress, all fifty governors, mayors of all large cities and many smaller cities have issued proclamations calling upon us all to remember. We are to remember one of the two major events in recent centuries of Western civilization — an event not only in the death and life of the Jewish people, but an event which speaks to every person of conscience and perhaps particularly addresses the condition of Christendom.

Two days ago the spiritual underworld — the revisionists, the neo-Nazis, and those who sympathize with them — celebrated a birthday. I saw him once in the flesh. I was travelling through Germany with a group of Methodist youth on our way to the First World Christian Youth Conference in Amsterdam, in the Netherlands. We stopped with a little Methodist congregation in Nuernberg, and the son of the family invited me — the only one of the group who had had enough first-year and second-year German to make a little headway with the language — to come with him that evening. So I excused myself, and he took me to the stadium, the stadium where American boys later, during the Occupation, played football. At that time it was the central place for the Nazi Party rallies. Since we were late, he led me up back stairways to the rim of the stadium, and we looked out over a crowd of approximately one hundred thousand people.

The stadium was domed with the "Cathedral of Light," which Albert Speer later said he invented. The technique involved the placement of huge spotlights, which created an awesome, eerie, evocative, primitive emotion, perhaps reminding some of those old druids and their human sacrifices. Down on the green some kind of a religious play was going on. Dozens of pretty little girls with flowing pastel-colored robes — pink and blue and green — were doing some kind of a choreographic pageantry, somewhat like what we see between the halves of a football game in this country now. The action was very well done. And suddenly

Presented by Dr. Franklin H. Littell, Ida E. King Distinguished Professor of Holocaust Studies at Stockton State College, on April 22, 1990, at an area service at Beth Judah in Ventnor, New Jersey.

there arose, out of a hole in the green, the figure of evil: the Leviathan, the Satanic figure. They scattered. Then there came, clad in shining armor, Siegfried, the hero of Teutonic folk myth, and he slew the dragon. And after this religious — or was it political? — pageant of heathenism, all the lights went out.

I found myself in this eerie setting, with all these tens of thousands of people, in total darkness. And then the lights came on, pointing at the podium. There he was! The whole crowd jumped to its feet: Sieg Heil! Sieg Heil! Sieg Heil! — in that monstrous litany which meant self-destruction to so many Germans and murderous deaths to so many of their victims. I cannot adequately describe to you the evocative power of the moment, its centerpiece this demonic creed, this semi-religious political blend which was Nazism in its arrogance.

The next day we ran into another little group of American students, one of them a Jewish girl, and she said she jumped to her feet too! The crowd was as people possessed! I say truthfully for my own sake: I was looking for a hole, something to crawl into. It was so unclean! — this Moloch, this idolatrous dictatorship, this Fuehrerstaat! — this pride, this arrogance, this misuse of religion, this murderous politics with its programs of genocide. The Jewish people were the first target. Whether individual Jews were believers or not, whether they were devout or atheist, whether they were Communists or Social Democrats or pacifists, they reminded the Power of Evil of the god who is God. So they were targeted for destruction, and they died *Kiddush Hashem.*

How could this happen in the heart of Christendom? This is the question which has come back to haunt some of us again and again and again, and it has shaped my work now for years. I remember a few days later talking with the bishop of my church, the Methodist Episcopal Church of Germany. He was a good man. Hitler's no conceptual problem; Himmler's no conceptual problem; Goebbels is no conceptual problem. We have the symbols or signs of evil for the demonic individuals in history. But what do you do with good people — who do the wrong thing when the time of decision comes. Otto Melle was a good, old-fashioned, Methodist preacher, and he told our little group how Germany's youth had been going to the devil. They were staying out late nights, and they were smoking, and some of them were drinking beer, and they were dancing.... Along came a *Wundermensch,* a worker of miracles, who inspired them and gathered them up and taught them discipline and directed them to sacrifice for the *Volk.* Those of you who understand German will understand with me the pathos the word *Volk* carries, or did carry. Nation? Sometimes. People? Sometimes. Race? Sometimes, especially under the Nazis. Race...

He told us what a wonderful work Hitler had done. Understand, this was almost a year after Kristallnacht declared to the whole world — those who would see — what Hitler meant. It was three and a half years after Martin Niemoeller, who was after all a Christian pastor, had been in a concentration camp. And the bishop of my church concluded his little sermonette, "Adolf Hitler is God's man for Germany." I tell you, every few days now — for more than fifty years — that statement has come back to my mind. How could it happen that Christianity over centuries should have defined itself so much in terms of contempt for the Jewish people? — so much in terms of alienation from the Jewish people rather than the affirmation of love and service and fraternity that a good man, not a vile contemptible vulgar antisemite, could take that track? How could he allow his people, unshepherded, to rush like lemmings to their own destruction, taking on the way under the hand of Cain the Jewish people, two-thirds of all the Jews who lived in Europe at that time, to become victims in Hitler's *Festung* Europa?

Thank God there were a few, not many, church leaders — not the pope, not most of the Protestant bishops, not many of the deans and superintendents, but a few good people who did the right thing at the right time. Some of you certainly saw the program last Sunday night, which Rabbi Schulweis and his people presented over *60 Minutes:* "Rescuers and Those They Rescued." Our friend Felix Zandman of Philadelphia referred to those who saved him and kept him and his immediate family alive in a small hole for more than two years, at risk of their own lives, as "saints." That they were, certainly, but to use that word makes it a little too easy on the rest of us. I like to think those who stepped in when their neighbors who were Jews needed them to be ordinary people who did the right thing at the right time. That puts the question to you and me: probably none of us in this room is a saint.

I think of Marian Pritchard. Marian Pritchard was a Dutch woman. A Jewish man and his children came to her out of the night — (she didn't even know them) — in a little village in the Netherlands. She welcomed them and prepared a hiding place for them. A German occupying army group came by and searched: there'd been a rumor. They didn't find the hiding place. So they let the group out to get some fresh air and a Dutch policeman, who was a collaborator, came back and caught them. Then he tried to blackmail Marian Pritchard. The interviewer in the film "Courage to Care" said, "What did you do then?" And this calm little woman said, "I shot him." Just like that. When the interviewer recovered from this calm statement, he said, "What did you do then?" She said, "The undertaker in our town was a good man, and he took the body and put it in a casket with another body that was being buried that afternoon." Thus disappeared a collaborator from off the face of the earth. And then she said something that was very important. Speaking forty years later, she said, "It still bothers me. But I'd do it again."

This simple affirmation of the importance of life is vital. When it is necessary to kill, never affirm it; affirm life. In the presence of death, even when someone like that collaborator deserved it — still, do not rejoice in death. Do not allow death to win.

I think of another simple woman who worked with a group in Berlin that saved many Jewish lives. There were twenty-six hundred Jews who wintered through in Berlin the whole span of the war, with all the destruction, who were saved by ordinary people who did the right thing at the right time. When the newspaper people came rushing around to ask the question which they didn't understand, "Why did you do it?," Frau Klein said: "Out of self-respect." A wonderful human answer! Saintly, if you wish, but I prefer "human." I think of that wonderful Yiddish word *menschlichkeit* — just to be genuinely human.

Or I think of Daniel Trocmé. Daniel Trocmé was the nephew of André and Magda, who were the pastor and his wife in that French village of Le Chambon. There's a movie now circulating in the regular theaters, directed by Pierre Sauvage, who was saved there: he was just six weeks old when his parents brought him to Le Chambon. The village saved five thousand. These facts are all authenticated at the Avenue of the Righteous and in the files at Yad Vashem. Daniel was engaged in studying for the Ph.D. at the Sorbonne. You can imagine how privileged a position that was, and how happy he was to be on his way. But then he decided he couldn't go along that track in a time of need, so he went back to help in the rescue. He was caught, and he died in a concentration camp. But when he came home to help he wrote a letter to his family, which we still have. He said, "Don't feel sorry for me that I'm giving up my study. I'm doing it so that in time to come I'll not have to be ashamed."

Again, they were persons who expressed what it is to be a man, what it is to be a woman, what it is not to be a lemming following a mad leader and a false religion into destruction.

Why do we talk this way? Why do we remember? Time is running out on my generation — survivors, rescuers, liberators, and spectators. We speak for the sake of our grandchildren and our great-grandchildren and those yet to come. We hope that they will not see such terrible years as the years 1933–39 and '39 to '45, the years of the Holocaust.

We remember too in order to honor those who perished and to affirm life. You will remember Anne Frank, who never reached her sixteenth birthday. You will remember the million and a quarter Jewish children who perished in the Holocaust. If you ever have the chance, you must go to the Children's Memorial at Yad Vashem, one of the most beautiful and moving sights of remembrance on the face of the earth. You will remember, I hope, Sophie and Hans Scholl — two German students who were Christians, who passed out flyers condemning the brutality of the Nazi regime, and who were caught with some of their confederates and beheaded. I hope you will remember also Hannah Senesh. I notice that your booklet has her famous poem "Blessed Is the Match." I'll read you a poem which was brought out by a teammate. They were parachuted into either Hungary or Yugoslavia and Reuven Daphne, who is now Deputy Director at Yad Vashem, brought this poem out after the team split up. She was caught and tortured, and she died.

> To die, to die in youth, no, no, I did not want it.
> I loved the warmth of sun, the lovely light.
> I loved song, shining eyes, and not destruction.
> I did not want the dark of war, the night.
> No, no, I did not want it.

It's for the sake of the youth that we remember and that we speak. We speak now so that we in our season and they in theirs to come shall so live with each other that in the latter days, we shall not have to be ashamed. Amen.

28

Holocaust as Holocaust,
Holocaust as Symbol

Lawrence A. Hoffman

By way of introductory illustration, I am drawn to a personal anecdote, dating only to last week, when I went skiing for the first time. From my wife to my friends and students, everyone assured me that the risks to life and limb were overrated; I would enjoy it, they said; I needed a vacation. So away I went. The ski range — Killington by name — turned out to be universally acclaimed among ski advocates, and for good reason. From the moment of my arrival, I found an army of smiling experts devoted to my welfare there. With indescribable ease, my family and I were shunted from line to line, where without exception yet another polite smiling agent saw to our needs, all the while assuring us that we were well taken care of. One man measured me for boots; a woman demonstrated how to fasten them; another man gave me skis. Several lines ended in mere paperwork related to the renting procedure, and without even reading the small print, I (like the queue of people before and, I suspect, after me) quickly signed my acquiescence to whatever it was they were doing. At last, I reached the slopes, where I was quickly directed to my group. My daughter of ten, immediately spotted as a child, was removed from her family and taken with the children for their own lesson. She would rejoin us happily at noon, we were assured; not to worry. We adults then boarded a crowded open-air truck where, instead of sitting, we stood packed together holding stationary poles for support; the wind whipped bitter-cold against our faces while we trundled over the hills on our way up the mountain to that unknown destination called "the slopes."

None of this was unenjoyable. And yet, I may never return. From the first unruffled and unruffling agent to the last, Killington's model of bureaucratic efficiency reminded me of other long lines moving effortlessly toward happy smiling people trained to offer guarantees that no one was to worry. Not that I ever saw them myself. My haunting recollection is a montage of others' fleeting images. But their images are real enough, too real, and, come to think of it, not very fleeting: children removed "temporarily" from parents; another frigid truck ride, where the less fortunate passengers were outfitted with no polyester ski clothes, but for whom the sub-zero gusts of wind would, by bitter comparison, still be one of the more comfortable things they would feel for the rest of their all too short lives.

I elaborate on this private nightmare, which I have admitted to no one until now, only to demonstrate how much Jews live with the Holocaust still. It is central, pivotal, in our lives.

Rabbi Hoffman is professor of liturgy at Hebrew Union College–Jewish Institute of Religion in New York City.

Everyone you meet either lost family or knows of those who did. Internally, at Jewish gatherings, one hears whispered, "She's a survivor, you know," or "He's second-generation." There is never any need to explicate survivor-of-what or what the first generation was. From Hollywood to Madison Avenue, from Broadway to Doubleday, the entertainment industry trades on the Holocaust with a greater or lesser degree of ethical sensitivity, with the effect that we need not depend even on memory and conscience to assure that it is always before us.

If you would know, then, that fulcral experience of every thoughtful Jew you meet, remember that we are, all of us, each in his or her own way, survivors — by the grace of God, that is; not by the grace of the civilized Western world. If there is responsibility still to bear, it is this: the silence or complicity of those we set in power, and our own failure to cry foul, when murder most foul it most assuredly was, and we the murderers (at least by proxy), who equally with Cain must now abide the charge of God, "The blood of your brothers and sisters cries unto me from the earth."

In the Reform Movement's post-Holocaust liturgy, a Yom Kippur confession reads:

> For the sin of silence
> For the sin of indifference,
> For the secret complicity of the neutral,
> For the closing of borders,
> For the washing of hands,
> For all that was done,
> For all that was not done,
> Let there be no forgetfulness before the Throne of Glory,
> Let there be remembrance within the human heart,
> And let there at last be forgiveness.... [1]

You see, I by no means wish to imply that the "dangling responsibility" for the Holocaust — "dangling" because it dangles and drags and pursues us relentlessly, no matter how we twist to avoid it — is exclusively a Christian problem. It is a problem for all who take their stand in transhistorical faith communities that could have done more than they did. Jewish liturgy is only now coming to terms with the Holocaust; and it is an appropriate Christian liturgical response on which I have been asked to comment this morning. In that regard, Father John Pawlikowski makes three points:

a. First, he identifies the Holocaust as a paradigm for evil in general, but evil on a new scale, "a new era in human possibility," the ultimate assertion of "human autonomy and power" when death becomes the final solution to "the universal crisis of the human person." [2] This recognition of the Holocaust as meaning more than itself — an identification to which I shall return later — leads to our speaker's second point.

b. He insists that Christianity's task is to "channel the realization of human freedom into constructive outlets" by "recovering a fresh sense of transcendence," this being the liturgist's

---

1. Chaim Stern, ed., *Gates of Repentance* (New York: Central Conference of American Rabbis, 1978), 439. For parallel liturgy from the Conservative Movement, see Jules Harlow, ed., *Mahzor for Rosh Hashanah and Yom Kippur* (New York: Rabbinical Assembly, 1972), 581: "We have sinned against You, and them [sic!], by refusing to hear...by hesitating...by useless conferences...by being overcautious...by not using our power...by theological rationalizations."

2. John T. Pawlikowski, "Worship after the Holocaust: An Ethician's Reflections," in *Worship* 58, 317–18.

task, insofar as "the realm of the symbolic remains our only viable hope in this regard."[3] So John urges us to replace the reason-dominated Kantian ethic with an experiential grounding in the personal encounter with the living God, which "first and foremost" is the function of "the symbolic experience of the liturgy."[4] Toward this end....

c. John isolates a variety to thematic elements appropriate to a contemporary liturgical response, including a novel accent on (1) hope, (2) community, and (3) human co-creational responsibility for the world, which we must learn to evaluate positively in and of itself.

I should like to respond to this fine contribution in two ways: first, as liturgist, and then, as a Jew.

As a liturgist, I welcome the newly found accent on all the items John mentions as part of his third point, especially the three I have cited. As John himself notes, the positive evaluation of creation is to be found in classical Jewish liturgy, and I add that the notion of our enjoying co-creator status with God is equally familiar to that prayer tradition, it being, in fact, a significant postulate of classical Jewish theology. "Hope," too, is worth our emphasizing in a post-Holocaust context, toward which end, I note (not at all parenthetically) that the national anthem of the State of Israel is *Hatikvah*, "The Hope"; as I shall point out shortly, this "two-thousand-year-old hope" (to cite the anthem's lyrics), which is bound up with the guarantee of Israel's continued secure existence, is not irrelevant to Holocaust theology.

Above all, however, my liturgical perspective leads me to herald John's emphasis on "community." As I argued yesterday in the ritual action study group, I understand the notion of community to represent for us a psychosocial construct which serves as a fulcrum around which experience in our time may be artistically, orderly, and coherently structured. "Community" thus becomes what I have been calling the new Master Image of our age, a Platonic ideal, if you like, according to the likeness of which, real human groups may be constructed. Such groups present foci in which we, the members, act out ritually (that is, liturgically) our determination to be liable one to another wholly and unreservedly, not, that is, simply according to a limited list of discrete expectations, but along the lines of Buber's *I-Thou* relationship, and in accord with the common determination that we act together to apprehend, and to live, a life modeled on God's will. In this way, "community" is nothing less than the locus in which the numinal presence of God is to be found. So from a liturgical perspective, John is entirely correct to place a rediscovery of "community" at the top of the priorities that must be met if the ethical mandate he outlines is to be satisfied.

He is similarly correct in emphasizing "symbol" as the predominant mode of communication particular to the liturgical arena. It is through shared symbolic discourse, or not at all, that we will further the victory of the spirit. I suggest, however, that sign and symbol should not be differentiated according to Rollo May (as our speaker would have it),[5] but along the lines suggested first by C. G. Jung, and then, each in his own discipline, by Irwin Goodenough and by Victor Turner.[6]

---

3. Ibid., 320.
4. Ibid., 323.
5. Ibid., 328).
6. See Victor Turner, *A Forest of Symbols* (Ithaca, N.Y.: Cornell University Press, 1970), 26, where Turner quotes Jung directly, with the same words that I include in the next paragraph; and Irwin R. Goodenough, *Jewish Symbols in the Greco-Roman Period* (New York: Pantheon, 1953–65), 12:69.

Unlike signs, which Jung calls "an abbreviated expression for a known thing," symbols "are the best possible expression for a relatively unknown fact."[7] I argue elsewhere that symbols function liturgically in that they are "items in the worship service which direct the community of worshipers, immediately and with absolutely no commentary or explanation, to an awareness of an experience or value which they hold in common: one to which they are either attached or repelled strongly; but whose exact significance they cannot verbalize."[8] Thus, the cross, for example, positively symbolic to Christians, can generally be but a sign to Jews, whose lack of Christian experience prevents their comprehending the full depth of emotion invested in it by Christians. Similarly, but in a diametrically opposite sense, the swastika can be identified as the best example of a *negative* symbol for Jews, while, for most Christians, not all, certainly, but those, at least, who were not themselves persecuted by the Nazis, it will probably have only sign value. One may be very serious about signs, of course; Jews learn to show reverence toward the cross, and Christians despise the swastika, without, however, either item attaining the status of a symbol whose depth of denotative power (by definition) transcends the very scope of verbal description.

But it is symbols, not signs, that change our lives. We read highway *signs* telling us not to speed and to fasten seat belts; but we race down highways, our belts unfastened. No one changes behavior patterns because of signs. Insofar, then, as the Holocaust demands changed behavior, we must encode that message in symbolic discourse, and this the liturgy does, precisely because regularized liturgical experience shared with one's community reinforces the symbol as a connective bonding element in the ritualizing group. Its members are socialized into sensing that deeper message which makes a symbol what it is. They then have no need for words, which they recognize never to go far enough anyway. When called on to explain their symbols, they manufacture linguistic equations "explaining" them to outsiders, but insofar as outsiders memorize the explanations, they master only what is now the sign-content, not the symbol-content which arises out of shared experience, and goes beyond verbal equation. If, therefore, we wish the Holocaust to symbolize evil in general (as John argues we should), we have no recourse but to begin on the level of symbol, knowing that it is through regularized, liturgical, community note-taking that mere signs are given symbolic force.

But we cannot manufacture symbols out of logical equations, simply by saying they are so. Also, symbols demand the specific, not the general. Evil in general, then, is not symbolically resonant. If we wish to achieve the end which our speaker puts nobly before us we have no choice — and I say this as liturgist — but to represent that one particular paradigmatic example of evil itself, the Holocaust, as itself, the Holocaust, not as something broader or more general than what it was.

To be sure, I have no intention of negating the significance of other tragedies so readily called to mind: the drowning of boat people, torture in Central America, slaughter in Sabra and Shatila. But I said before I would return to our speaker's identification of the Holocaust as meaning more than itself. The problem is that it will never mean more than it was until it first "means" what in fact it was. When people react viscerally and absolutely to Holocaust as negative symbol, they may find it possible to react equally painfully to that which the

---

7. Carl G. Jung, *Psychological Types* (London: Routledge & Kegan Paul, 1949), 601.

8. *Gates of Understanding*, ed. Lawrence A. Hoffman (New York: Central Conference of American Rabbis, 1977), 1:137.

Holocaust symbolizes, but not until then. So as liturgist, I have this single important critique of John's otherwise superb paper: he generalizes the specificity of the Holocaust until it loses that very immediacy it requires to speak to us as a symbol. What emerges from John's remarks is Holocaust as sign, Holocaust as a mathematical construct, an algebraic "X" that is arbitrarily said to equal evil in general; not Holocaust as demanding symbol, summoning us from our very depths to change our ways.

Before us should be the task of displaying Holocaust as symbol in the liturgy. As liturgists, we ask, How can we construct our worship so that Holocaust appears as symbol?

Toward this end, I have one suggestion, at least. It is "the calendar." Surely, as liturgists, we know that worshiping communities impose their symbolic universe of reality first and foremost on their structuring of time. Christian time is Epiphany, Good Friday, and Easter Sunday; Jewish time is Rosh Hashanah, Yom Kippur, and Passover. More than convenient markers of months, these days bespeak symbolic realities for us. What we value most and what we fear greatest we encode with temporal specialness. What is not so reserved for community memories to ponder is relegated by our worshipers to relative insignificance in our scheme of things. So it happens that the Jewish calendar now designates one day as Yom HaShoah, "Holocaust Day." Is it too much to ask that Christian calendars mark it as well?

Yom HaShoah is already in the official Christian calendar in some places. It should be so universally, and not only as one of the many days added through the centuries as options (usually disregarded), but as a demanding event to which Christians are called after Auschwitz. For Jew and Christian alike, Yom HaShoah offers the opportunity for more than the expression of guilt. It calls for a ritual rehearsing of memory, appropriate confession before God, affirmation of the "saved remnant," and dedication toward those tasks which our Holocaust memory demands.

In the interests of time, let me pass over some other, more obvious, similar extensions of John's paper: a discussion of the Reproaches, which should be dealt with in some manner that does justice both to liturgical integrity and to human reality — the solution offered recently by the Methodist book of prayer may be one way; and some means of counteracting the potentially harmful message derived from the Holy Week lectionary.[9] I must, however, turn to what is my second major suggestion today, a theological consideration of the State of Israel.

The fact is that Jewish liturgy is well-nigh universal in its post-Holocaust liturgical linking of the birth of Israel the State with the near extinction under the Nazis of Israel the people. Reform High Holy Day liturgy, for example, extends the medieval poetic epic called the *Avodah* beyond the traditional chronological confines of Creation to Second Temple. Instead, this volume of 1978 offers us an entire rubric called "From Creation to Redemption," in which recollection of the Holocaust is succeeded by "Rebirth," when, even as Ezekiel 37 foresaw, "After the suffering we rose up...in one land especially the Land of Zion."[10] Similarly, the Conservative Movement's Passover Haggadah of 1982 presents an alternative *Maggid* section where — to cite the book's accompanying introduction, "the Holocaust and the rebirth of the State of Israel are mirrored — for they shape our own Exodus from

---

9. For short discussion, see Eugene J. Fisher, *Ecumenical Trends* (March 1981): 37–39.
10. *Gates of Repentance,* 442–43.

our own Mitzrayim [Egypt]"[11] and the Grace after Meals here calls on God explicitly to "bless the Land of Israel, *the dawn of our redemption.*"[12]

For reasons that need not occupy us here, I find myself in the minority when it comes to linking the State of Israel theologically to the Holocaust, a fact which I mention only to underline the obvious observation that if I, as a recalcitrant objector to this pervasive view, still posit the need to take Israel's link to the Holocaust seriously, imagine what the majority who hold the general perspective would say. At the very least, I suggest it is incumbent for Christian liturgy to approach the State of Israel with the realization that it has such theological reality for Jews. Israel is, at least, the Jewish Land for the saved remnant. Its very soil is, at least, one of the prime sources of Jewish spirituality. We should not confuse Zionism as a theological category that has historical consequences in terms of a living, functioning Jewish polity with any particular government of that polity, whose policies even Zionists may be ethically obliged to eschew and to counteract as contrary to the very same post-Holocaust ethic that mandates Christian communities to take the State of Israel seriously.

I have offered all of the above merely as liturgist, that is, as observer of how liturgy functions — through such specifics as symbol and calendar — and what current liturgies (in this case, Jewish ones) say about Israel the State, especially. I would be remiss, however, if I did not end as I began: as a Jew.

As a Jew, I ask two questions of seriousness, seriousness of Jewish-Christian dialogue, to start with. I remember well the convention I attended seven years ago, when I first discovered the Academy. There were times when it seemed as if you, my colleagues, were continuing in the middle of old conversations, in which I, both newcomer and outsider, had difficulty even ascertaining the subject of the discussion that seemed to me to be mere predicate of some subject stated long before. But you opened yourselves and your world to me, and through the years, I have come to know you, to share with you, to celebrate with you, to deliberate with you, and to pray with you. So I owe you nothing short of absolute candor now, as you do me the honor of inviting my comments on worshiping after the Holocaust.

I must say then that if our discussion goes no further than this room, we would both be guilty of dialogic dilettantism. The lived liturgy, after all, demands not the mere bread of "bread and circuses," the momentary dabbling at life's crises. The memory of the Holocaust claims me as a Jew; I ask that you let it claim you as Christians.

So I turn to the second area of seriousness, seriousness of self, of myself as Jewish self, of yourselves as Christian selves, and of our Academy, as a community of such selves, where together we may present the awesome potential of mattering in a world where sceptics argue that nothing matters any more. The question is whether in ten or fifty or a hundred years, we will really have mattered.

Those very same sceptics to whom I allude say that no one can change things in the complex world of institutional behavior, that the church, some putative monolithic entity "out there," for example, is beyond the cries of individuals. But you have said that the real church is not "out there" at all, that the real church is yourselves. Appropriately coincident with this holy day for you [Epiphany], then, I sense the prophetic call that summons you and me alike to lives that matter.

---

11. Rachel Anne Rabinowicz, ed., *Passover Haggadah: The Feast of Freedom* (New York: Rabbinical Assembly, 1982), 94–99, and Introduction, 8–9.

12. Ibid., 85 (emphasis added).

If our discussions in the Academy remain limited to academic debates, we will not have mattered, nor shall we imagine we have. If we effect liturgical change in nonessentials, altering the outward gloss of liturgical words and actions alone, while leaving human relationships themselves the same as they were before the changes, we may delude ourselves into thinking we have mattered, but we shall not have made any difference at all. We shall matter only when we heed that prophetic call to take the risks and effect real changes that assuredly will not happen without us, and, despite our best efforts, may not even succeed with us. We may not know it in our own lifetime, but in the sight of God, at least, it may then (and only then) be said that we will have mattered.

29

What Did Pastor Martin Niemoeller Really Say?

One of the most misquoted citations of the Holocaust is the "confession of guilt" by Pastor Martin Niemoeller. A highly decorated commander in World War I, Niemoeller as a preacher later attracted large congregations. He held one of the most prestigious pulpits in Germany, Berlin-Dahlem.

We include it here in its proper form for use and also to stress the importance of accuracy in matters as sensitive as the Holocaust. All primary sources should be cited with precision, and certainly not rewritten at will to suit special pleading or the interests of a particular occasion.

Martin Niemoeller became the most prominent leader of the anti-Nazi Confessing Church in Germany. He had been unsympathetic to the Weimar Republic. He at first welcomed the "national renewal" the Nazis promised. However, when Hitler was made dictator he saw his error and recognized the evil in the dictatorship and its programs.

In 1934 he took the lead in forming the Pastors Emergency League. When the church struggle intensified he was arrested for "attacking the state." The court set him free, but the Führer overruled the court and sent him to concentration camp as a "personal prisoner." From July 1937 until the end of the war he was held in prison and concentration camp, including over three years in solitary confinement (at Sachsenhausen and Dachau).

When he was released from concentration camp he helped prepare and release the "Stuttgart Confession of Guilt" (October 1945), through which in the presence of ecumenical leaders from abroad the leaders of the German churches confessed their failure as Christians adequately to fight against Nazism.

Niemoeller became president of the Church of Hesse and was for a time one of the presidents of the World Council of Churches. His confession of shared guilt was always included in his sermons after the war. A popular preacher and speaker, he was much sought after to address congregations in North America.

According to his widow, Sybil Niemoeller, these are his exact words:

First they came for the Communists
and I did not speak out —
because I was not a Communist.

Then they came for the Socialists
and I did not speak out —
because I was not a Socialist.

Then they came for the trade unionists
and I did not speak out —
because I was not a trade unionist.

Then they came for the Jews
and I did not speak out —
because I was not a Jew.

They they came for me —
and there was no one left
to speak out for me.

30

For You Who Died I Must Live On...
Reflections on the March of the Living:
Just Like Me

Poland

Jody Kasner

Those victims of man's hatred
  were children just like me.
Those who once had normal lives
  were children just like me.
Those uprooted from their lives
Those dragged from their homes in the middle of the night
  were children just like me.
Those robbed of everything they had
  were children just like me.
Those locked behind a ghetto wall
  were children just like me.
Those struck by pain and poverty
  were children just like me.
Those taken by starvation and disease
  were children just like me.
Those forced to brave the endless winters
  were children just like me.
Those who never saw the outside world
  were children just like me.
Those left orphaned in the streets.
  were children just like me.
Those robbed of their childhood
  were children just like me.
Those robbed of their smiles
  were children just like me.
Those who never even had a chance
  were children just like me.

Those ripped from the arms of their mothers
  were children just like me.
Those shipped in from far-off lands
  were children just like me.
Those forced to stand for days on end
  were children just like me.
Those killed before their time
  were children just like me.
Those marched unwillingly to their deaths
  were children just like me.
Those stripped and shot and gassed and burnt
  were children just like me.
Those buried in pits, in unmarked graves
  were children just like me.
Those all too young to die
  were children just like me.
Those flickering lights in a cold dark world
  were children just like me.
Those silent soldiers who fought off the darkness
  were children just like me.
Those one and a half million innocent souls
  were children just like me.
Yes, those children of the Holocaust
  were children just like me.
And you, who killed my neighbors, my friends and my family
  you too, were children just like me.

—Jody Kasner, age sixteen
Toronto, Ontario

A Parable

PAUL M. VAN BUREN

I should like to close with a "rabbinic" tale, as far as I know it. There was a man who had two sons, his well-beloved first-born, and, years later, a second whom he also loved and who learned almost all he knew from his elder brother. One day the younger son said to his elder brother, "It is with us as with Jacob and Esau: it is I who have become the preferred son." They quarrelled, and the younger son gathered all he could lay his hands on and took his journey into a far country. There he gave himself out as the only son of a rich man and ran up a staggering debt. The elder son, hearing of this and wishing to protect his father's good name, labored hard and suffered grievously in an attempt to lessen the indebtedness. Finally, his credit rating slipping, the younger son came to himself and resolved to return and repair the damage he had done, saying, "My father and my brother, I have sinned against heaven and before you both, and am no longer worthy to be called your son and brother. Let me become your agent to restore your fortune, your health, and your noble name throughout the world...."

I have heard it said that the tale concludes with the younger son carrying out his resolution, but I cannot vouch for the authenticity of that ending.

—*The Burden of Freedom,*
New York: Seabury, 1976

Hardly Ever Again

Words and Music by

HANK KNIGHT AND TOM PAXTON

In for- ty five re - mem - ber when the world said, "Nev - er nev - er a-gain!" Nev - er a-gain six mill - ion lost; nev - er a-gain: The Hol - o - caust. "Nev - er," we said, "Nev - er a - gain." But this is now and that was then.

The T V re-port-ers stand out in the street; their cam-'ras pan the dead at their feet. With a but-ton the im-age is at our com-mand,_____ and the "Lords of the Earth" carve up the land. Oh, "Nev-er," we said, "Nev - er a-gain."_____ But this is now and that was then. "Hard - ly ev - er a-gain." ·Is that what we meant to say? "Hard - ly ev - er a-gain."_____ Will be turn and walk a - way?

Hank Knight and Tom Paxton

What Can We Say?

Rabbi Irving Greenberg

Judaism and Christianity do not merely tell
of God's love for humanity.
They stand or fall on their fundamental claim
that the human being is of ultimate and absolute value.
The Holocaust poses the most radical counter-testimony
to both Judaism and Christianity.
No statement, theological or otherwise,
should be made that would not be credible
in the presence of burning children.